A CULTURAL HISTORY OF PEACE

VOLUME 2

A Cultural History of Peace
General Editor: Ronald Edsforth

Volume 1
A Cultural History of Peace in Antiquity
Edited by Sheila L. Ager

Volume 2
A Cultural History of Peace in the Medieval Age
Edited by Walter Simons

Volume 3
A Cultural History of Peace in the Renaissance
Edited by Isabella Lazzarini

Volume 4
A Cultural History of Peace in the Age of Enlightenment
Edited by Stella Ghervas and David Armitage

Volume 5
A Cultural History of Peace in the Age of Empire
Edited by Ingrid Sharp

Volume 6
A Cultural History of Peace in the Modern Age
Edited by Ronald Edsforth

A CULTURAL HISTORY OF PEACE

IN THE MEDIEVAL AGE

Edited by Walter Simons

BLOOMSBURY ACADEMIC
LONDON • NEW YORK • OXFORD • NEW DELHI • SYDNEY

BLOOMSBURY ACADEMIC
Bloomsbury Publishing Plc
50 Bedford Square, London, WC1B 3DP, UK
1385 Broadway, New York, NY 10018, USA
29 Earlsfort Terrace, Dublin 2, Ireland

BLOOMSBURY, BLOOMSBURY ACADEMIC and the Diana logo are trademarks of
Bloomsbury Publishing Plc

First published in Great Britain 2020
This edition published in Great Britain, 2024

Copyright © Bloomsbury Publishing, 2020

Walter Simons has asserted his right under the Copyright, Designs and Patents Act, 1988,
to be identified as Editor of this work.

Cover image: *Allegory of good government, peace* © DEA / G. DAGLI ORTI / Getty Images

All rights reserved. No part of this publication may be reproduced or transmitted
in any form or by any means, electronic or mechanical, including photocopying,
recording, or any information storage or retrieval system, without prior permission
in writing from the publishers.

Bloomsbury Publishing Plc does not have any control over, or responsibility for, any
third-party websites referred to or in this book. All internet addresses given in this
book were correct at the time of going to press. The author and publisher regret
any inconvenience caused if addresses have changed or sites have ceased to exist,
but can accept no responsibility for any such changes.

A catalogue record for this book is available from the British Library.

A catalog record for this book is available from the Library of Congress.

ISBN: HB: 978-1-4742-3847-2
        PB: 978-1-3503-8577-1
        Set: 978-1-3503-8603-7

Series: The Cultural Histories Series

Typeset by RefineCatch Limited, Bungay, Suffolk
Printed and bound in Great Britain

To find out more about our authors and books visit www.bloomsbury.com
and sign up for our newsletters.

CONTENTS

LIST OF ILLUSTRATIONS	vi
GENERAL EDITOR'S PREFACE	ix
ABBREVIATIONS	xiv
Introduction: Was there Peace in the Middle Ages? *Walter Simons*	1
1　Definitions of Peace 　*Jehangir Yezdi Malegam*	13
2　Human Nature, Peace, and War 　*Gregory M. Reichberg*	33
3　Peace, War, and Gender 　*Katrin E. Sjursen*	51
4　Peace, Pacifism, and Religion: A Universal Longing Unfulfilled 　*Anne Marie Wolf*	65
5　Representations of Peace: Heavenly Dreams, Earthly Needs 　*Walter Simons*	81
6　Peace Movements: Peace in the Communes 　*James A. Palmer*	101
7　Peace, Security, and Deterrence 　*Jenny Benham*	119
8　Peace as Integration: The Many Sides of Medieval Peace 　*Geoffrey Koziol*	135
NOTES	149
BIBLIOGRAPHY	153
CONTRIBUTORS	177
INDEX	179

ILLUSTRATIONS

INTRODUCTION

0.1   St Francis arranging peace between a wolf and the citizens of Gubbio, by Sassetta.   2

0.2   Cross with inscription *Pax-Lux/Rex-Lex*.   8

CHAPTER 1

1.1   Division of the Carolingian Empire at the Treaty of Verdun, 843.   16

1.2   The *Deditio*: Henry IV of Germany kneels to seek forgiveness at Canossa in 1077, before Queen Mathilda of Tuscany.   19

1.3   Laon Cathedral, France, West Front.   24

1.4   Frederick I Barbarossa, German emperor.   29

CHAPTER 2

2.1   Triumph of the Catholic Doctrine embodied by Thomas Aquinas, by Andrea Di Bontaiuto.   34

2.2   Thomas Aquinas, Commentary on Aristotle's *Ethics*.   41

2.3   Statue of Averroës, Cordoba, Spain.   43

2.4   Portrait of Pope Innocent IV, writing.   45

CHAPTER 3

3.1   Women following Peter the Hermit on Crusade.   53

3.2   Marriage of Margaret of Anjou and King Henry VI of England, to signal peace between England and France.   55

3.3   Women besieged in a fortified town.   57

3.4   Joan of Arc at the siege of Orléans.   61

CHAPTER 4

4.1   Maimonides' draft of his legal code, *Mishneh Torah*, in his own hand.   70

4.2   Knight of the Order of Knights Templar during the battle of al-Bocquee or Buqaia (Lebanon) in 1163.   77

4.3   A knight, probably a crusader, in a gesture of homage.   78

ILLUSTRATIONS vii

CHAPTER 5

5.1	Pax overseeing the flight of *Labor* (suffering), *Metus* (fear), and *Fraus* (deceit), in a manuscript of Prudentius, *Psychomachia*, about 1000 AD.	82
5.2	"The Good Tree" (*Ecclesia*), displaying the fruits of the Spirit, including Peace (*Pax*), in autograph manuscript by Lambert of St Omer.	83
5.3	Antiphon for Peace (*Da pacem, Domine, in diebus nostris*) in a Book of Hours.	85
5.4	The Heavenly Jerusalem in the Book of Revelation.	86
5.5	Heavenly and earthly communities compared in Augustine, *City of God*, after a fifteenth-century engraving.	87
5.6	Celestial Jerusalem in Guillaume de Deguileville, *The Pilgrimage of Human Life*.	89
5.7	Hieronymus Bosch (*c.* 1450–1516), *The Wayfarer* or *Peddler*.	90
5.8	Crusaders besieging Jerusalem.	91
5.9	Judas' kiss, by Giotto.	96
5.10	Ambrogio Lorenzetti, *Peace and War*. Detail: Virtues of Good Government.	98
5.11	Ambrogio Lorenzetti, *Peace and War*. Detail: Peace.	99
5.12	Ambrogio Lorenzetti, *Peace and War*. Detail: Effects of Good Government.	100

CHAPTER 6

6.1	St Francis' exorcism of demons from the city of Arezzo's.	104
6.2	A preacher's audience.	105
6.3	The Kiss of Peace.	108
6.4	A Bianchi procession, depicted in 1401.	113
6.5	San Bernardino of Siena, preaching in the Campo, Siena, by Sano di Pietro.	117

CHAPTER 7

7.1	Emperor Louis the Pious treating for peace, and the sack of a town.	120
7.2	King John I of England does homage to King Philip Augustus of France.	125
7.3	Charlemagne receives hostages of Tassilo of Bavaria.	126
7.4	King John II of France as a hostage in London.	128
7.5	Drawing up of a treaty between France and England.	131

CHAPTER 8

8.1 An idealized depiction of an ecclesiastical council in the Utrecht Psalter of *c.* 830.   137

8.2 The Peace and Truce of Lillebonne, Normandy (1080).   143

8.3 Swearing an oath on a reliquary in the *Sachsenspiegel Landrecht*, Landesbibliothek Oldenburg, Germany, 1336.   144

GENERAL EDITOR'S PREFACE

RONALD EDSFORTH

When people learn that I study and teach peace history, they often look puzzled and ask me, "Does peace have a history?" *A Cultural History of Peace* is an emphatically positive response to that question. Yes, peace has a history. The original scholarly essays collected in these six volumes clearly show that peace always has been an important human concern. More precisely, these essays demonstrate that what we recognize today as peace thinking and peace imagining, peace seeking and peace making, peace keeping and peace building have long recorded histories that stretch from antiquity to the twenty-first century. All of us who have contributed to *A Cultural History of Peace* believe that present and future generations should have the opportunity to recognize and understand the importance of this peace history.

Very few universities and colleges had faculty who taught and researched peace history before the end of the Cold War. Even today, most professors who do peace history moved into it from other specializations in History or other academic disciplines. Most contributors to *A Cultural History of Peace* are professional historians, but Anthropology, Sociology, Political Science, Journalism, Art History, Religion, and Classical Studies are also represented. These fifty-six contributors work on four continents in thirteen different countries. Their participation in this project tells us that peace history has earned a global recognition in academia that not so long ago was unimaginable. Their essays build upon prior scholarship, but they also introduce new research and new interpretations. As a whole, *A Cultural History of Peace* highlights our humanity, something that has been for too long overshadowed in history by the inhumanity of war and other forms of violent conflict. Pursuing answers to new and seldom asked questions, these collected essays expand our knowledge of when, how, and why people in the past pursued peace within their own societies and peaceable relations with people from other societies.

The South African novelist Nadine Gordimer wisely observes, "The past is valid only in relation to whether the present recognises it" (2007: 7). In other words, what happened in the past is not necessarily history. History is made when scholars produce meaningful answers to the questions they ask about the past. The past cannot change, but history can and does change when scholars ask new questions, and when they use previously undiscovered or ignored evidence to develop new interpretations of the past. Evidence of what people said or did, or said they did, are basic materials out of which scholars shape answers to questions like "Does peace have a history?" Of course, to answer this particular question about the past, we must have in mind some definition of peace. Like most people, we probably immediately think of peace as *not war*, a classic definition that describes peace in negative terms, as an absence of the type of violent conflicts that still loom so large over popular histories and stories about the past. The American psychologist and peace activist William James succinctly summed up this common way of framing of the past, simply stating, "History is a bath of blood" (1910: 1).

James' description of history still plays well in a world that during the last century experienced the massive casualties and devastation of two world wars, genocides, and numerous civil wars, as well the fears created by transnational terrorism and still-threatening nuclear arsenals. Significantly, a bath of blood framing of history continues to shape the priorities of most mainstream reporting of the news from around the world—"if it bleeds it leads"—when, in fact, most people today live in zones of peace where their lives are not threatened by violent political conflict. A human being's chances of dying in war have been historically low in this century, in striking contrast to the peaks of worldwide violence reached during the global conflicts of the twentieth century (https://ourworldindata.org/war-and-peace). Yet, so accustomed are we with framing history *and* the present as a bath of blood, most of us have difficulty comprehending these facts. Steven Pinker recently noted this problem in the preface to *The Better Angels of Our Nature: Why Violence Has Declined,* saying "Believe it or not—and I know that most people do not—violence has declined over long stretches of time, and today we might be living in the most peaceable era in our species' existence" (2011: xvi). It is not just a coincidence that the rapid growth and globalization of peace studies has happened since the end of the Cold War. Undoubtedly, some of questions raised in *A Cultural History of Peace* have been influenced by the extraordinary recent decline of interstate warfare and resolution of many longstanding civil wars.

A Cultural History of Peace demonstrates that for several thousand years peace has been regarded as a highly desirable social condition, perhaps most especially when the violence and cruelty of war have been in the ascendency. Describing this collection of peace history essays as a cultural history—rather than social, political, diplomatic, or international history—is appropriate because, throughout history, peace has emerged from the cultures of groups, societies, and nations that developed practical ways to peaceably settle serious conflicts. Here I employ the broad environmental definition of culture that psychiatrist and classics scholar Jonathan Shay uses in his brilliant book, *Achilles in Vietnam*: "Our animal nature, our biological nature, is to live in relation to other people. The natural environment of humans is primarily culture, not the 'natural world' narrowly defined as other species, climate, etc." (1995: 207). Surely no human culture is ever truly homogeneous or free from conflicts that arise from serious differences between individuals and groups. Murder and warfare are the bloodiest ways that humans have dealt with those with whom they have serious differences. Bath of blood history foregrounds these activities when we peer into the past. Peace history does something very different. It reveals the long unfinished task of making human cultures peaceable environments that encourage the expression of our most humane instincts: respect for all others who are human like us, and sympathy for those humans who are fearful and/or suffering.

In a remarkable book, *Humanity: A Moral History of the Twentieth Century,* philosopher Jonathan Glover describes respect and sympathy as "human responses" that although they are "widespread and deep-rooted" are often blocked. Frequently aggressive and cruel instincts find expression in warfare and encouragement in cultures that reserve the highest honors for warriors and their blood sacrifices. Yet, clearly, respect and sympathy have been absolutely necessary for the survival of our social species. Respect and sympathy are, in Glover's words, "the core of our humanity which contrasts with inhumanity." However, as Glover recognizes, "humanity is only partly an empirical claim. It remains also partly an aspiration" (1999: 24–5). *A Cultural History of Peace* presents strong evidence for the empirical claim, as well as the aspiration. It focuses on the many people in the past who worked to establish peace within their own societies and peace with other societies by institutionalizing respect and sympathy; people who are unlikely to be highlighted as heroes in bath of blood histories.

GENERAL EDITOR'S PREFACE

As General Editor of this title in the Bloomsbury Publishers' cultural history series, I have had to follow two major guidelines. The first one required six volumes of essays that follow the same chronological order as other titles in the series. Accordingly, *A Cultural History Peace* is presented in volumes focused on Antiquity, the Medieval Age, the Renaissance, the Enlightenment, Age of Empire, and the Modern Era since 1920. This chronology order is Western-oriented and something of a barrier to producing a truly global history of peace. Nonetheless, some of the essays in the first five volumes of *A Cultural History of Peace*, and all the essays in Volume Six, present peace history in a global perspective. Indeed, those essays show that envisioning a more peaceful interconnected world and finding ways of realizing that vision is a crucial component of the complex of historical processes we today call "globalization."

Bloomsbury's other major guideline required the eight topical essays in each volume of *A Cultural History of Peace* to concentrate on identical themes in peace history. My first task as General Editor was developing the eight major themes for these collected essays. Developing the major themes was difficult particularly because I recognized that a kind of "translation" problem arises when applying modern ideas about peace to the study of peace history in earlier eras when those ideas, or at least modern formulations of them, were absent. I only started doing peace history in 1998 after two decades of teaching and writing concentrated almost exclusively on American history. Not surprisingly, I remained focused on the modern era when preparing my first peace history courses and new research projects. That focus on the modern era was reinforced by what I learned in a peace research seminar at the University of Oslo in the summer of 2007. Thus, I knew that my initial selection of themes for this collection could be criticized as present-oriented. Many hours of discussion with my colleagues in Dartmouth's History Department convinced me that this "translation" problem was not insuperable and that, after significant revision, my original ideas would be viable focal points for *A Cultural History of Peace*.

These six volumes validate this conviction. Each one contains an introductory overview of the historical era written by its editor and eight thematic essays written by specialists. They develop the following themes: Definitions of Peace; Human Nature, Peace, and War; Peace, War, and Gender; Peace, Pacifism, and Religion; Representations of Peace; Peace Movements; Peace, Security, and Deterrence; and Peace as Integration. This structure facilitates long views of key subjects in peace history. Anyone interested, for instance, in putting together a chronologically ordered history of how peace has been defined from antiquity to the modern era can achieve this goal by reading, in order, each of the first chapters in the six volumes of *A Cultural History of Peace*. When they do so, they will discover the distinction between "negative" and "positive" definitions of peace that are commonly used in peace research today is useful when formulating questions about pre-modern definitions of peace. They will also see that the modern distinction between negative peace and positive peace is a simple model that may hinder understanding the variety and richness of what people since antiquity actually meant when they spoke and wrote about peace.

How people in different times and places have understood what we usually call "human nature" has deeply influenced what they said and did about making peace and war. Human nature is, of course, a tricky term. Does it even exist? If it does, is it an endowment of fixed characteristics, or malleable and evolving? And if by human nature, we mean "instinctual," does this mean "inevitable," or are instincts better understood as potential behaviors that have been repressed or expressed depending on environmental influences produced by particular cultures at particular times in the past. The essays in this collection that develop the theme "Human Nature, Peace, and War" make clear that prevailing beliefs about human nature, whether faith-based or secular, have always played an essential role in how people understand what kinds of peace are possible in their imperfect material world.

Peace and war are among the most clearly gendered historical categories, as Chapters Three in *A Cultural History of Peace* make abundantly clear. It has been common all over the world for women to be regarded as "life-givers" and men as "life takers." Of course there are deviations from this global historical pattern. The Truong sisters of Vietnam and Joan of Arc are among the most famous transgressors of the male monopoly of military power. However, women like them have been exceptional. More commonly, women have provided material and psychological support to male warriors. And, perhaps most significantly, some of them have been peace thinkers and peacemakers. Indeed, the widespread idea that peace is feminine has been a source of political legitimacy for women, not just a barrier to achieving political power.

Although pacifism in Western democracies is now usually understood as a principled and often religiously inspired refusal to engage in violence, in other historical settings people who could justify certain violent actions and some wars were still considered "pacifists" whenever they opposed militarism or an ongoing war. On such occasions the deeply subversive cultural implications of nonviolence—its resistance to the idea that history must be written in blood—have been manifest. The essays herein that develop the theme "Peace, Pacifism, and Religion" enable readers to better understand the ambiguous role of religious faith in peace history. They describe religious traditions that link faith and peace, but also ancient and enduring traditions that link religion to the promotion of war.

Since antiquity countless artists, sculptors, composers, poets, playwrights, and writers have produced representations that reflected, but also shaped, understandings of peace in their cultures. Ancient symbols of peace like the olive branch and the dove that were incorporated into religious iconography have never lost their currency, even when used by secular peace activists. Many other representations of peace created during the last two millennia have also survived. Chapter Five in this collection presents a long history of these representations of peace. These have often been of peace imagined because their creators could not find real peace in contemporary political cultures. The accumulated representations of peace now form a vast and priceless cultural reservoir, much of it easily accessed via the Internet. Currently, new representations of peace are being produced and deposited in this cultural reservoir every day, while old ones are revived and reconfigured by peace activists around the world.

Peace and anti-war movements have always produced and deployed representations of peace, but they have not been a constant presence in the past. Chapter Six of *A Cultural History of Peace* describes collective efforts to prevent wars, or to stop them from continuing, as well as organized opposition to militarism. Throughout history peace movements have been condemned as subversive, especially when they resisted ongoing wars authorized by political authorities. Even when they have failed to achieve peace, as they have frequently done in the past, peace movements extended the contemporary cultural bases for challenging militarism and the glorification of warfare. Peace movements have, over the long run, produced traditions of anti-militarist thinking that in this century are mobilized by peace activists whenever interstate warfare threatens global peace.

Today most global peace activists regard the achievement of security via the threat of force as itself a problem, partly because this kind of negative peace has so frequently broken down in the past. The six essays in this collection that explore the theme "Peace, Security, and Deterrence" nonetheless demonstrate the strong and enduring appeal of this approach to peace. Although the perception problem modern political scientists call "the security dilemma" has been recognized since antiquity, the political practicality and immediately recognizable results of deterrence have almost always prevailed in the face of building threats made by military rivals. Enshrined in the modern era as a form of political realism, deterrence policy shaped the nuclear arms that saw rival superpowers each deploy tens of thousands of nuclear weapons that, if used, would have certainly destroyed civilization. Yet today, most national governments still equate peace with security and produce deterrence policies that create military alliances and threaten adversaries with war.

The last chapters of each volume of *A Cultural History of Peace* address a theme that many people mistakenly identify as a modern phenomenon: peace through integration, as if it must be something resembling the European Union. These chapters show that the social order imposed by expanding empires, kingdoms, and nation states has long been proclaimed as a form of peace, even when peace was not the reason for the warfare that preceded it. Moreover, its principal beneficiaries have often identified their empires as an expanding civilization, most famously Pax Romana and more recently Pax Americana. Yet, since the medieval age, another kind of peace achieved by nonviolent agreements built upon shared characteristics of identity has been imagined, and occasionally implemented.

Christianity's claim to be a universal church that could bring all people together in a brotherhood of Christ opened the door for identifying "humanity," a word first used during the Renaissance. Then science, especially eighteenth-century taxonomy, provided a secular path to a similar end: the recognition that all humans are, in very important ways, a single unique species of life. In the modern era, threats to the continued existence of this humanity in the form of global catastrophes such as nuclear warfare and climate change have contributed to an unprecedented "species consciousness" and the claim that all humans have rights that must be respected. Unprecedented communications technologies that today allow us to see and hear people from all over the world in real time have facilitated the expansion of global peace and human rights networks. Although during the five years that *A Cultural History of Peace* has been in the making, politics that divide people into hostile groups have gathered strength in many countries, the long history presented in this collection suggests the cultural foundations for peace, so long in the making, will weather the present storm, and humanity will continue to make itself a global reality.

ABBREVIATIONS

MGH: *Monumenta Germaniae Historica*, Hanover: Hahn, since 1826, multiple volumes in several subseries.

PL: *Patrologiae Cursus Completus, Series Latina*, ed. Jacques-Paul Migne, Paris: Migne, 1844–1864, 222 vols.

INTRODUCTION

Was there Peace in the Middle Ages?

WALTER SIMONS

In the latter half of the thirteenth century, the following tale about St Francis (d. 1226) began to circulate. When Francis was visiting the city of Gubbio in Umbria, people told him of a ferocious wolf who terrorized the countryside and had killed many victims, both animal and human. The citizens of Gubbio were so afraid of the wolf that nobody dared to venture outside the walls except armed "as if going to battle." Francis resolved to help them. Ignoring the entreaties of the people convinced that the wolf would kill him, and protected only by God's aid, Francis went out to meet the wolf. As he approached the animal, he explained that he came to make peace between the wolf and the people of Gubbio, his mortal enemy. If the wolf were to accept that peace, Francis said, the citizens would feed him daily for as long as he lived, and he would never be hungry again—and was it not hunger that made him commit so much evil? In return, the wolf must promise to never again attack a human or animal. The wolf agreed. He followed Francis back into the town, where everyone gathered in the central square heard the conditions of the pact. Both parties confirmed their commitment to peace: "with one voice," the townspeople swore to feed the wolf while the wolf raised his paw and put it in Francis's hand to signal that he would observe his part of the agreement. After the pact was concluded, the wolf came to live in Gubbio, where he went door-to-door while residents provided all his needs. He never hurt anyone, and when "brother wolf" died of old age two years later, the citizens of Gubbio were saddened (*Francis of Assisi* 2001, 3: 482–85, 601–4; Cobianchi 2009; Jansen 2018: 31–34).[1]

The story fits into a well-known tradition, celebrated throughout the Middle Ages, of holy men and women fulfilling social needs through extraordinary deeds. Since the days of Irish monks spreading the faith in the British Isles, those miracle workers supposedly vanquished the dangers of the natural world, always associated with paganism, to demonstrate the superiority of the Christian God. But the story of St Francis and the wolf of Gubbio differs from the genre in important ways. Francis meets with the wolf not so much to subdue nature in the name of God and humanity as to establish peace among all of God's creatures: his mission is one of harmony and inclusion, bridging all social gaps, including those between humans and animals—a goal illustrated famously by the many stories and art works that depict him preaching to birds and other animals (Vauchez 2012). Chapter Six in this volume explains how his disciples, the "friars minor" or Franciscans, followed in his footsteps as a peacemaker to settle disputes in contentious cities or as propagators of peace movements, along with other religious figures. The story of the wolf of Gubbio actually reflects quite closely various aspects of such peace efforts: the crucial role of mediators, often men or women imagined as liminal (i.e., outsiders because of their special way of life and reputation); the recognition of harm done and needs unfulfilled as causes for strife, and conversely, the association of peace with balance,

FIGURE 0.1: St Francis arranging peace between a wolf and the citizens of Gubbio, from the Altarpiece of Sansepolcro, 1437–44, by Sassetta (Stefano di Giovanni di Consolo), c. 1400–50. London, National Gallery. Photo by DeAgostini/Courtesy of Getty Images. Credit: DEA/G. NIMATALLAH/Contributor.

justice, and moral righteousness; the foundation of peace on social consensus and compromise; and finally, the swearing of oaths in public to establish lasting pacts that feature in Chapters One, Three, Five, Seven, and Eight of this volume. Late medieval depictions of the tale sometimes even added details drawn from real-life peace practices, as in the Sansepolcro Altarpiece by Sassetta, which shows a notary recording the proceedings on the central town square—an essential element of Italian civic pacts of the thirteenth through sixteenth centuries.

Readers unfamiliar with medieval history may be surprised to learn of such peace processes, or that peacemaking was a valued social good in this age. After all, the prevailing view of the Middle Ages is dominated by images of war and pestilence, harsh punishment and brutal oppression, where might is right and human life holds little value. Those stereotypes are kept alive by modern fiction and non-fiction alike, from *Game of Thrones* to popularizing works of psychology and neuroscience, which, unhindered by actual historical research, seem to dismiss medieval people as hopelessly cruel (Pinker 2011). They remain powerful by the persistence of outdated narratives that posit the modern, national state (which largely postdates the Middle Ages) as the sole vehicle of human progress—a view that even professional historians find difficult to shake and which still dominates the teaching of history in secondary education across the globe. Before we learn more about the concepts of peace and actual peace practices in the medieval age that are analyzed in the following chapters, it thus may be helpful to briefly sketch a history of that long and poorly understood period.

A VERY BRIEF HISTORY OF THE MEDIEVAL AGE

However one wishes to define the Middle Ages, one usually starts with the recognition of important changes that occurred in the world of classical antiquity between the fifth and eighth centuries AD. Where imperial Rome used to rule, that is to say from the Iberian peninsula to Mesopotamia, and from the coast of North Africa to northern England, there now existed a variety of political units of unequal power. In the southeast, a "Byzantine" empire centered on ancient Byzantium (or Constantinople = modern Istanbul) maintained Roman law and institutions more or less uninterrupted until the end of the Middle Ages, albeit in an area that shrank considerably over the centuries. This old empire was pressured increasingly by the sprawling new territories of Arab Muslims who expanded their reach from Mecca and Medina in the Arabian peninsula to Persia and westwards across north Africa into Spain. Most of Europe was dominated by Germanic and Slavic peoples, originally migrant, who settled in smallish units, which we sometimes call kingdoms, but which might be understood better as zones of influence exerted by clans and their chieftains. In the late eighth century, one of those peoples, the Franks, under the leadership of Charles the Great (Charlemagne), crowned as emperor in 800, established a new "Roman" empire which covered a large part of continental western Europe. Although this "Carolingian empire" (named after Charles's lineage, the Carolingians) in no way matched the governmental capacities of its ancient Roman model and partly disintegrated after 843, it did revive, however briefly, important elements of classical statehood, such as the concept of the ruler as legislator, centralizing ambitions, and imperial sponsorship of education and the arts. Of the three "civilizations" one could perceive in Europe around the Mediterranean in the year 800—of "western" Christendom (the Carolingian Empire and the British Isles), "eastern" Christendom (the Byzantine empire and Slavic lands under its religious influence), and the Muslim world—western Europe was by far the poorest and least developed, held back by a subsistence-level economy, absence of trade and industry, and very low levels of literacy. Those challenges were aggravated in the ninth and tenth centuries by invasions of Northmen (Vikings) and Magyars, which further fragmented public authority.

An important turning point arrived around the year 1,000 AD, when—probably under the influence of a warming climate and certainly with the help of technological innovation—agrarian production began to expand, long-distance trade and urban life rebounded, and the European population started to grow after centuries of decline or stagnation. A reorganization of political and jurisdictional authority in western Europe by an aristocratic and military elite linked by ties of vassalage (in what we used to call "the feudal system") brought a degree of stability at the local and regional level. New material gains poured into improved systems of education, raising levels of literacy significantly, especially in cities, where substantial numbers of children—boys and girls alike—received primary instruction. Also, for the first time in European history, an international body of (male) students attended universities, where they became acquainted with classical works of philosophy and politics. By around 1200, noble families who had secured claims to kingship also benefited from expanded resources that enabled them to extend authority over large areas and to lay the foundation of early modern nation states, first in England and France (to a lesser extent in Germany, central Europe, and Spain), led by the crown, assisted, in turn, by a professional administration of royal officials trained in Roman law and Aristotelian political philosophy, who were dispatched to represent public authority in the provinces. In Italy and the Low Countries, the most urbanized parts of Europe, cities gained and retained considerable autonomy until the end of the medieval period. This story of economic expansion and growing political maturity was interrupted, but not ended, by a series of crises (economic, social, demographic, political, and ecclesiastical) from around 1275 until around 1450, a period marked by epidemics and war, from which the Italian city states appear to have recovered first, giving rise to their artistic and intellectual "Renaissance". European expansion into the Americas, Africa, and Asia around 1500, and the advent of the Reformation around 1520 further transformed the medieval world into an early modern one.

PUBLIC AUTHORITY, PEACE, AND VIOLENCE

All of the above should indicate that a vast gap, in terms of economic, social, intellectual, and material development, separated people living at the beginning of the medieval era from those living at the end of it. However, change across this long period did not follow neat, linear patterns, and historians sometimes disagree about causes and effects of several developments sketched above. One particularly knotty problem concerns the history of the "state" and "public authority" in the Middle Ages, and since it directly impinges on questions of war and peace, we need to address it in some detail.

Modern readers should be aware that for much of the medieval period, the "state" did not play the role it normally fulfills in the twenty-first century. Indeed, the demise of the Roman state in the fifth century and the relative weakness of state authority after its temporary revival in the West under the Carolingians has contributed much to the perception of the Middle Ages as a time of anarchic violence. According to the traditional view, prominent since the nineteenth century but rooted in the rhetoric developed by late medieval monarchies, private warfare was not curtailed until the rise of centralized kingship in the late twelfth century. In monopolizing violence and the administration of justice at the expense of feudal lords, the medieval crown thus planted the roots of the modern state (Strayer 1970).

Current scholarship, however, significantly complicates this picture. Much of the debate has concentrated on the so-called "feudal revolution" around the year 1,000, which since Georges Duby's influential work on social order in central France (1953) assigned a prime importance to new forms of local lordship established by aggressive "castellans" (holders of castles and the land around it), who appropriated juridical powers, thereby erasing what was left of Carolingian governmental structures (Bisson 1994, 2009). After more than sixty years of fine-tuning by two generations of medievalists, the model is now generally found to be in need of thorough revision or even repeal: some historians have moved the decisive transition backward to the era around the year 900 or forward into the twelfth century; others, questioning the model's methodological premises, cast doubt on the relevance of a "feudal revolution" over the longer term. Informed in part by anthropological usage, historians working in this vein emphasize remarkable continuities in the settlement of disputes in western Europe from the Carolingian into the post-Carolingian era and onward into the twelfth century. Rather than being generated by any breakdown of public authority, feuds and reconciliation during the tenth through twelfth centuries then appear as conventional mechanisms to preserve social order; sustained upticks in violence or perceived large-scale transformations may largely reflect a changing source base (Gluckman 1955; Barthélemy 1999, 2004, 2009; West 2013; White 2016; Moore 2016).

As Charles West (2013: 258–9) has observed, this line of argument carries the risk of exchanging one dogmatic framework (the state is the only guarantor of order), for another one (social relations are always regulated by conflict) just as reductive. The "feudal revolution" – model and the revisionism it engendered were also excessively Francocentric: conditions in Germany and Italy, not to mention the rest of Europe, were different (Wickham 2016: 78–9, 99–120). If the future course of these discussions thus remains uncertain, they at least have yielded remarkable results for the study of peace and peace processes, for they encouraged extensive research into conflict resolution at various levels of society and the multiple agents involved in the peacemaking process: bishops and monks, "holy men and women," "popular opinion," and, starting around 1100 but more powerfully after 1200, urban communities.

We are now also looking with new eyes, more alert to hidden continuities, at state formation by feudal monarchies from the twelfth century onward. Rulers who extended governing authority in burgeoning nation states often usurped or coopted instruments of peacemaking that were developed before and independently from them, by cities, the populace, the clergy. Greater security was not simply the crown's work but relied on broader societal changes: the birth of a profit economy and the expanded tax base; increased literacy and systematic record keeping; the impact of Roman law and Aristotelian concepts of the common good studied at universities. Those developments explain why state formation successfully overcame the "crisis" of the late Middle Ages in many parts of Europe. True, the rising costs of warfare drained the monarchy's resources (or rather: *everyone's* resources) for a good part of the fourteenth and early fifteenth centuries, but somehow their administrations carried on to emerge stronger and better equipped than ever. In the midst of the political crisis, new political institutions such as parliaments became quasi-permanent instruments of government in several areas of Europe, providing a forum for crown and subject to discuss fiscal and other issues of common concern, including the preservation of peace (Blockmans 1998). Even though participants in these deliberations formed a relatively small elite, the growing role of parliaments extended the political arena to a size not seen in previous centuries. Chris Wickham has recently argued that, more generally, the late medieval body politic relied on a greater number of political actors than before and benefited from a deeper engagement by these partners, fostering wider debate about the theory and practice of government (Wickham 2016: 235–51).

Since the pioneering work of the sociologist Norbert Elias (1897–1990) it is also a historical commonplace that monopoly of force by the state resulted in increased self-control of individuals, including control of violent impulses (Elias [1939] 2000), which took centuries of conditioning to achieve. This belief fits well with the common preconception of medieval people as "childlike" in their emotional presentation, prone to aggression at the slightest provocation. Given the relative weakness of state authority in the Middle Ages, one would then expect high levels of daily violence, and this is indeed the impression left by most histories of violence in the premodern age. A survey of cultural history in the preindustrial period, based on Elias's theories and written by his disciple, Pieter Spierenburg, in 1992, took it for granted that medieval people lived in constant "existential insecurity" and were thus hyper-aggressive: "medieval society was without doubt much more violent than ours," Spierenburg maintained (1992: 194). Writing more recently, in 2006, the French historian of early modern Europe, Robert Muchembled, less directly inspired by Elias but implicitly adopting his assumptions, came to the same conclusion: "Everybody was violent at the end of the Middle Ages and in early modern Europe" (Muchembled [2006] 2008: 21). Numerous other examples could be cited: the historical judgment of these generalists appears unanimous, and statistics on violent crime presented in those surveys do seem to indicate a continuously high level until the twentieth century.

Few of those statistics, however, date from the Middle Ages. Specialists of crime in the medieval period, well aware of the fact that reliable statistics are few and far between, tend to be more circumspect in drawing broad conclusions. Medieval crime rates have been called "high," but we might ask: "high, compared to what?" As Warren C. Brown points out, homicide rates in thirteenth-century Bristol, England, seem higher than those in the European community today, but they are below the U.S. average (2011: 4–5). Is the United States, then, an example of a "failed state"? (Opinions differ.) It is also not true that medieval people were "used" to violence and universally condoned it. Although examples of violent behavior that are abhorrent to the modern observer are not hard to find, specialists of the medieval period emphasize that only certain codified and ritualized modes of violence were deemed legitimate, at best. As for overall levels of violence, it may be wise to remind the reader that the Middle Ages form a very long period, of seven to ten centuries (depending on one's starting point) and that periods of crisis with a high incidence of violence may have alternated with others that saw lower levels (Linklater 2016: 148; see also Dean 2001). Medievalists question—even more than did Elias himself—to what extent the "civilizing process" followed a universal and linear pattern; on the whole they find his model of growing self-restraint and its relationship to violence difficult to apply to the medieval period.[2]

The role of the medieval state in securing internal peace, or its failing to do so, raises another issue, too often overlooked. When examining levels of violence in medieval society, we simply cannot ignore the forms of institutionalized, state-sponsored violence that became more prevalent in the later period and are characteristic of the early modern and modern state. Historians working in the wake of R.I. Moore's influential *The Formation of a Persecuting Society* ([1987] 2007) call attention to the state as an agent of violence rather than of peace, for instance through the systemic persecution of religious and other minorities from about 1200 onward. Moore's analysis of this dark underside of the "twelfth-century renaissance"—the development of a machinery of state control, riding the tide of economic expansion to suppress perceived threats—could therefore be seen not (or not only) as a decisive step toward greater internal stability but rather as the beginning of a long history of European state-aggression against its own subjects and the subjugation of colonial populations within its reach (Moore 2007: 144–96).

A similar argument could be made regarding the scale of war in the Middle Ages compared to later centuries. As is well known, medieval armies were small, battles were relatively brief affairs, and fighting normally did not involve the civilian population (although important exceptions existed). The transformation of warfare under the New Monarchies of the late fifteenth and sixteenth centuries (widespread use of artillery, professionalization and massive expansion of royal armies) made war far more destructive in the early modern age; that devastation, in turn, pales in comparison to the havoc wreaked by total warfare in the industrial age (Parker 2008).

All of this is not to claim that the Middle Ages were a period of peace and happiness preceding modern carnage, but rather to posit that comparisons between the two periods result in a balance sheet of wins and losses; projecting onto the medieval age all kinds of barbarisms that are, at least in part, invented, while ignoring very real horrors on "our side" of the divide, does not serve the historical enterprise.

THE MAIN THEMES: RELIGIOUS BELIEF, WAR, HONOR, AND GENDER, COLLECTIVE ACTION

Translating the eight themes selected for the *Cultural History of Peace* series to the medieval period naturally involved a change of perspective. In a world without modern technology, international institutions, truly global political and economic empires, or, as we have seen, nation states comparable to those of today, several questions of war and peace necessarily take on a different meaning. The contributors to this volume have used the general framework of the series to investigate concepts of peace that made sense to medieval people and were employed in practices of peace they cherished for many centuries. Together, the essays may be gathered under three main themes that I want to briefly introduce and situate in their context.

It will surprise no one that religious belief and practice form a major subject in studies of peace in the Middle Ages. They are the focus of Chapters Two and Four which, in different ways, discuss the three major religious systems of the period (Christianity, Islam, and Judaism), but religion can be said to permeate all of the essays. The reason is obvious: in this age, virtually everybody was religious in the sense that they believed in an afterlife and regarded questions of salvation as paramount. Although the precise incidence of unbelief is uncertain, historians agree that the numbers are relatively small (Hamilton 2003: 118–26; Arnold 2005). Few doubted the existence of a divine entity who judged over good and evil and intervened on earth. Whether revealed truth trumped human experience at all times and at all costs was a different matter about which opinions might diverge, but scripture and theology informed decisions on war and peace to one degree or another throughout the period. This is not only because faith was strong or pervasive, but also because religious thought infiltrated all other areas of life to the extent that the spiritual and material world became inseparable. Accordingly, in both Islam and Christianity (Judaism hardly knew this problem), secular and religious powers competed on multiple terrains, including in matters of both "church" (religion) and "state" (politics). The contest between the two formed the background of prolonged political disputes in Western Christianity. The basis for this struggle was laid in Late Antiquity, when Christian emperors of Rome intervened in decisions of the Church, while St Augustine (354–430) theorized that secular authority derived its justification from divine sanction; it received a new impetus when Pope Leo III crowned Charlemagne as "emperor of the Romans" in 800, as we have seen, sealing an older alliance between the papacy and the Carolingians but giving rise to centuries of conflict between pope and emperor; and it continued into the late Middle Ages and early modern period, when kings found themselves, in practice if not always in theory, as heads of national Christian churches. Western Europe never became a theocracy, but religious authority affected secular action at all levels of society throughout the period.

A strong faith did not always imply close adherence to the Church's wishes—assuming it was clear at all times what those wishes might be. Beyond the basic doctrinal principles (the fourth-century Nicene creed offered a summary of beliefs to which each Christian should subscribe; see Hamilton 2003: 15–32), there was often room for disagreement within the same faith, even among the laity and the relatively uneducated. The idea that ordinary people blindly followed Church officials into war is a modern misconception, while secular rulers probably rejected requests from religious leaders as often as they

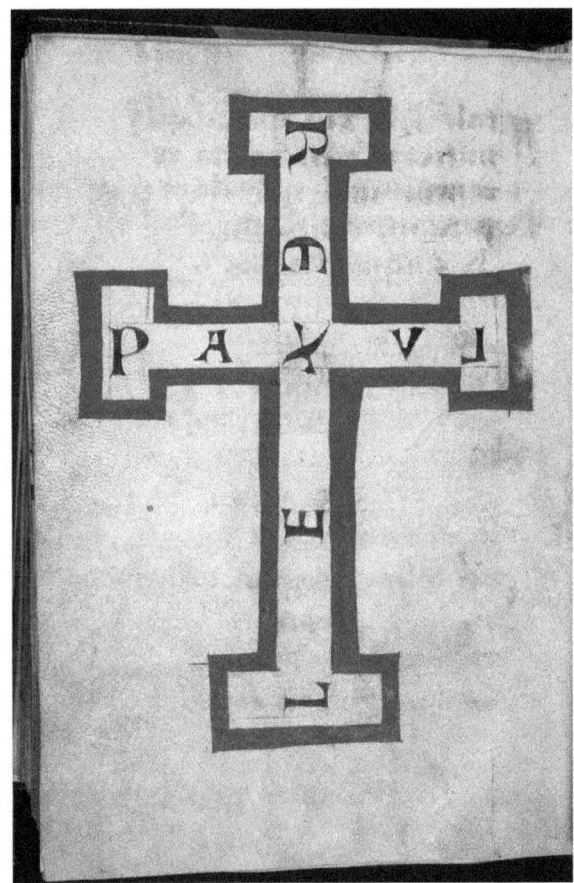

FIGURE 0.2: The cross in this twelfth-century manuscript from Moissac, France, bears two intersecting inscriptions in Latin (partly in mirror-script), formed by two monosyllable epithets commonly applied to Christ, with the letter x as the nexus: *Pax-Lux/Rex-Lex*, or "Peace-Light/King-Law." The phrases, probably of Carolingian (ninth-century) origin, enhanced the protective powers of the cross but also reminded Christians that their religion should be one of peace, following Eph. 2:24 and Jn 14:27. London, British Library, MS. Harley 2893, fol. 268v. Public domain image available from the British Library: http://www.bl.uk/catalogues/illuminatedmanuscripts/ILLUMINBig.ASP?size=big&IllID=37469

accepted them. Besides, clerics are known to have mobilized (on occasion) religious sentiment against war and for peace rather than the other way around, as did, for instance, Guibert of Gembloux (c. 1124–1214), a monk in Brabant (in the southern Low Countries) who, in a letter to the archbishop of Cologne in Germany, argued that given their role as spiritual shepherds, clerics should always favor peace among Christians rather than war for feudal or political reasons (Cottiaux 1995).

Indeed, as several essays in this volume demonstrate, medieval concepts of peace often drew on religious authority, whether Jewish, Christian, or Muslim. As we will also see (Chapters Two and Four), few reservations were raised when it came to violence against non-believers (Jewish attitudes on this matter differed from those of most Christians and Muslims), and crusades unquestionably were waged, legitimized, and even celebrated on religious grounds (Mastnak 2002; Gaposchkin 2017). However, it would be simplistic to think they were waged *solely* on religious grounds. Not all religious warfare was universally condoned, and there is some evidence of inter-faith tolerance. Cary Nederman and his collaborators, in particular, have challenged in numerous publications the notion that religious tolerance is distinctively modern, tracing important principles of it to medieval thought (Nederman 2000, 2013). When we look at relations between Christians and Muslims "on the ground," we find that, for centuries, Christians made up the majority of the population in various Muslim-controlled areas, and that even in the much-contested lands of twelfth-century Syria and Palestine, dominant Christians exercised what Christopher MacEvitt (2008) called "rough tolerance" over religious minorities.

Weighing the impact of religious attitudes on war and peace in this "age of faith" is made even more complex when we consider change over time. While passion for religious war waned among both Christians and Muslims later in the period, the treatment of Jews in Christian lands followed the opposite trajectory. Distributed widely (albeit thinly) throughout Christendom in the early Middle Ages, Jewish communities were subjected to violent attacks at the start of the Crusades around 1100 and eventually expelled from England, France, and the rest of Western Europe (with the exception of Italy and parts of the German empire) in the later Middle Ages. As mentioned above, religious deviance among Christians was also punished more severely and more systematically in the West after 1200. In a few cases, persecution of such Christian "heretics" led to armed campaigns as, for instance, in the "Albigensian Crusade" against "Cathars" in southern France, from 1209 to 1229, or in the campaigns against the Hussites of Bohemia in the fifteenth century (Bull 2009; Limor 2009; Moore 2007; Nirenberg 1996, 2009). Surely, that trend continued into the early modern age, and it might be argued that, among Christians, religious conflict triggered outright war more often in the sixteenth and seventeenth centuries than in the Middle Ages.

Several essays in this volume highlight another prominent feature of medieval society, the cultivation of martial prowess, rooted primarily in Germanic warrior codes but celebrated in ancient Mediterranean and Middle-Eastern customs as well. The thirst to prove oneself in battle remained strong throughout the period among the noble aristocracy, whose self-identity evolved around war: to be a nobleman was above all to be a fighter on horseback. The aristocracy was therefore usually "the party of war" in medieval political debates, with merchants and craftsmen of urban communities as well as farmers more readily opposing war: in the view of the latter groups, fear of war's economic consequences usually outweighed all other considerations. Legal customs and practices reflected the social divide. It was long the prerogative of a nobleman accused of a major crime to prove his innocence by challenging the accuser to a duel, but cities of northern Europe, which had few noble residents, banned the judicial duel in favor of rational forms of evidence as soon as they gained legal autonomy, in the twelfth century, well before higher authorities in Church and state attempted to curtail the duel (Van Caenegem 1954: 139–47).

Such recourse to physical violence was also closely tied to notions of male honor, of singular importance in medieval patriarchy (for gender roles in medieval society, see Bennett and Karras 2013; Karras 2003). A man slighted or threatened might respond violently and was often expected to do so if he wanted to maintain the honor of his person or that of his family—which amounted to the same thing in noble milieus. In such circumstances, non-aggression carried the risk of losing one's public reputation, which might lead to legal jeopardy and social degradation (Fenster and Smail 2003). Again, the threat was greatest for members of the aristocracy, who had the most honor to defend; men at the bottom of the social ladder possessed, in principle, little or no honor, although the need to uphold their very masculinity might push them to violent action. The extent to which male aggression, idealized above all by nobles, crossed over to other social groups is illustrated by the autobiography of Peter Abelard (1079–1142), the logician and theologian best known today for his relationship with a private student, the extraordinary Heloise (d. 1164). Born as the oldest son of noble family, Abelard was destined to follow in his father's footsteps as a knight; instead, he made an early decision to renounce his inheritance of the family estate and become a cleric and academic, or, as he put it, "I . . . withdrew from the court of Mars [war] to be educated in the lap of Minerva [the goddess of wisdom]. I preferred the weapons of dialectic [logic] to all the other teachings of philosophy, and armed with these I chose the conflicts of disputation instead of the trophies of war." The bellicose phrasing reappears in several other passages (in turn corroborated by many contemporary sources) that describe his debates with other logicians as quasi-violent confrontations for supremacy. When later in his memoir Abelard recalls the moment when Heloise's vengeful uncle hired two thugs to castrate him, exposing his affair and ending his teaching at Notre Dame of Paris, thoughts of shame and humiliation as a male dwarf all other feelings (*The Letters of Abelard and Heloise* 2003: 3 and 17–18).

The influence of the heroic warrior code, combined with the public concern for male honor, also explains why feuds were so common and had the potential to turn into private warfare or even civil war, even though those directly responsible for the fighting formed a small minority. Feuding was endemic among the landed aristocracy (two or three percent of the total population) and non-noble elites in cities (by the late Middle Ages those families often had merged with the landed aristocracy, especially in Italy) but those few families might engulf in their conflicts others in their employ as servants or otherwise dependent on them. If unchecked, those feuds posed a threat for several generations.

The response to this social plague in urban communities illustrates a crucial point of peacemaking in the Middle Ages: like waging war, making peace "worked" by mobilizing concern for (male) honor. In urban peace efforts, heads of families swore to maintain peace, thereby engaging their clans and partisans; any breach of the peace thus reflected poorly on the patriarch's authority over the clan, which was the very foundation of his honor. The same logic governed peacemaking in other cases as well. As Chapters One, Three, Seven, and Eight show, whether concluded at the highest level, between emperors and kings, or at the level of counts and barons, lords and cities, formal peace pacts were often sealed by personal oaths, which held real power in politics since public authority and honor were inseparable. The fact that divine retribution would punish oath-breakers further enhanced their significance.

If men waged war, did women work for peace? Chapter Three demonstrates how gender concepts, in principle, delineated well-defined tasks for the sexes. War was to be an almost exclusively male domain, though women (or a "woman's honor") might be invoked as a *casus belli*, like other objects of conquests. Yet, as with all other aspects of gender, masculine and feminine tasks should not be imagined as simple mirror images: women might serve as peacemakers both in fictional narratives and in real-life practice, but being a woman was not, by itself, a sufficient qualification to act in such matters, since femininity also evoked passivity and the realm of the private home rather than the public theater of peace. To function successfully as a mediator, a woman must have gained some form of prior authority, for instance as a charismatic religious leader, as did St Catherine of Siena (1347–80), who intervened at the highest levels of Church and state conflict in Italy (Muessig 2011), or, in the midst of actual war, the enigmatic beguine (lay "religious" woman) *Paupertas*, who mediated between French and Flemish camps in 1297–1302 (Field 2019). That said, exceptions to conventional gender roles can be found, as we read in the same Chapter Three (see also Kumhera 2017: 201–26). In any case, it is fair to say that the reality of gender in medieval Europe was diverse and evolved across the millennium. Whereas patriarchy severely restrained women of the upper classes everywhere, women of the middle and lower classes appear to have made some gains in cities of northern Europe during the central Middle Ages, particularly in cities, where they enjoyed considerable economic autonomy and more favorable inheritance systems; greater female agency in matters of war and peace was then not unheard of. Changing attitudes in cities also helps to explain why, if male honor remained important and might trigger violent action at all times, such action would not be met with quite the same understanding in German cities of the fifteenth century as it did among Germanic warriors of the seventh.

Finally, the essays in this volume underscore the importance of collective action and consensus, the main subject of Chapter Six and a leitmotif in many others. When medieval people reflected on "waging peace," they naturally sought the help of secular or religious leaders—anyone, really, with the power to stop war and violence. However, given the nature of conflict in this age, solutions might not always be sought at the top. Peace started at home, within the family, the clan, and the local community, and of course, within the self and one's relationship to God. Even in the midst of seemingly endless internecine warfare among the Franks in the sixth century, bishop Gregory of Tours reminded his readers that shedding the blood of kinsmen was always a crime, and that no one could receive God's grace who did not maintain the peace among his own people (2006: 20–21, 76). When eleventh-century town-dwellers banded together to rebel against feudal lords, they called their association a "peace": it was founded on the assumption that its members would observe peace amongst each other. There is no need to take the ideal at face value, it will be argued throughout this volume, nor should we ignore the violence which such "communes" inflicted upon those whom they regarded as outsiders. It is important nevertheless to be conscious of the institutions and practices those communities created to regulate and maintain peace, like the "peace-makers" known in many cities from the twelfth to fifteenth centuries and the procedures they deployed to resolve conflict in those same centuries (Van Caenegem 1954: 302–23; Rousseaux 2007; see also Chapters Five and Six).

Clearly, the historical evidence discussed in this volume does not lend itself to easy generalizations, and more work needs to be done. This is not surprising: the history of peace and peace practices is certainly thriving and yielding new insights rapidly, but it is a relatively young branch of the historical discipline still sharpening its tools to weigh what can be gathered from the sources. The essays collected in this volume formulate the "state of the question" in peace studies of the medieval age based on primary and secondary sources, collected and examined by specialists, some of whom may count themselves rightly as pioneers of the subfield. While the essays are organized around the eight themes selected for the collected essays of *A Cultural History of Peace*, and thus treat questions that will be familiar to readers of the other volumes, their main goal is to direct attention to concepts and practices of peace particular to the Middle Ages.

We started our overview with one such procedure, laid out in the story of St Francis and the wolf of Gubbio. Stripped from its miraculous traits, the reconciliation of the two warring parties depicted in the tale was surely replicated, in one form or another, throughout the Middle Ages, from the lowest village to the courts of kings and queens. Along with the essays in this volume, the tale may serve to remind modern readers, whether scholars or activists of peace today, that peace requires work, a willingness to take risks, and acceptance of the other—the former enemy.

CHAPTER ONE

Definitions of Peace

JEHANGIR YEZDI MALEGAM

In 833 at Soissons, the Frankish king and Roman emperor Louis the Pious performed a public penance at which he decried himself as the reason for the breakdown of all peace in his kingdom (on the penances of Louis, see recently De Jong 2009). Louis said that he had broken faith with his sons when he rescinded a sworn agreement on the division of his legacy. By breaking his oath, the king had effectively destroyed all fidelity so that every breakdown of law and order was singularly due to him.

As presented, Louis's confession conveys a notion of peace particular to his time, place, and political setting. The king as font and cornerstone of social order was in a powerful position, assuming the role of Christ, the cornerstone of concord. As peacemaker he not only made peace but also embodied it. Yet, as a man and prone to sin, the mandate of peacemaking also limited the king, and made him vulnerable to charges well beyond his own actions.

As Christ's ambiguous legacy to humanity, peace in the Christian tradition encompassed a range of demands, responsibilities, claims, and chastisements. These changed with political, social and even economic transformations so that we cannot speak of definitions of peace as static. Nonetheless, scripture and tradition *had* provided a finite vocabulary with which to describe and impose the demands of peace. What changed was who appropriated the language of peace and which templates of peacemaking they sought to emphasize.

The bulk of medieval writing on peace comes from a small group of authors, some priests and monks, others courtiers or scholars. Although they trained on many of the same religious sources, they came from a range of backgrounds and their discussions of peace do respond to the exigencies of the worlds in which they lived; for many, genuine peace demanded such responsiveness. We may also perceive in several darkened glasses discussions of peace contrary or even alien to our authors, highlighted by the confusion or disgust their combination of familiarity and difference aroused. Sometimes we learn the most from these misunderstandings of the peace of others.

Exploring definitions of peace between 800 and 1400 thus allows us to understand transformations in authority and obedience, in imaginings of self and other. These were changes in what it meant to be a person but also in the range of social actors gradually allowed to become persons. In this chapter I will trace over five centuries how, in the medieval Christian west, the heavy burden of peacemaker, once monopolized by a Carolingian king, devolved onto all European subjects.

CAROLINGIAN LEGACIES

In the era of Charlemagne and his successors, courtiers and scholars focused on peacemaking mainly as the attribute of the ruler. Through liturgy, capitularies, exegesis, and historiography, the king-emperor Charlemagne emerges as a pastiche of peacemaking imagery. Very little of this imagery was standardized and we should speak more of a set of ideas that revolved around the image of the king than any single message (Davis 2015: 293–94). At his imperial coronation in Rome in 800, the liturgy refers to Charlemagne as *rex pacificus* (peaceful/peacemaking king), while the accompanying *laudes regiae*, songs of popular acclaim, hail him as a new Solomon, whose very name means "peaceful."

In Carolingian royal discourse, peace is treated as a self-evident benefit rather than the mere absence of war ("negative peace"; for a complete treatment of the Carolingian kings as peacemakers, see Bonnaud-Delamare 1939 and Kershaw 2011: 132–234). The multi-chapter proclamation (capitulary) *Admonitio generalis* of 789 lays out a program of societal reform, with a substantial explanation of what peace should be in this society: love, piety, blessedness but also religious orthodoxy and uniformity of observance, all of which were essential to the divine sacraments (see Kershaw 2011: 141; *Admonitio* 2012: preamble, p. 180; c. 53, p. 206, c. 59, p. 208, and especially c. 61, p. 210–12). As Donald Bullough points out, while Charlemagne and his son Louis the Pious made arrangements of *pax et amicitia* with other Christian rulers, they used no such language for their engagement with pagans (Bullough 2003: 366). This does not mean that the Carolingians did not war against other Christians—we know they did—but rather that they understood *pax* as exclusively an arrangement among Christians. It could include fighting because the meaning of Christian *pax* was more expansive than abatement of individual conflicts.

Possessed internally of this peace, the king could sustain himself in war. The *rex pacificus* also had to engage in negative peace, fighting to abate conflict. His advisor Alcuin of York (who may have framed the *Admonitio*) opposes positive peace to a negative peace necessitated by Charlemagne's incessant wars (Kershaw 2011: 145–46). Like his father, Pepin, Charlemagne is presented as diplomatically pacific, which is to say warring only when pushed by more belligerent opponents: an early conflation of non-aggression with peace. In the *Vita Karoli*, written after the emperor's death, Einhard characterizes Charlemagne's regular opponents, the pagan Saxons, as haters of peace, embellishing the image of a king who would go to war only in defense of peace (Einhard 1911: 1.7).[1] Yet Carolingian writings complicate easy distinctions between positive and negative peace. Looking back from 890, the poet Saxo describes a possibly fictional peace pact that Charlemagne supposedly made in 803 with the Saxons at Salz. The treaty ended thirty-three years of fighting, but it also specified that the Saxons abandon their pagan worship, pay tithes to the Church and submit to their bishops, essentially an act of conversion (Poeta Saxo 1899: 138; Leyser 1979: 6).

As Charlemagne's kingdom faced strains in the years after his death, peace infiltrated new conversations. Like his father and grandfather, Charlemagne's son Louis designated successors while still alive, and divided the kingdom between them. However, during his lengthy reign, his mature sons rebelled and, with the exception of one son, they survived to rule their inheritance. Louis divided his kingdom several more times, prompting rebellion from his sons and—following a vicious circle—responding to rebellion with new divisions.

As if to forestall critique, the language of these divisions privileged peace. In 817, through an *ordinatio imperii*, Louis divided his kingdom on the strength of a state of peace achieved at that year's synod in Aachen. After performing a three-day fast intended to clarify his decisions and avoid rending the unity of the kingdom, Louis decided on the imperial coronation of his son Lothar and installed his other sons, Louis and Pepin, as lesser kings. The provisions for the division, which included regular meetings, were to ensure "perpetual peace" between the brothers, and by this means to secure the safety of the Church. Aided by divine grace, all subjects were enjoined to honor these terms to maintain "perpetual peace" amongst themselves and all Christian people (*Ordinatio* 1883: 271).

While the *ordinatio* borrows from similar provisions made by Louis's father when he divided his imperial legacy in 806, its preamble stands out. Louis's slippages between personal discipline, fraternal peace, the peace of subjects, the safety of the Church and divine grace foreshadow the terms of his self-censure at Soissons years later. This constellation of ideals associated with peace reappears in various political and theological discussions of the central and later Middle Ages. It is the closest we come to a medieval "definition" of peace (see also Renna 1979).

A culture of admonition and correction during Louis's reign produced a rich trove of writing on peace. In his *Via regia*, Smaragdus of St Mihiel counseled that peace was God's covenant with Israel reflected in the New Israel, the kingdom of the Franks. Agobard of Lyons equated the peace of the kingdom with the peace of Christ's body (Kershaw 2011: 177–80, 189–97). Humanity participated in this peace through the oaths that it made and kept: Agobard even supported rebellion against any king who broke his oath. In 831, Louis divided the Frankish inheritance again, this time between his sons Pepin, Louis and Charles—but omitting Lothar. Claiming to be showing faith by warning him of the danger that lurked, Agobard blamed Louis for causing discord, since he could have "led a tranquil and quiet life" had he wanted to (cf. 1 Tim 2:1–2). Even worse, Louis had besmirched the earlier oaths on which he had based the 817 divisions. Agobard feared that these empty oaths would cause widespread distrust through the kingdom (Agobard of Lyons 1981: 1, 2 and 4). In his general penance at Soissons, Louis echoed this explanation for discord, saying that he bore responsibility now for all disrupted sociopolitical bonds.

While Charlemagne's contemporaries had seen the reign of a peacemaker even in the midst of regular territorial wars, later writers exhibited greater pessimism. They turned to Augustine who had cautioned against confusing earthly peace with ideal peace. Alcuin of York had flirted with Augustinian ideas when arguing that wars made with pacific intentions were a form of peacemaking. However, it took an atmosphere of perceived threat and disruption, evocative of the backdrop to Augustine's own *City of God*, to make those ideas resonate.

The Annals of Saint-Bertin and the Annals of Fulda recount regular intrafamilial conflicts in the period after 840 in East and West Francia (Buc 2001: 55). Ruling West Francia, a kingdom surrounded by strong Christian enemies and the threat of pagan Viking assaults, Charlemagne's grandson Charles the Bald had to be content with only a modicum of peace. From Reims, threatened by Normans and rival Frankish kingdoms, Archbishop Hincmar warned against mirages of counterfeit peace. For Hincmar, peace meant protection of the Church and its privileges, even by the sword.[2]

To sustain this conflict-ridden search for a real and final peace the king must cultivate inner tranquility, closer to the Greek *eirene* than the Latin *pax* (Bullough 2003: 368). Lupus of Ferrières counseled the king to find peace in intimate daily moments, while assuring Charles that a greater kingdom of peace lay beyond his fraught earthly realm. Paul Kershaw argues that Sedulius Scottus was also writing for Charles the Bald when he "collapsed the distinction between the [peaceful] court and the inner life of the king" (Kershaw 2011: 227).

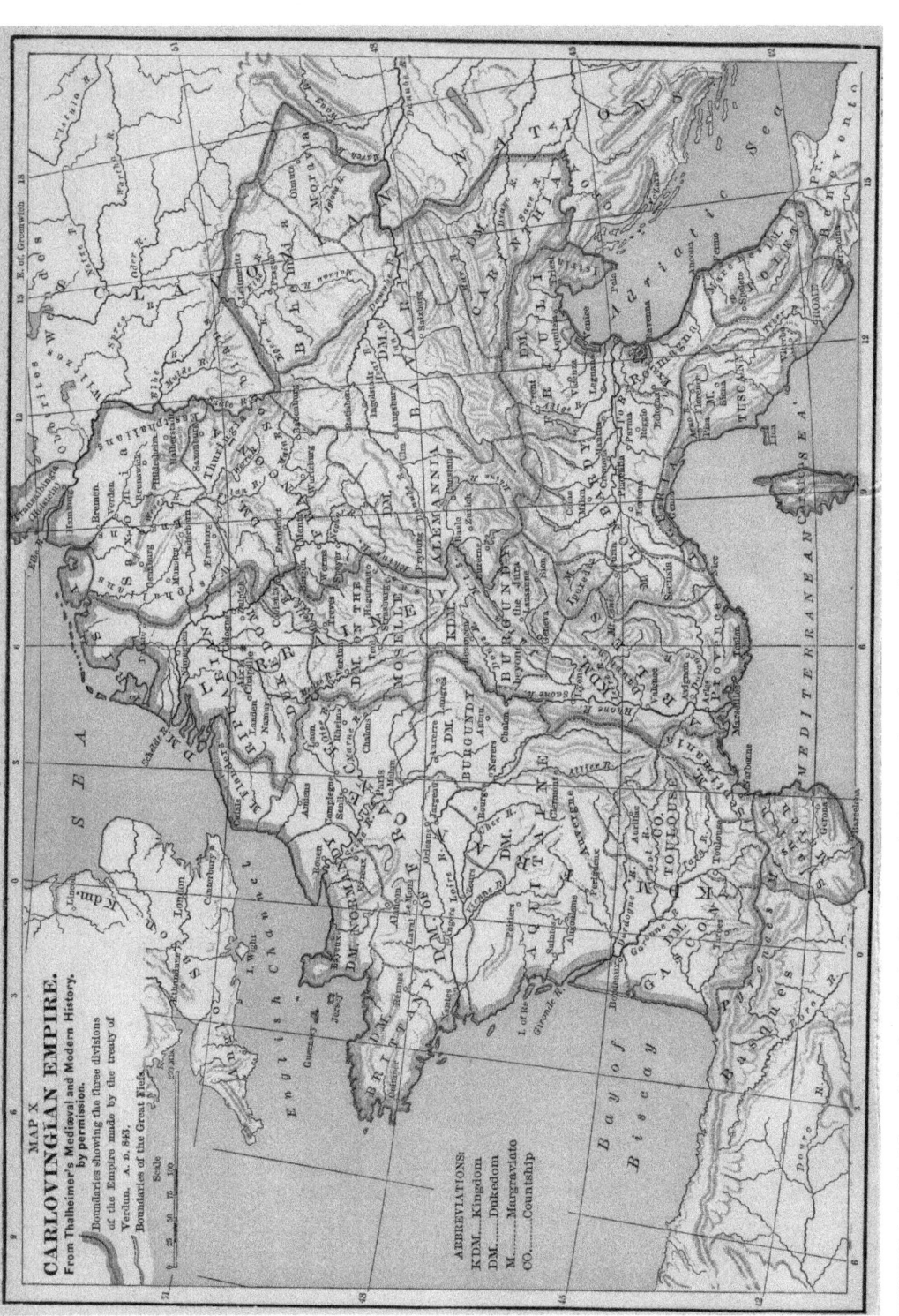

FIGURE 1.1: Division of the Carolingian Empire at the Treaty of Verdun, 843. Public Domain. Source: Wikimedia, https://commons.wikimedia.org/w/index.php?curid=1479391.

As the Carolingian kingdom divided into East and West Francia, friendship and oaths dominated the conversation around peace. After Louis's death, his three surviving sons, Lothar, Louis the German, and Charles the Bald held numerous meetings and created a series of agreements (*conventus* or *placita*) to secure *pax* and *amicitia*, terms that would be used interchangeably for friendship. By the Treaty of Verdun (843), Charles the Bald received Septimania, Neustria, and other parts of the west, Louis Austrasia and Bavaria in the east, and Lothar the Rhineland, Provence and northern Italy. Charles also made internal accords, notably the Treaty of Coulaines (843) for which lords of his kingdom came together "in a concord of peace (*pax*) and friendship (*amicitia*)." These were not contracts, but socio-political bonds: Charles's assent to an accord made him part of a peace collective, which the Carolingians called *convenientia* (Kosto 1998).

Accords of *amicitia* were easy to deride as mercenary, misguided, or simply hypocritical. While Louis the Pious had specified that they were for the sake of "perpetual peace," critics had a different view of the *amicitiae*, especially in light of their general inability to secure lasting accord (Buc 2001: 24–8 discusses royal *amicitia* as a moral problem). The peace councils were celebrated against the backdrop of churches, emphasizing the orderly manner in which accord had been reached. Nevertheless, writing in the 840s, Florus of Lyon called these peace agreements a masquerade (Kershaw 2011: 199–203). And the irascible critic of Carolingian rule, Liudprand of Cremona, paired Carolingian accords with vulgarity, bacchanalia, and overindulgent feasting (Buc 2001: 52). As Louis the German and Charles the Bald made alliances after 843 against their elder brother and his heirs, observers compared *amicitia* to *coniuratio*: a sworn plot, peace against others. Such anxieties about false peace became part of a broader critique of *amicitia* that would harden lay-clerical identities in the eleventh and twelfth centuries.

AMICITIA, PACTA, AND PERFORMANCES OF PEACE

In the wake of Carolingian discord, new dynasties came to power. The Saxon duke Henry the Fowler founded the Ottonian royal line *c.* 919. Hugh Capet, a descendant of the West Frankish Robert the Strong, replaced the last Carolingian king in 984. Neither dynasty had an easy time, and chroniclers of the period present political life more nakedly than before. Widukind of Corvey, Thietmar of Merseberg, and Liudprand of Cremona were keenly aware of the fragile and fluctuating alliances that maintained the kings' power. Peace for Ottonian chroniclers was quiescence first, only then followed by harmony under just rule (Fasoli 1968; Benham 2011). It was discipline born out of fear appropriate for a world in which, according to Liudprand, "it is more honorable to fight with spears than with pens" (2007: 252). The same holds for the Salians who succeeded the Ottonians in Germany. The chronicler Wipo addresses King Henry III as "well suited to both peace and war" (2000: 52). Peace also had positive definitions as the harmony that came with just, paternalistic rule (Widukind 1935: 2.36), but negative peace must precede positive peace if we go by the writings of Widukind (1935: 1.36) and Liudprand (2007: 48).

On an embassy to Constantinople in 968, Liudprand defended King Otto I's brutal reign from those who accused him of "faking peace." Liudprand's rebuttal highlights what made an Ottonian king a peacemaker. He noted that Otto had freed Italy from tyrannical yoke: the result of lax rule that led to violations of the Church, desertion, and rebellion. As a restorer of peace, Otto was simply returning the Church to its former privileges (see Liudprand 2007: 241–42 and 252, on forceful reprisal of heresies as cauterization).

The Ottonians also restored peace by personally resolving disputes. Despite the claims of emperors like Henry II to "sacral" kingship that raised them above other nobles, the Ottonians and Salians were, in fact, very much a part of the cut and thrust of everyday politics. While nobles might accost each other through depredations or calculated insults they also denounced each other before the king (Leyser 1979: 98–102). Widukind describes how Otto I summoned a meeting of quarreling groups to the royal estate at Steele in 938. He had initially planned arbitration but in the interest of minimizing injury to the notables gathered (perhaps these arbitrations often resulted in violence) the king settled on trial by combat (Widukind 1935: 2.10). Widukind derides as "disturbers of peace" those who rejected royal justice and conducted their feuds separately. He chastises the king for being merciful towards the backsliders because that gave others implicit permission to commit murder, pillage, and arson without regard for good or evil.

The Ottonian and Salian kings nurtured a courtly culture based on *familiaritas*, an informal friendship not as binding as *amicitia*. This enabled what some historians call "consultative" lordship, meetings of friends and kinsmen to determine courses of action or even how to feel in specific situations (Althoff 1997). Gerd Althoff suggests that these consultations were stage-managed ahead of time, but we have literary accounts of more contentious councils, where lack of consensus equates to criticism of the ruler. Political opposition could be signaled by criticism of the prince's bearing, his emotional display or his deployment of gestures.

Politics and performance were closely intertwined. Ceremonial acts preceded and followed negotiations. They established parity between principals or gave early clues regarding intentions. One of the most prominent was a performance of appeasement (sometimes known as *deditio*) in which the petitioner put down his weapons, prostrated himself, and begged pardon of the opposing party. It took from the penitential ceremonies revived by Louis the Pious and continued among Carolingian princes: Lothar I before his father Louis, and Lothar II and his mistress (and future queen) Waldrada before popes Nicholas and Hadrian II.[3]

Much of the peacemaking performance was what Althoff calls "frontstage" to negotiations "backstage" (Althoff 1997: 229–57). Jenny Benham has studied these background activities, including the use of envoys and choice of location—which varied according to the status of those involved and their desire for visibility. She rightly argues that successful peacemaking was peacemaking that was *perceived* to be successful, the public "liminal" event for which all the preparation had taken place. By the twelfth century, actual terms had come to matter as the basis for future negotiation (see Benham 2011: 117–37 on envoys and 209–10 on the relative importance of perception and terms). However, such participants in negotiations might still refer to the memory of a performance.

Bodily gestures of sorrow and joy during peace ceremonies conveyed transitions from hostility to friendship among enemies; these gestures were subject to assessment by those around, and we know this because chroniclers thought it necessary to record those assessments. The memory of consensus covered a range of elements in the performance, including how well each participant had calibrated the emotional tenor of the proceedings. Disputes could, therefore, be continued by means of conflicting accounts of how past peacemaking ceremonies had proceeded (Buc 2001: Ch. 1). Was a gesture of placation or remorse well-timed or inappropriate? Did it indicate a peacemaker or one whose weakness and lack of sensibility could lead to greater discord?

In this reliance on gesture and memory of gesture, Ottonian princes and their chroniclers were not so different from bishops in northern Italy or nobles in West Francia.

DEFINITIONS OF PEACE 19

A Milanese author represented the archbishop of Ravenna's slight manipulation of the Salian king Conrad's imperial coronation procession as violence, in order to then inscribe the memory of a consensus among other metropolitans against Ravenna and in favor of the priority of the see of Milan. A favorable peace in the face of *violentia* became the touchstone for Milan's future claims against its longstanding rival (Malegam 2011). Karl Leyser argues that the sacral kingship of the Ottonian and Salian kings suffered a blow during the minority and early reign of King Henry IV, not as commonly supposed during the Investiture Controversy but rather through a series of discords at key ceremonial occasions. The princes of the kingdom were treated to accounts of their young king

FIGURE 1.2: The *Deditio*: Henry IV of Germany kneels to seek forgiveness at Canossa in 1077, before Queen Mathilda of Tuscany, pope Gregory VII's ally, with abbot Hugh of Cluny advising. Miniature from *Vita Mathildis*, manuscript, Italy, twelfth century. Rome, Biblioteca Apostolica Vaticana. Photo by De Agostini/Courtesy of Getty Images.

unable to maintain order during Easter, Whitsun, and Christmas courts: he was kidnapped; bishops and abbots fought over seating precedence; and in 1071, monks of Stavelot registered a complaint over lost properties by breaking the shrine of Saint Remacles on the king's dinner table (Leyser 1979: 96–7). Henry's inability to respond appropriately—in this case punitively—diminished his claim as *rex pacificus*.

Literature emerging out of the West Frankish kingdom plays with many of the same tropes of disputation and peacemaking. The Old French epic *Raoul de Cambrai* features several confrontations of lords with their king or with kinsmen who express anger and grief according to a social choreography. Reconciliations take place before a social group that comments on the nuances of performance. Raoul burned alive the mother of his friend Bernier, who then denounced him in front of friends. Yet it was Bernier who received censure when he refused to accept Raoul's overly humiliating penance. While historians like Althoff have argued that participants at these face-to-face settlements observed "rules of the game," more likely politics determined perceptions of right and wrong in any performance.

Such informal peacemaking mechanisms also have continuities with treaties and extra-udicial peace agreements such as the *convenientia*. An agreement not to sue or simply a non-judicial pact, in Roman law, this interpersonal diplomatic form is best known from extant, written eleventh- and twelfth-century examples. Adam Kosto argues that the presence of charters of *convenientia* by 1000 indicates a strengthening of public institutions. However, it might indicate equally that a form of collective accord, once considered extra-judicial and private, had become a primary basis of peacemaking: friendship underwrote law (Kosto 1998).

Fighting and friendship went together in this system. To be at peace one had to honor a web of alliances with someone else as the target. Peace was forged and then reiterated through conflict. As Richard Barton has shown, aggression often prepared the ground for negotiation or renegotiation of alliances (Barton 1998).[4] The pliable memory of the emotions in play during the forging of these relationships bolstered further negotiations and demands, including in future generations. Thus, even words like "hatred" or "enmity" refer to long-standing associations rather than simple enmity; hostilities drawn out over periods of time drew in multiple friendships and alliances and became the nodes of new social networks (Bartlett 2010; Smail 2001).

Yet this system had brakes. Fighting in the course of these enmities was rarely the result of what some historians have seen as "hot" vengeance, retribution taken immediately after an offense, without care and reasoning (White 1996). It was an opening gambit to negotiations or a carefully calibrated complaint; problems arose when complainants wrongly calibrated their responses. Commentators harshly criticized unreasoned fighting, while commending the same bellicose activities when carried out under what they portray as the guidance of zeal, honor or craft (Gauvard 1999). Additionally, words that seem to refer to a lack of cognitive input are actually quasi-judicial assessments of the merits of a particular complaint. Thus, where we find accusations of impulsive or "insane" assault, the message is that it is unmerited, excessive, or dishonorable in the judgment of peers.

PEACE AS PROTECTION AND REFORM OF THE CHURCH

With peace and friendship so imbricated in bellicose political practice, the term "violence" requires examination. In western Europe, *violentia* was sparingly used in texts that otherwise seem to overflow with what modern readers would describe as violence. The isolated abstract noun is even rarer: persons act "violently" or "with violence" when their gambits are underhanded or subversive to friendship and love (Malegam 2011). Where it is opposed to peace, *violentia* refers to activities calculated to subvert love at the highest level, *caritas*: the peace of the Church.

Between the late tenth and the late twelfth centuries, refined constructions of the peace of the Church made *violentia* a threat to ecclesial unity, sacramental purity, and the universal mechanics of government in medieval Europe. In 975 at Saint-Germain Laprade in the Auvergne, and again in 993, Bishop Guy of Le Puy held a church council where he imposed an oath of peace on knights and peasants of the surrounding region. As was common with peacemakers of the time, Guy had soldiers at his disposal to emphasize the message. The Auvergnat meetings number among the first of what historians call the "Peace of God" movement. The "Peace" in "Peace of God" refers to a range of concerns, including local welfare, clerical protections, reform of monasteries and clerical behavior, and control over periods of fighting, etc. The limited early councils focused on local Church demands for privilege and protection. Certain categories of persons deemed powerless, *pauperes*, also came under the protection of this Peace. By 1020, councils in Aquitaine, Burgundy and the Auvergne could collectively merit the term "movement," and lay princes began to take an active role in declaring and protecting the Peace of God.

On the heels of the peace councils came narrative descriptions of the activities around them, people thronging to the croziers of their bishops, monks bringing relics for general adoration (Rodulfus Glaber 1989: 195–98). Some of the narratives assert that peace would not have been possible without the grace of this or that saint, or they contrast the bumbling attempts of laymen to make peace with the virtuosity of monks carrying relics. They also criticize peacemaking according to a criterion that was novel for these years: the endurance of peace (Malegam 2008).

If one had to point to a model of peace for the conciliar activity, it would be the peace that powerful monastic houses like the Abbey of Cluny were demanding for themselves and their subsidiary churches around 1000. The Peace of Cluny protected the abbey from incursions including, most importantly, obligations of hospitality to princes. By conferring this immunity, West Frankish princes enhanced their own prestige while improving their relationships with the abbey's patron Saint Peter (Mehu 2001; Rosenwein 1999). Iogna-Prat argues that in the long term, this exclusionary arrangement contributed to a suspicion of outsiders, including heretics, Jews and Muslims (2002).

Similar forms of peacemaking took place in the late tenth century among a group of monasteries in Lotharingia, a movement collectively (if incompletely) named the Gorzian reform, after the energetic cellarer of Gorze abbey, John of Gorze. Of middling birth, John worked closely with Lotharingian aristocrats like Bishop Adalbero of Metz to protect and rebuild houses in the region. Much like the friendships of lay aristocrats, this peace thrived on occasional conflict and threat between bishop and abbey. Peace also required bricks and mortar building, sound administration, and military defense exemplified by two charismatic leaders, Abbot Richard of Saint-Vanne and later, Bishop Bruno of Toul, the future Pope Leo IX (on Lotharingian reform see Vanderputten 2015, Nightingale 2001, Jestice 1997). But reformist peacemaking in monasteries was also a shaking up, a refusal to allow protection and tranquility to become inertia. While organizing the military defense of his diocese, Bruno also replaced unsatisfactory abbots with his own hand-picked candidates. Despite their use of military force and the oppositional stances they often took toward less-energetic abbots, interventionist bishops were thought of as "lover[s] of peace and restorer[s] of monasteries" (*Gesta* 1852: 543).

In 1049, anxious to reform the Roman Church, Emperor Henry III installed Bruno of Toul as pope. According to his *vita*, Pope Leo IX met a nun at the gates of Rome who told him to say, "Peace to this house and all who live in it" upon crossing the threshold of the apostles (*Vita* 1997: 76.) The reformers around Leo certainly conceived of their activities as peacemaking. Humbert of Silva Candida, a legate and close advisor, bemoaned violence done to Christ's body by clerical abuses like simony, the buying and selling of Church offices (Remensnyder 1992). Simony was a labile accusation that could be leveled equally against reformers and opponents of reform. In terms of eleventh-century political realities, simony was an assault on two connected guarantors of peace, faith and fidelity, both termed *fides* (Robinson 1978). Reformers like Humbert worried that simoniacal bishops lacked the power to convey the Holy Spirit in the sacrament, which meant that any congregants who took Mass or had been baptized by these bishops had endangered their souls (Blumenthal 1988: 74–6).

Theologians were not the only ones affected by fear of false sacraments. To local communities, even clerical unchastity meant sacramental pollution, fears that reform leaders encouraged when they supported urban rebellions against unpopular bishops (Cowdrey 1968). Leo's initial well-meaning measures against simony also produced fears that any priests ordained by simoniacs would lose the power to convey the Holy Spirit: a devastating trickle-down effect. Suspicion of Church leaders began to endanger the peace of communities. The reformers had fulfilled their own dire predictions.

Simony also meant another disruption of peace. In 1056, Henry III died, leaving his kingdom to a six-year old son. For fifteen years, Henry IV's mother and courtiers patched together the Salian political order, and after he reached maturity, Henry had to make good on the favors that had sustained his rule. He also continued the Ottonian-Salian policy of granting *honores* (offices) to friends and kinsmen, notably installing them in politically sensitive bishoprics. According to one historian, Henry mismanaged these friendships, unable to fully exploit the "rules of the game" (Althoff 2006).

According to his critics, especially Pope Gregory VII, the king's ill-judged *amicitiae* portended his downfall. When Henry went against the wishes of the Milanese people and the papacy by installing his own candidate, one Tedald, as archbishop of Milan, he became guilty of simony in Gregory's eyes. His continued support for simoniacal clergymen that Gregory had excommunicated meant that the king was bound to his bad friends by "chains of anathema." His hatred of true peace also became evident to Henry's opponents when the king supposedly turned against the pope immediately after making peace and taking Mass with him at Canossa (Bonizo 1891: 610).

According to partisan biographers, Pope Gregory had decided that the Church had spent too long in an enervating peace with empire. It was time for its defenders to take a more militant stance (Paul of Bernried 1862: 513). He often used Cyprian's favored biblical phrase: "Cursed is he who withdraws his sword from bloodshed." More often used to refer to episcopal censure, the prospect of real bloodshed became more acute, when Gregory started to recruit lay princes to oppose and unseat the king of Germany (Robinson 1978: 95–100; Malegam 2013: 72–3).

The papal espousal of sacramental concerns and this peculiarly militant version of peace alarmed bishops in the empire and the Italian city-states. They denounced the pope on behalf of King Henry, upon which Gregory excommunicated him and urged Christian subjects to redirect their *fides*. Some of the most virulent anti-Gregorian rhetoric of this period is from cardinals, who accused Gregory of destroying the peace by usurping the papacy and flouting the divine will conveyed through kinship.

The intra-ecclesial conflicts drew heavily from the vocabulary of peace and violence. Monks from the abbey of Saint Hubert of Amdain complained to Pope Urban II against the administrative interference of the bishop of Liège, who also happened to be a friend of King Henry. Urban denounced the *violentia* done to the monks, called the bishop's hand-picked abbot an invader, compared him to a diabolical falsification of the Host that would enter and devour them, and urged the monks to resist violence by breaking their vows of obedience (*Chronicon* 1848: 624). A few years later, Sigebert of Gembloux criticized Pope Paschal II for raising armies against bishops in Liège and Cambrai who opposed him. Paschal had reversed his assigned role as a preacher of peace (*predicator pacis*) where peace was "*regnum* and *sacerdotium* [coupled] into a single cornerstone of concord." He had failed to perform a key function, which was to ensure that all creatures remained subject to the higher powers embodied in kingship. As Agobard had against Louis the Pious, Sigebert invoked the book of Timothy: "Through the deserts of our sins, the apostle, who should even now pray for the king, even if he is a sinner, so that we may lead a tranquil and quiet life, directs us [instead] in fighting, so that we may not lead a tranquil and quiet life" (cf. 1 Tim 2:1–2) (1892: 461).

THE PEACE OF CITIES

Not all churchmen desired simple tranquility. Guibert, abbot of Nogent, argued that in those who "lived well" spirit and flesh must refuse to be content with peace. The canon lawyer Rufinus of Sorrento derided peace between wicked persons as "the sleep of Behemoth, who hides in reeds and swamps" (1997: 76). Sometimes, conflict and social disturbance were the only antidotes to pernicious tranquility, because they signaled that something was wrong.

As proof of the usefulness of disorder, Guibert interpreted the uprising of the commune of Laon as divine reproof. He and his fellow churchmen had been unable to recognize threats to peace within the Church, or to see their bishop for what he truly was: a lay warrior and a simoniac. Rather than cause a disturbance, they had persuaded the pope to accept a leader that they suspected was unfit. To shake them out of this insensibility, God had allowed a commune to form within the city. When the bishop betrayed the commune and rescinded its charter in 1112, the communards erupted in full-fledged rebellion. In the subsequent massacre, his own servants murdered the bishop. Social and even gender hierarchies were reversed as men dressed as women and women as men in order to flee. For Guibert, writing in 1115, the commune was a scandal and a rebuke but it was also simply the social body enacting the hatred of peace emanating from the spiritual head. But why should a commune stand in for perversions of peace?

In Guibert of Nogent's words, *communia* was a "novel and the worst possible name" for oath-communities that had begun to emerge in France and northern Italy (1981: 322). Most prominent in cities (although there were rural communes) these associations formed around an agreement among members to protect one another. In times of attack they would form a militia. They served as compurgators in legal disputes and some communes put collective pressure on lords to secure justice for clients who were oath-members. The problem lay in the shared semantic space between communes and other associations based on a vow of peace, such as monasteries and commonwealths.

Harmut Hoffmann and Dolorosa Kennelly have demonstrated the relationship between the peace language of the communes that emerged around 1060, and Peace movements that had begun a century earlier (Hoffmann 1964; Kennelly 1962). The Peace of God

FIGURE 1.3: Laon Cathedral, France, West Front, early thirteenth century. Photo by DAVID ILIFF. License: CC-BY-SA 3.0. Source: Wikimedia, https://commons.wikimedia.org/w/index.php?curid=40026220

movement had siblings in diocesan peace associations. Archbishop Aimon of Bourges convened an armed "Peace League" in the 1030s and 1040s. In 1069, Bishop Odo of Toul assembled an oath community that refuted Count Arnulf's claims over the city. He justified this overthrow as a return to justice, so that God might be recognized as "true peace" (*pax vera*) (*Miracula* 1858: 192–98).

The Peace movement also gave rise to a mechanism for controlling fighting, which was called the Truce of God (*treuga dei*). Its secular variant in Germany was the *Landfriede* or lord's territorial peace. Thanks to its legislation of times without fighting, the Truce became a way to create armies: to organize, discipline, and then deploy a united band of knights, who would stop fighting when told to do so. In the 1040s, before his war with

King Henry III, Baldwin of Flanders declared a Truce of God. Even Pope Urban II's famous call to Crusade in 1095 was couched in the language of a general Truce among Christians. Like the communes that developed out of them, these oath associations were born in equal parts from peace and war.

The communes had names like the *Pax* of Valenciennes or the *Institutio Pacis* of Laon. Used for the boundary within which members enjoyed protection and followed the Rule of the city, the urban *Pax* had more than a superficial resemblance to the protective and exclusive *Pax* of abbeys like Cluny. In some cases, it protected members of the peace of a city even when they were traveling outside it. But though *Pax* may have been "a harmless synonym" for "commune," as Charles Petit-Dutaillis has claimed, to critics, most of them clergy, the term suggested *a coniuratio* or plot, inversions of Christian community (1970: 78; see Oexle 2001 and Malegam 2013 on plot and inversion). The bloody insurrection of the Laon commune of 1112 had seemed to fulfill this, at least as Guibert told the tale: leveling of ranks, compulsion of masters by servants, enforced conspiratorial oaths taking the place of sacraments.

The earliest chartered commune, Le Mans, set the pattern for anxieties about perverted peace. In 1070, the townspeople revolted against Duke William (the Conqueror) and their bishop Arnald, who, as the son of a priest, embodied clerical unchastity. Rather than create its own government this early commune invited the margrave of Este to rule over Le Mans. Forbidden entry to his own city, Arnald made an accord with the populace—a peace against the margrave—who fled. Then the townspeople swore an oath (*sacramentum*) of mutual aid and demanded a charter from the absent margrave's ally Godfrey who had taken over the city. Finally, they made the bishop lead them against Duke William and force him to accept the charter. According to its critics, by forcing local rulers to cooperate, the Le Mans commune enacted violence in the guise of peace. The violence inhered in their collective oath, *coniuratio*, but manifested in mockeries of judicial process followed by summary blindings and executions (*Gesta* 1901: 376–81).

That the oaths should provoke so much concern is surprising, since they echo language from the Peace of God: peace that pleases God, directed toward good, with enmity toward the wicked. Personifications of peace adorned the communal seals. But critics worried that the communal oath only bound communards to "peace against everyone else" (Oexle 2001). In 1127, the citizens of Lille attacked Count William Clito for violating the terms of peace. The 1114 charter of Valenciennes states: "There is sanctity and stability" in peace but that only meant protection for merchants having business with the city, and it even excluded those from neighboring Douai (*La Paix* 1981: 103). The shared semantic field made churchmen even more sensitive to what they saw as betrayals of true peace.

Most horrifying may have been when lay rulers agreed to grant communal charters. In 1115, Ivo of Chartres rebuked King Louis the Fat, who granted several charters that would later be ratified by his son and grandson (1854: 99). According to Ivo, the king should defend the bishop of Amiens against the commune. He warned Louis not to violate the divinely mandated peace of the kingdom because of bad friendship. The mercenary oaths that the commune invited were false sacraments, binding persons not to God but to mammon, and by extension, to the devil. Worried that clergy would be forced to accept communal rule, Stephen of Tournai (1128–1203) echoed Isidore of Seville's denunciation of congregations that come together without emotional and spiritual commitment. Stephen warned of living among dragons (*dracones*) and ostriches (*strutiones*), beasts with scaly (or feathered) hides: "Scale will cleave to scale among them, so that no breath escapes through" (1893: 299; Oexle 2001: 290). Several of his contemporaries also used this description of Leviathan from the book of Job as a marker for wicked confederacy, the mockery of peace.

Anxieties about commune presaged general fears of groups that claimed to be held together by peace. Marked by dubious oaths, peace became a reversal of social order: even heretical and seditious groups announced themselves as champions of the true peace. After initial support, Bishop Hugh of Auxerre anathematized an anti-nomian group led by Durand of Le Puy, whose followers claimed that Mary had urged them to bring back peace and eradicate "violence." Called Capuciati or "White Capes," they banded together under a common oath, and forcibly drafted "men of peace" under the badge of the Virgin and Child. They also executed dissenters. After victories against the "enemies of peace" in 1183, the peace men entered the royal domain of France, where, according to some accounts, the movement degenerated into rebellion against seigneurial lordship (Malegam 2013: 240–42).

The language of exclusive peace is less marked in the Italian communes. In Italy, communes formed in cities that were at war with their neighbors, and these became an important part of their origin stories and insignia. The mid-twelfth century Roman commune suggests that at the heart of the communards' concerns lay a peace more in keeping with imperial discourse. Otto of Freising relates a letter that the communards sent to Conrad III of Germany, assuring him that the Roman citizens desired peace and justice with those who were like-minded. As guardians of historic Roman liberty, they were keeping the imperial city safe from the treachery of the pope and his Sicilian allies. However, the association of commune with diabolical peace was strong enough that Otto, when describing the Roman commune, blamed its emergence on an accused heretic, Arnold of Brescia, even though he was a relative latecomer to the movement (Otto 1978: 48).

While they may have provided a backdrop for disruptions of religious and social peace, cities also became venues for acts of mass peacemaking to rival the Peace of God movement. During the Great Devotion of 1233, Franciscan and Dominican preachers visited the Italian communes and spread a message of reconciliation. The Dominican John of Vicenza and the Franciscan Gerard of Modena brought peace to the cities through a combination of performance and imposition of general penances and oaths on the populace. As a result, various city governments turned over their municipal statutes to the mendicants for revision. Peace and justice became the theme of new urban legislation guided by the Franciscan peacemakers (Thompson 1992). Even if the faction-ridden Italian cities did not cease their internal disputes, over the long term, the mendicants had made an impact on laws and judicial institutions, the secular instruments of peace.

Soon, in the Low Countries, France, and Lombardy, as lay and ecclesiastical princes realized they could use communal support to offset rivals, the communes gained in prestige. Commune had become an expression of freedom and harmonious coexistence that a city could use as its point of origin. Communal origins meant unity and an internal peace against outside invaders. The city of Milan, for example, dates its commune to conflicts with Emperor Frederick Barbarossa in the second half of the twelfth century. Eventually, these communal aspirations stood in for the commune in civic foundation stories. Giovanni Codagnelli (c. 1230) opens the history of Piacenza in February 1090: when knights and the *popolo* resolved a "great sedition." Otto Gerhard Oexle argues that the city's commune emerged during this civil war, but as Chris Wickham notes, the author does not use the word "commune" (Oexle 2001: 302; Wickham 1994: 309). Instead of implicating the commune in the violence, Codagnelli speaks of a mass conversion that produced the foundational accord. Suddenly, through God's will, both sides stopped fighting each other and exchanged mutual embraces and remorseful tears, all the while crying: "Pax, pax!" (Codagnelli 1901: 1–3). The city founded itself on this memory of reconciliation.

The emerging cities of the high and later Middle Ages afforded novel opportunities and backdrops for a uniquely urban violence: crimes of opportunity committed by persons outside the familial networks that might otherwise restrain them. At least, that was the fear the cities conjured up. But as Claude Gauvard suggests, the same population forces also produced peculiar forms of urban solidarity committed to the prevention of crime, the maintenance of peace and the safeguarding of honor (Gauvard 1993). Neighbors perforce got to know each other and ensured the criminal elements could not sneak in undetected. City charters had specific safeguards around entrance and egress from the city. Even as communes evolved autonomous municipal institutions these sometimes complemented local seigneurial authority. Laon's second commune committed to maintaining the *ius* of members (i.e., their ability to secure justice from *traditional* lords in the first instance (*Charte* 1974: 14.17)).

Regardless of how its early opponents saw it, then, the peace of the commune could be a socially conservative instrument, upholding local lordship rather than undercutting it. The same cannot be said for the political theory of secular monarchy that evolved from the late twelfth century onwards. Borrowing liberally from the religious experiments of the central Middle Ages, the secular language of peace made extraordinary claims for the singular authority of the monarch.

PEACE AND SECULAR POLITICAL THEORY

By the twelfth century, via refinements of Eucharistic theology, medieval exegetes and canon lawyers had developed a corporate understanding of the Church, by which they now meant not just the king and his priests but all Christians. The Church as corporation was imagined as a body in a state of complete peace, specifically peace between head and members, an old Pauline image. On the basis of peace, therefore, different orders in Church and society functioned in a coordinated but distinct manner. The bonds of all other community must measure up to the peace of the Church. In 1118, the Liégeois canon Alger wrote that while the Host was always Christ's body one could only be nurtured in this body through genuine acceptance of the Church's peace (1855: 739–854).[5]

In the middle of the twelfth century, however, John of Salisbury repurposed the Pauline image of a body that must live through the peace of head and members to describe not church but commonwealth. Its antithesis was a collective of persons aggregated scale upon scale, the terrifying Leviathan image that churchmen used for any group of persons bound by wicked sacraments (John of Salisbury 1855: 591). By the thirteenth century, thinkers such as Vincent of Beauvais and Gilbert of Tournai were making clear analogies between the mystical body of the Church and that of the commonwealth (see Kantorowicz 1997, and my departure from him below). With this sacralization, the peace of the commonwealth became equivalent to and, in some ways, even superseded the peace of the Church.

By the late fourteenth century, jurists were speaking of several sociopolitical bodies as *corpora mystica* in the universal sense: domains that ranged from village to kingdom and world. It could also be used non-specifically for groups of persons and polities. For Ernst Kantorowicz this usage was "a levelling down and a banalization" of complex liturgical notions (Kantorowicz 1997: 210). However, it is also possible to see it as the logical elaboration of a peaceful collective modeled on twelfth-century imaginings of the Church.

The ideal type of collectivity was a community that cherished the peace of its members, a body subject to moral evaluation in terms of the authenticity of its peace.

The corporate images of peace reflected changes in the political and social order of the late twelfth century. With the imperial coronation of King Frederick Barbarossa in 1155, the king-emperors of Germany began to speak of their realm as the "Holy" Roman Empire. Frederick's step-uncle, Otto of Freising, crafted an image in which Frederick embodied peace. In one sense, Frederick fulfilled the promise of Otto's earlier work, *The Two Cities*, in which he departed from Augustine to present an eschatological vision of peace (on the question of whether Otto specifically envisioned Frederick as the endpoint of history, see Bagge 1996: 348n). In the *City of God*, Augustine had spoken of material Rome and spiritual Jerusalem as inextricably interwined; peace allowed reason to distinguish between the two in daily life. For Otto, two cities, earthly Babylon and celestial Jerusalem, were separate and in conflict until the end of time, when the latter's triumph would mark eternal peace. The empire would make concord with the papacy during the final age once there was a German king strong enough to maintain it (Otto 1912).

Perhaps Otto hoped Frederick would be this king. Consecrated alongside his namesake, the bishop of Muenster, Frederick's coronation represented a conjunction of New and Old Testaments, of kingship and priesthood. Barbarossa brought real peace by pacifying warring duchies in the Rhineland, Bavaria, and Denmark, declaring a *Landfriede* in the empire, and settling a disputed episcopal election in Cologne. If forced to do battle to pacify his subjects, Frederick ensured that he first had made peace with God. Following the old Carolingian model, Frederick modulated his emotions, bringing peace to others only after he himself had attained it. When roused to anger, he became not irate, but indignant, and to an appropriate degree; unlike his retinue, he avoided the madness (*furor*) of the fighting orders. When insulted by papal legates at an imperial diet at Besançon, Frederick restrained his own men and sent the legates home safely, while writing to the pope of his "merited indignation" (Otto 1978: 113).

However, Frederick's peacemaking came at a price. Certain interventions caused anger in Rome, and as part of his plan to pacify Christendom before embarking on an eschatological quest to the Holy Land, Barbarossa fought several wars with northern Italian cities. His biographer claims Barbarossa was correcting the violence within the Italian communes, so that once he had broken the political network of Milan, he outlawed all pacts save the overarching Peace that he bestowed on the city. This Peace was in effect a conditional protection—from himself.

The Italian campaigns and Frederick's eventual interference in papal elections removed any prospect of concord with the papacy. Instead Pope Alexander III spent much of this rule in exile, cultivating the protection of the secular monarchs of England and France. He governed through correspondence, much of which opposes a papal vision of peace to that offered by Barbarossa. In the face of Frederick's implacable and militant vision, Alexander developed peace as "discretion": the clerical and secular spheres should be subject to different standards of restraint (Malegam 2013: 281). While clergy policed their own, they must abstain from secular affairs except in so far as these affairs affected them. Alexander's discretionary peace definitively distinguished between clerical and secular domains. The third Lateran Council (1179) that he summoned codified these standards under the name of peace. While forbidding tournaments, they granted clerics, merchants, and even peasants, immunity from attack by knights. Arms could be used in defense of the peace (i.e., against brigands). Armed servants of peace received the same spiritual absolution as Crusade, and, most significantly, it was *incumbent* upon secular

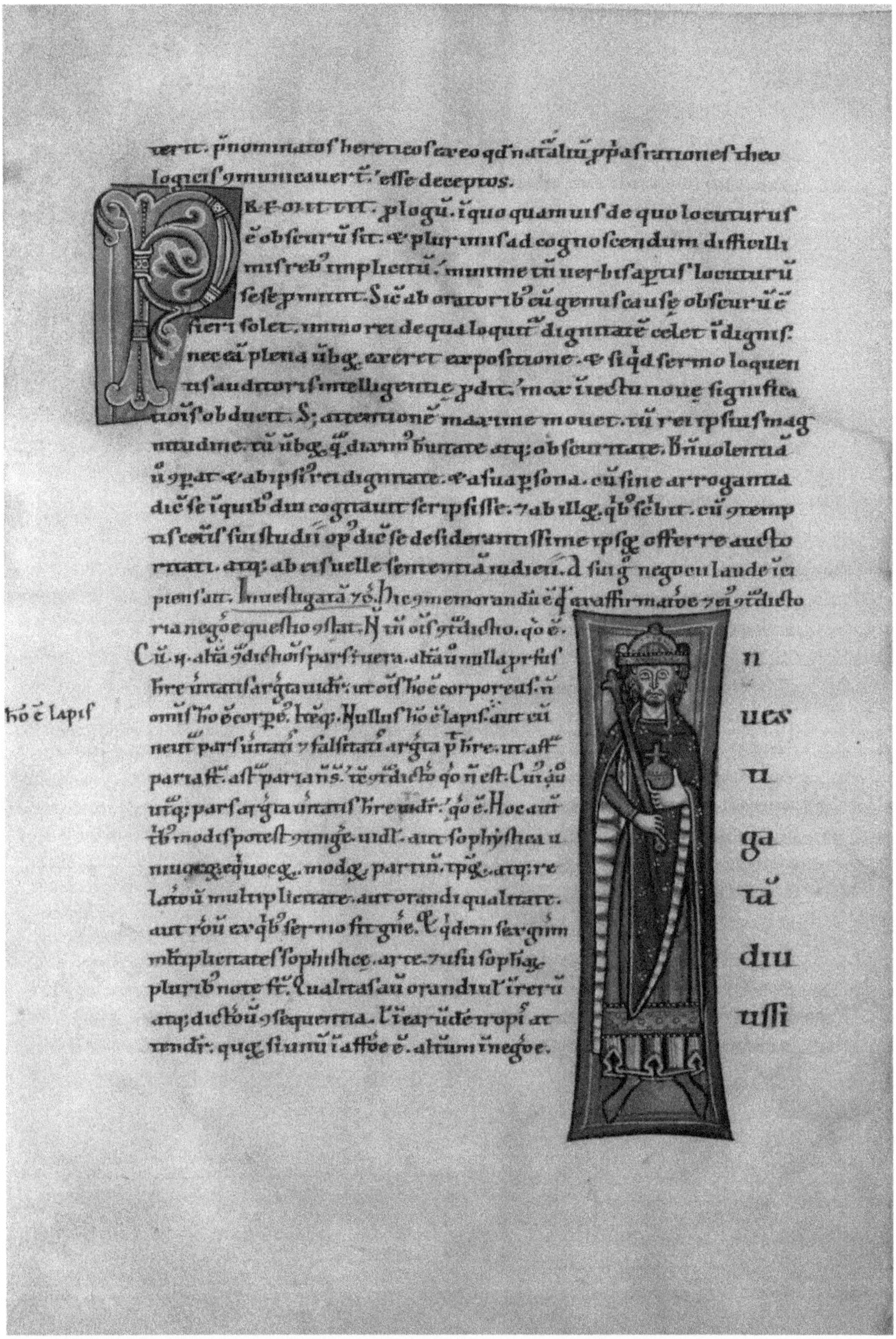

FIGURE 1.4: Frederick I Barbarossa, German emperor, in a twelfth-century manuscript. Freiburg im Breisgau, Germany, Universitätsbibliothek, Handschrift 367, fol. 4v. Public Domain image available from Wikimedia, https://commons.wikimedia.org/w/index.php?curid=59807611

rulers to help coerce heretics in the name of peace (*Concilium* 1973: canon 27, 224). Lateran III's provisions for peace thus created mechanisms that papal inquisitions would eventually adopt.

Alexander's tenure saw a rehabilitation of peace that was imperfect and relied on mundane instruments, politics, and friendships. In fact, by the late twelfth century, the greatest threats to social order were coming from "apostolic" lay religious movements who aspired to peace that was not of this world. When accused of heresy these laymen responded that clerics had been seduced by the peace of this world. A participant at the Lateran council, Rufinus of Sorrento, explicitly embraced the peace of the world in his treatise *On the Goodness of Peace* (c. 1180).

The bulk of Rufinus's treatise concerns the peace that human beings should pursue with one another, since humanity experiences peace as modules of divine, diabolical, or angelic peace. The only peace applicable to an earthly commonwealth (*respublica*) is that of the merely good but not blessed, which he calls the Peace of Babylon. Babylonian peace ensured the authority of the householder and the steadfastness of domestic relationships, which translated to peace in the town square and religious places, and respect for laws and customs. At the broadest level of "the orb," civic and domestic peace turned into the community of kingdoms and regions, connected by travelers, commercial instruments, markets, and languages. These groups had to communicate with one another or descend into barbarism. At all levels of this peace, a tacit pact between ruler and subject guaranteed mutual respect and an ordering of roles. The enemies of the peace of Babylon were enemies of the sociopolitical body, of an accepted "decorum" of authority and obedience (Rufinus 1997: 114–30).

As Rufinus's treatment of peace soothed anxieties about the rise of new collectives, the growing influence of Aristotelian logic provided validation for mundane peace. Humanity was by nature sociable, inclined to peace in the first cause. In his *Summa Theologica*, influenced by Aristotle's *Nicomachean Ethics*, Thomas Aquinas assured his readers that there was virtue in natural friendships that developed for human benefit outside of the "divine good." The greatest good that human beings could attain on earth was peace which took the form of *concordia*, friendship based on mutual charity. In Aquinas's *Summa*, the ruler's use of force—including warfare—is sanctioned *studio pacis*, peace, in this case, meaning the benefit of the commonwealth.[6]

Around 1300, two treatises made the peace of the commonwealth the sole responsibility of the secular monarch. In *De monarchia*, a furtively circulated text written against the overreach of the Avignon papacy, Dante imagined peace as singular dominion that subjected persons, communities, and kingdoms according to a hierarchy of who should serve and who should govern. The prime cause, the monarch, produced a peacemaking momentum that spread to the entire world. As proof, Dante argued that Christ had chosen to appear only when the world had submitted in perfect tranquility to a single ruler, Augustus (1916: 1.11, 345).

Both Dante and Marsilius of Padua based their arguments on Aristotle's *Politics*, in which the philosopher counseled that the end (and thus final cause) of all government was peace. As Dante put it, paraphrasing Aristotle, peace enabled humanity "to attain most freely and easily to its proper function which is almost divine" (1916: 1.4, 343). Only in peace could humanity achieve its greatest potential, and only in tranquility could the various components of the state function effectively. Marsilius dismissed clerical interference in the secular sphere as a threat to this peace. Although Christ had refused earthly dominion for himself or his apostles, ambitious popes were usurping secular prerogatives of coercion and subjugation (1928: 1.19.9–11, 105–107).[7] They had prevented Ludwig of Bavaria from being instituted emperor, the just regulator of civil society, and preserver of peace. Without a model of diplomatic and civil conduct, people and polities in Italy had started to fight.

In secular political theory, then, true peace was the sole prerogative of the secular monarch, manifested as social tranquility, a condition in which human being, household, and state could perform their most appropriate functions in accordance with the dictates of reason. Marsilius insisted that peace and tranquility could come only when the secular ruler governed both clergy and laity unobstructed. He accused the popes of furthering their secular ambitions through the pretense of peacemaking. With this defense of secular monarchy, the specter of false peace that clergy had summoned up in the eleventh and twelfth centuries now reversed upon them.

CONCLUSION

In 1304, King Philip IV of France issued the third of four *ordonnances* restricting warfare within his kingdom. While in the first two, Philip had prohibited internal wars during times when the king was at war in a manner consistent with the old Truce of God, the 1304 ordinance declared that "regardless of local custom" *all* internal wars were forbidden (Firnhaber-Baker 2010: 52–3). By doing so, Philip announced himself as a keeper of the peace, which is to say one who prevented all warfare but at the same time who reserved the prohibition of warfare only to himself. Was this the ideology of secular kingship in practice?

Perhaps not. As Justine Firnhaber-Baker argues, the French kings rarely stopped wars based on the peace ordinances they promulgated, choosing instead to treat these wars as trespasses upon their authority as lords. Breaking the peace did not refer to the act of fighting but to fighting on a lord's land without his permission, or, usurping a lord's authority to declare peace or war on his land (Firnhaber-Baker 2010: 51, 58, 60; Firnhaber-Baker 2014). The Truce of God and the German *Landfriede* had similarly made provisions that limited or prohibited warfare on a territorial basis.

In one sense, then, the French monarchical claim to peace could be considered only a kind of supra-lordship. The king as lord magnified had been a feature of German constructions of kingship since the later Carolingian period, exemplified by Notker of Saint Gall's representation of Charlemagne as caretaker and overseer of church administration (Goetz 1981). By asserting lordly prerogatives over peace, then, secular monarchs like Philip and Louis IX were implementing practical if traditional measures to curb fighting.

However, at some point, lordship and sovereignty overlap. Medieval lords were possessed of a certain peace that they could extend to subjects and clients on their land. Medieval religious houses had their peace that lords honored to mutual benefit. Even townspeople carried peace with them. As did Jewish communities although, in their case, peace was seen as a shameful mark of exiled status. By the thirteenth century, however, the king's peace had become uniquely redemptive. In England, Jews received protection under royal peace, while by the fourteenth century in France and later in Burgundy, the prince (king or duke) conferred peace through pardon.

By means of pardon, princes could shore up extra-judicial settlements of redemption. They could also promote social peace through cohesion of communities, and reintegration of miscreants who had been alienated from them. But as Walter Prevenier suggests, they could also assert their power of discretion, ignoring the extensive judicial machinery around royal pardons to make arbitrary decisions, often undercutting the demands of lordly opponents. It also allowed princes to "make truth" out of conflicting claims, thanks to their position as peace-givers (Prevenier 2010: 180–82; 194). The resistance to the royal monopolization of pardon itself shows how powerful was this exclusive claim over peace (Gauvard 1991: 907–34; Prevenier 2010: 187–88).

Royal pardon highlights the dual mandate of peace in a secular monarchy. Marsilius wrote that the office of the monarch must have the full prerogative of coercion because it embodied law. At the same time, the prince who occupied this office should possess more subjective qualities, such as a sense of equity that would allow him to function in areas outside the ambit of the law. This left the monarch open to the kinds of calumnies and friendships that had guided medieval political process for centuries yet made those mundane instances of conflict and concord part of a process that assured social cohesion and peace. While in 833 Louis the Pious had excoriated himself because personal lapses had destroyed the peace of his kingdom, the peace of the commonwealth was far better served. Its "mystical body," held together by a perfect ordering of head and members, enabled a mutual exchange of benefit, a call and response in which all components made peace possible.

CHAPTER TWO

Human Nature, Peace, and War

GREGORY M. REICHBERG

If one considers the theme of peace as it was taken up by medieval thinkers, a paradox emerges. Few words have such a constant presence in the Old and New Testaments, as well as the Qur'an, but not often was this term in its various meanings made the subject of systematic analysis. It usually figured as a topic of spiritual meditation or scriptural exegesis, and unlike, say, the categories of "goodness" or "truth," the metaphysical and moral dimensions of "peace" were rarely discussed in their own right. A notable exception was the philosopher/theologian Thomas Aquinas (*c.* 1224–1274). This learned saint did not take himself to be a theological innovator; his stated aim was to sum up and organize into a coherent whole the insights of his predecessors, Christian thinkers certainly, but also the philosophical thought of selected Jews and Muslims. Although he did discuss the metaphysics of peace (how "peace" stands in relation to "unity" and "goodness," and whether it can be deemed an attribute of God), he took special care to examine the implications of peace for human nature. The ethical dimensions of this question were of special interest to him, leading him to consider how dispositions opposed to charity—the chief source of peace—can result in war.

Taking Aquinas as a guide into the metaphysical, human, moral, and political dimensions of peace, as they were understood in the high Middle Ages (1100–1300), we will begin by mapping out his thoughts on this subject. Afterwards we will consider peace in relation to war, and here the views of several other medieval thinkers will be considered.

The sources for Aquinas's reflection on peace were fourfold (on the historical background, see Renna 1979, Erb 2007, and Shogimen 2010): First of all, he sought to explain certain key passages from the Hebrew and Greek Scriptures, for instance Isaiah 26:12 "Lord, you establish peace for us," or the words of Jesus "my peace I give you" (Jn 14:27); second, the writings of the late Roman Christian thinker St. Augustine, who famously defined peace as the "tranquility of order," and who was one of the first of the Latin theologians to discuss the nature and status of just war ("bellum iustum"); third, the Greek philosopher Aristotle, who had noted how concord within states is premised on a special kind of relation between citizens, which he termed "political friendship." Finally, there was the neo-Platonic treatise *On the Divine Names*. Written in the late fifth or early sixth century by a Christian author, Pseudo-Dionysius the Areopagite (most likely a Syrian disciple of the Greek philosopher Proclus), chapter eleven of the work was devoted to the metaphysics of peace.

FIGURE 2.1: Triumph of the Catholic Doctrine embodied by Thomas Aquinas, fresco by Andrea Di Bontaiuto, 1365–67. Spanish Chapel, Church of Santa Maria Novella, Florence, Italy. Photo by DeAgostini/Courtesy of Getty Images. Credit: DEA/S. VANNINI/Contributor.

THE METAPHYSICAL BACKGROUND

In seeking to identify the essential characteristics of peace (*pax*), Aquinas emphasizes how this concept bears a close association with the related terms "goodness" (*bonum*) and "unity" (*unitas*). On a par with the most general and fundamental of all terms, "goodness" and "unity," strictly speaking, cannot be defined. Both are coextensive with being (Aquinas 1970–1976, q. 1, a. 1; primary sources are cited according to the standard textual divisions). In this connection, Aquinas cited the Persian philosopher Avicenna (980–1037), who had affirmed that "being" is among all concepts the most evident, the first conceived, and to which all the others are reduced (Avicenna 2005: I.6) and for this reason it, along with unity and goodness, transcends all possible genera and species. "Being," Aristotle, had similarly written, "is not a genus." (Aristotle 1984a: 998b22). Because "peace" is so closely associated with unity and goodness, and through them being itself, we should not be surprised at the difficulty we typically encounter when trying to explain exactly what peace is.

As the good designates that toward which all things tend, and because to tend is to desire, *goodness* denotes the terminus of desire, namely that in which desire (also termed "appetite") finds its completion or fulfillment. By extension, in desiring the good, a thing likewise desires peace. Hence Aquinas writes that by the very fact of tending to a good a thing at the same time tends . . . to peace. Peace implies the removal of disturbances or obstacles to obtaining what is good. By the very fact that something is desired, the removal of obstacles is also desired. Consequently, at the same time and by the same appetitive tendency that a good is sought, so too is . . . peace.

—Thomas Aquinas 1970–1976: q. 21, a. 1, ad 1

On this very broad metaphysical understanding, peace has three fundamental characteristics: (1) it is a terminus of appetite or desire (Aquinas uses these two terms interchangeably); (2) an appetite which obtains its good without obstacle or hindrance, hence in tranquility (in other words "with security"); and (3) in such fashion that no contrariety (conflict or incompatibility) arises between multiple desires. Aquinas sums up this last point when he notes how "peace implies that . . . our desires rest altogether in one object."[1] Peace thus implies a multiplicity that in some manner has been reduced to unity.[2] Aquinas sums this up when he says that "peace is the 'tranquility of order'" (Thomas Aquinas 1895: II–II, q. 29, a. 1). "Order," in turn, denotes a "kind of relation and unity of parts based on a reference to a common good that organizes and unites them . . ." (Mienert 2016: 1196). Umberto Eco put this well, when he noted that "peace is the perfection achieved when [a] being is subjected to an order" (Eco 1988: 199–200).

Having identified these three characteristics of peace, Aquinas proceeds to consider its scope. To what sort of things does the term *peace* apply? To what can it be predicated? In response, and borrowing from St. Augustine and Dionysius, he makes a surprising claim: "all things desire peace" (*omnia appetent pacem*) (Thomas Aquinas 1895: II–II, q. 29, a. 2). Every single entity that exists—whether mineral, vegetal, animal, or rational—has an innate tendency (a "natural inclination" or "natural appetite") to its completion. Hence each has an inclination to obtain, without obstacle or hindrance, the good to which it tends. Some things do this on their own volition. These are the rational (intellective) beings that direct themselves to their respective ends. Other beings, infra-rational (i.e., not possessed of rationality), have implanted in them an internal dynamism by which they are directed to their respective ends. To reinforce this last point, Aquinas contrasts two different ways an entity can be moved to some end. One way is "by violence,"[3] as when an arrow is aimed by an archer at a target (his example). A very different way of being moved arises when the mover implants in the thing moved a form—which I earlier referred to as an "internal dynamism"—by which it is inwardly inclined to the end toward which it is directed. "In this fashion," Aquinas writes,

all natural entities are inclined to what is suitable for them, having within themselves some principle of their inclination . . . so in a way they go themselves (*vadant*) and are not merely led to their due ends. Things moved by violence are only led and contribute nothing to their movement. But natural things go to their ends inasmuch as they cooperate with the one . . . directing them.

—Thomas Aquinas 1970–1976: q. 22, a.1

The upshot of this is that peace is not something that can be forced. Wherever it is found, on whatever level, it implies (in the words of pseudo-Dionysius) *consent*, or, at a minimum, *connaturaleness*. Aquinas explains that *consent* denotes a union of wills that proceed from knowledge—as when several human beings agree to pursue a common project—while *connaturaleness* implies a union of natural inclinations—as when the diverse activities of natural entities are coordinated in the unity of an ecosystem (1895: II–II, q. 29, a. 2, ad 1; see also 1950: ch. 11, §885).

These metaphysical reflections are very abstract, but they are important because it is on this foundation that Aquinas draws out implications of ethical and even political significance. For instance, from the fact that peace denotes achieving, without obstruction, what a being inwardly desires, and by extension, a consensual concord of wills from one person to another,[4] it follows that a condition of authentic peace is incompatible with violence, threats, and coercion. Thus, he notes that

> should one man enter into concord with another, not of his own accord (*non spontanea voluntate*), but through being forced (*coactus*) as it were by the fear of some evil that will befall him, such concord does not represent true peace (*non est vera pax*).[5]

Similarly, from the idea that peace is fundamentally about a concord of *desires* (appetites or wills), Aquinas deduces that an authentic bond of peace is possible among human beings, say in civil society, even when they hold different opinions. Differences of opinion, he writes, are "not [necessarily] an obstacle to peace, because opinions involve cognition . . . [while it is by reason of] appetite [that people] are united through peace" (1895: II–II, q. 29, a. 3, ad 2). Thus, on his understanding, people can be genuinely united in peace even if they disagree about secondary or non-essential matters. By contrast, disagreements over matters essential to the common good inevitably disrupt the unity of peace (see Schwartz 2007: 22–41).

THE PEACE THAT IS SAID OF GOD

In his commentary on *The Divine Names*, Aquinas emphasizes how the peace that is predicated of human beings, angels, and indeed the whole cosmos, has its source in the peace which is said of God. Or, to use his terminology, these created actualizations of peace represent so many ways of participating in uncreated peace, *divina pax*, the peace of God (*pax Dei*) (1950: ch. 11, §§901ff.). These words occur in a text that is mainly concerned with explaining how peace flows from God to creatures. Curiously, however, as far as I can see, Aquinas never explicitly addressed the question, neither in this commentary, nor in the *Summa of Theology* (or elsewhere for that matter), in what way exactly peace should be predicated of God. While it is clear that this predication is more than merely metaphorical (as for instance when scripture refers to God's anger), it remains unclear whether peace is said of God solely by relation to creatures, namely insofar as he is the causative source of the peace which is found in us, or (other alternative) whether peace may be said of God as he is in Himself irrespective of his relation to creatures. As an example of the first sort of predication, Aquinas mentions attributes such as goodness and wisdom. In his terminology these are said "absolutely" and "affirmatively" of God. To say that God is "good" is not simply to affirm that he is the supreme cause of goodness in things, but moreover, by this term we wish to characterize something about God's very substance (Thomas Aquinas 1895: I, q. 13, a. 2 ad 6).

Other names are said of God affirmatively but relatively to creatures (see especially Thomas Aquinas 1895: I, q. 13, a. 7), either insofar as God acts on creatures (hence we speak of his "power" or "justice"), or because he is the source of some perfection that is found in creatures. In the latter case, the perfection is found *formally* in creatures but *eminently* in God. My hunch is that the logic of his argumentation requires Aquinas to view "peace" as a name of this sort. Recall what was said above about how peace denotes the *removal of obstacles* to the fulfillment of desire, and the reduction of *diversity* into unity. This reduction of diversity to unity is implied when it is said that peace is the tranquility of order (that the tranquility of order implies a diversity that is brought into unity is stated in Thomas Aquinas 1950: ch. 11, §891). But God's being is such that no obstacles can stand in the way of his fulfillment—hence none need be removed—nor is there any diversity in God's nature that can be brought into unity. He is purely and simply One, and for this reason, it would seem that peace can be said of his being, not formally, but only in relation to creatures.

Still, although it would seem that peace cannot be said formally of God, it remains that the idea of security, of inviolability, of flourishing without being subject to any threat or harm, does indeed characterize God's being. And insofar as these notions are part and parcel of peace, there can be good reason to say that God is peace itself (just as it is said that God is goodness or truth itself). On occasion, Aquinas does speak this way, as in his commentary on the *Divine Names,* where he writes first that God is to be praised as peace (*Deus, laudatur est pax*) (1950: ch. 4, §516) and then attributes to Dionysius the view that insofar as this peace is divine it exists in itself (*in se est*) (1950: ch. 11, §880), in other words not just relatively to creatures. Usually, however, Aquinas does not go this far and contents himself with statements such as "peace ... is found first and foremost in the source of order, namely in God (*scilicet in Deo*) or that from the "profound source," which is "the peace that is in God" (*in Deo ... in quo est pax*), "peace flows" into us (both statements appear in 1953b: 4:7, §159).

Among the texts I have surveyed, the closest Aquinas comes to affirming in his own voice that peace is an inherent attribute of God is in his commentary to Jn 14:27. There he explains how when Jesus said "my peace be with you," this phrase can have a twofold meaning. On the one hand, it may refer to the peace that is achievable in our present "terrestrial" condition, a peace that is not without opposition. However good this peace may be, it is nonetheless subject to disruption. Aquinas accordingly holds that Christ is the author of this peace but not its possessor (because there can be no imperfection in Christ insofar as he is God). By contrast, if "my peace I give you" is interpreted as a reference to the peace of the heavenly Jerusalem, where the blessed enjoy peace in perfect stability without the slightest opposition, then Christ may be termed both its author and possessor. This peace, Thomas adds, Christ possessed always (*semper*), a seeming allusion the condition of eternal and unassailable peace that characterizes his divine nature (Thomas Aquinas 1972: 14: 27, §1963). Note how, on Aquinas's Christian understanding, Christ is both human and divine, "true man and true God." By the first he is temporal and by the latter he is eternal. Thus, to say that Christ has peace *eternally* is equivalent, for Aquinas, to saying that he has this attribute by virtue of his identity with God. If, by his divine nature, Christ has peace, by inference we must say that God too is possessed of this attribute.

As an aside, it would seem on this basis that Aquinas would be little concerned with the problem of blasphemy, for if God's peace is inviolable, no acts can harm God. The contrary, however, appears to have been the case. Aquinas uttered strong words against blasphemy and thought that it could merit civil punishment. Taking the action of Jesus as an example, he noted how although Jesus patiently bore insults to his humanity (in other words he did not use force to defend himself nor did he allow others to forcibly defend him) he did not countenance insults directed against his divinity (Thomas Aquinas 1996: q. 12 lines 46–64, citing the story of Jesus and Beeizebul in Mt. 12: 22–32).

As Aquinas explained elsewhere (1895: I-II, q. 73, a. 8, ad 2), "no one can harm God in God's very substance." However, he immediately acknowledges that things pertaining to God can indeed be harmed, for instance, should someone seek to destroy human faith in God. In yet another passage (1895: II-II, q. 13, a. 3, ad 1), he examined whether blasphemy is worse than murder. His conclusion: "with respect to the harm done, murder is the graver sin, for it does more harm to the neighbor than blasphemy does to [things belonging to] God." But as regards the very object of the sin, blasphemy is worse, as it impugns God's honor, and for this reason blasphemy is a more grievous sin. He concedes, however, that murder should be more severely punished in the civil sphere.

KINDS OF PEACE AND ZONES OF PEACE

Leaving off this digression on blasphemy, let us now return to the main thread of Aquinas's treatment of peace (the description below of Aquinas's conception of peace draws on the more detailed account that may be found in Reichberg 2017: 3–4, 17–41). Above I summed up his teaching about the possessors of peace, which he identifies as human beings, angels, the cosmos, and God. Aquinas also took care to delineate different modalities or kinds of peace. These represent the various ways that authors in the Christian tradition may be found applying the term *pax*. Very common among these authors was to contrast the "perfect peace" of the Heavenly Jerusalem (Thomas Aquinas 1979: II, ch. 9, p. 204, lines 433–4: "in the future [kingdom of God] there will be complete peace," *omnimoda pax*), from the "true" but "imperfect peace" of our present condition.[6] Aquinas endorses this terminology and he explains how the first characterizes the peace of the blessed in heaven.[7] Having crossed the threshold of death, their communion in the vision of God renders them participants in the attribute of divine immutability. Peace at this level cannot be assailed by violence or in any way harmed by dissension,[8] and for this reason it is called "perfect" or "complete" (the Latin word *perfectus* conveys both meanings). By contrast, the "imperfect peace of the wayfarer"[9] is the condition of peace as it is found among the virtuous of "this world." This peace is vulnerable to attack, because the shared truth which lies at its foundation—and the communion of charity that flows from it—rests on belief, not intellectual vision; hence the threat of grave dissension remains a constant danger. But alongside the perfect and imperfect peace, both of which he considered peace in the proper sense of the term (hence he refers to them as "true" peace), he also recognized how there could be an appearance of peace even among evildoers, as when members of a criminal organization cooperate to carry out their crimes. This Aquinas termed a "false" peace. By contrast, he affirms that true peace necessarily presupposes virtue: "true peace is only in good men who are intent on doing good things. The peace of the wicked is not a true peace but a semblance thereof" (Thomas Aquinas 1895: II–II, q. 29, a. 2, ad 3). That peace requires moral uprightness and results from the close link between peace and goodness, and the insight that in human life peace is an effect of charity, the highest of the virtues. By charity, humans beings adhere to God as ultimate end, thereby inwardly affirming that in Him alone fulfillment may be found. Because this end encompasses all the other pursuits we might have, a right ordination to God ensures order in the multiplicity of our other desires. In this way, "[p]eace is obtained by submitting to and obeying God" (Meinert: 2016: 1199, paraphrasing Thomas Aquinas 1953a: 5, lectio 1, §382). Not only does charity have God for its chief end, but it comes about as a direct effect of God's action. This means that charity does not arise in us as a fruit of our own effort and initiative, but only by God working in us, lifting our nature to a mode of action that would otherwise be impossible for us to engage in. This means that peace likewise, insofar as it stems from charity, also arises in us an effect of grace. "Peace . . . is impossible without grace" (Shogimen 2010: 876).

Although peace arises in us as an "effect of charity," which is itself caused by grace, Aquinas is keen to point out that peace is not a merely passive condition. Vis-à-vis God we are indeed recipients of grace, but the effect of this reception of is to render us active; by means of grace we are able to assume a new form of agency. Aquinas can thus infer that "peace" is not so much a passive condition of "repose" or "contentedness," but more dynamically it names the action of being a "peacemaker."[10] Finally, Aquinas spoke of the "illicit peace" which can arise when the good, for the sake of concord, wrongly cooperate with the wicked. Commenting on the Apostle Paul's statement (Rom. 12:18) "if it be possible . . . have peace with all men," Aquinas explains how "sometimes other people's malice stands in the way of our having peace with them, inasmuch as no peace is possible unless we consent to their malice." "Such peace, he adds, is obviously illicit" (1953a: 12:18, §1010).

Much could be said about these distinctions. On the one hand, by acknowledging that the peace of this world is an imperfect one, he is, in effect, lowering our expectations about what can be achieved in our communal living, certainly within the civic order. We should beware of utopian attempts at replicating the perfect peace of the heavenly Jerusalem here below. Some of the worst forms of tyranny in contemporary society—I am thinking of, for instance, Cambodia under the Khmer Rouge—have resulted from an attempt to make society "pure," to purge it of all elements that do not fit "the ideal plan." Another pitfall would consist in placing an excessive expectation on our governments to make us perfectly secure. An expectation such as this can lead governments to adopt questionable measures, for instance a strategy of preventive attack, a strategy that Hugo Grotius (in line with the teaching of Aquinas) criticized as "abhorrent to every principle of equity." To this he added the wise reflection that "human life exists under such conditions that complete security is never given to us" (*De iure belli ac pacis*, II.I.XVII[1] in Reichberg, Syse, and Begby 2006: 405).

On the other hand, by linking the imperfect peace of this world to virtue (recall Aquinas's sentence that "true peace is only in good men who are intent on doing good things") he is telling us that coming together in society, and being governed well, involves more than being assured of our physical security. Instead, he framed the ultimate purpose of political society in terms of living a life of virtue together (Thomas Aquinas 1979b: bk. 2, ch. 2). But this high objective he tempered with the recognition that because the peace to be aimed at here below is an imperfect one "not all good acts should be commanded by law, nor all bad acts prohibited" (Thomas Aquinas 1895: I–II, q. 96, a. 3, ad 1).

Continuing his explanation of the words of Jesus, "my peace I give to you," Aquinas reverts to the famous Augustinian formula that peace is the "tranquility of order." "Peace," he writes, arises when order remains undisturbed (*ordo interbatus manet*) (Thomas Aquinas 1972: 14:27, §1962). Applying this formula specifically to human beings, Aquinas adds that just as there are three sorts of order, so too, for us, are there fundamentally three zones of peace ("triplex pax in homine"): namely when proper order is maintained (i) within an individual person ("hominis ad seipsum"), (ii) between a person and God ("hominis ad Deum"), and (iii) between a person and his neighbor ("hominus ad proximum").

There could be much to say about each of these zones of peace. Thus, for instance, Aquinas maintains that, of the three, the relation of human beings to God is the most fundamental, because it is only when we are rightly ordered to God that we are able to achieve order within ourselves (serenity or "inner peace") and between ourselves (interpersonal harmony). He frames this in relation to the fundamental Christian virtue, charity. By this virtue we are joined to God in friendship. This, in turn, is the basis for proper self-love, and, by extension, it renders us capable of loving each other effectively and appropriately. Aquinas sums this up when he writes that peace

> consists in two things, such that a man be in harmony with himself and with others. Neither can this be had sufficiently without God. For without God no one can have harmony within himself, much less with others, because a man's desires are in harmony in himself [and in concord with the desires of others] when what is desired by one suffices for all. Nothing but God can do this . . . For nothing other than God is sufficient [to quiet] all [desires] but God is sufficient.
>
> —1953c: 3, lectio 2, §89

Because peace is so closely linked to charity, and charity itself is a fruit of grace, should we infer that those not in a state of grace cannot be partakers in true peace? This would seem to be an implication of St. Thomas's argumentation. Does it accordingly follow that he could not acknowledge the possibility of a civic peace that would join within a single community Christians and non-Christians, under the assumption that the latter, by not having accepted the one true faith, are excluded from the circle of charity?[11] Aquinas does not expressly draw out this conclusion. For one thing, despite holding that charity gives rise to the best form of community (and a corresponding condition of peace), he recognized that "true" peace can rightly be said of other sorts of communities as well, based on natural ties of friendship. Moreover, apropos of sanctifying grace, he never claimed that it is the exclusive preserve of professed Christians. The grace that comes to human beings through the action of the Holy Spirit is, by hidden pathways, distributed beyond the boundaries of the visible Church to individuals of other faith communities (see the citations from Aquinas's writings that are collected in Bonino 2006).

SOCIAL AND POLITICAL DIMENSIONS OF PEACE

We have already seen how Aquinas maintains that there can be no true peace without charity (love of God and neighbor), and accordingly, no peace without true virtue (because love of God is the source of all other virtues). He sums this up by saying that peace is an "effect" (or "fruit") of charity (Thomas Aquinas 1895: II–II, q. 29, a. 3–4). He does recognize that justice has an important role to play vis-à-vis peace. Yet, he claims that justice (for instance, observing the rule of law) "removes obstacles to peace" but does not directly bring it about. Insofar as societal peace involves people having a shared attachment to the common good, a communion in the goods of virtue, this peace must have charity as its proximate root. Justice plays a necessary, but secondary role. Justice is premised on otherness (recognizing what is yours is indeed yours and what is mine is indeed mine) and as such does not join me to you. If anything, it leads me to recognize how we are distinct from one another. Love, by contrast, is the fundamental "unitive force" (1895: II–II, 29.3.3).

In reflecting on the social and political implications of this statement, Aquinas was struck by a line from Aristotle's *Nicomachean Ethics*, bk. 8. Upon enumerating the benefits that friendship brings to human life, Aristotle observed that its importance is not confined to the individual self, but extends even more crucially to the public sphere as well, "For polities (*civitates*), it seems, are held together (*continere*) by friendship" (Aristotle 1984b: bk 8, ch. 1, 1155a22–23). Reading this phrase in Latin translation,

Aquinas noticed how in the remainder of the sentence Aristotle linked the theme of friendship as a binding force within the polis to the related theme of concord:

> And legislators are more zealous about it [friendship] than about justice; this is evident from the similarity between friendship and concord [Greek *homonoia*, literally "oneness of mind"] for legislators most of all wish to encourage concord and to expel discord as an enemy of the polity.
>
> —1969: at 1155a 22–26

Aristotle's idea that "polities are held together by friendship" was made operative by Aquinas on two different levels. On the one hand, he applied it in the way that was

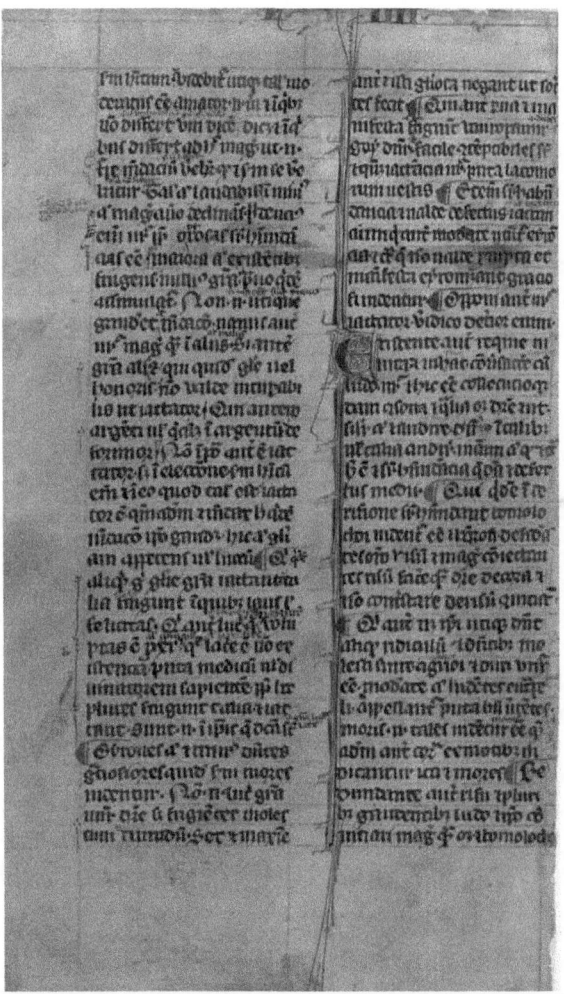

FIGURE 2.2: Thomas Aquinas, Commentary on Aristotle's *Ethics*, manuscript (fragment), copied not long after Aquinas's death (last quarter of the thirteenth century to first quarter of the fourteenth century), London, British Library, MS Sloane 1044, fol. 115v. Public domain image available from the British Library: http://www.bl.uk/catalogues/illuminatedmanuscripts/ILLUMINBig.ASP?size=big&IllID=14957

manifestly intended by Aristotle, namely internally (*ad intra*) to the members of a single polity, say within the ancient city-state of Athens or the medieval kingdom of Naples. On the other hand, Aquinas saw that it also could extend *ad extra* when one independent polity was joined in friendship to another. This distinction between the two kinds of civic friendship, namely intra- and inter-state, is explicitly made by Aquinas in *Super Ethic.*, bk. 9, ch. 6. Whereas Aristotle had referred solely to concord among citizens of the same polity, Aquinas discretely adds that it could also encompass the mutual relations of distinct polities:

> [Aristotle] Political friendship (*politica amicitia*), then, seems to be concord, as is commonly held; for it deals with affairs that advance their interests and concern their lives.
>
> —Thomas Aquinas 1969: at 1167b2–4
>
> [Aquinas] Next, at "Political then," Aristotle shows how concord is related to friendship among citizens. He notes that political friendship, either between citizens of the same polity (*civium unius civitatis ad invicem*), or between different polities (*inter diversas civitates*), seems to be identical with concord. And people usually speak of it this way: that polities or citizens (*civitates vel cives*) in concord with one another (*concordes*) enjoy mutual friendship (*habent amicitiam ad invicem*).
>
> —ibid., lines 74–80

Having explained how the social bond of peace derives from charity, Aquinas proceeds to consider the opposing sins (under the supposition that every virtue, charity included, has a set of contrary vices) (1895: II–II, q. 40–2). Among these he names: (i) schism, (ii) war, and (iii) sedition. Each of these vices is defined by reference to the specific type of social peace (concord) that it undermines. This leads Aquinas to elucidate in greater detail the different zones of societal peace. *Schism* stands opposed to the fellowship of believers who are joined together in charity; it thus disrupts the unity of the Church. For Aquinas this is the worst of all sins against societal peace. *War* ("bellum") disrupts the bond that unites one people to another; it violates the peace that is characteristic of the community of nations; *sedition*, finally, divides the unity of a single people or nation, leading it down the path of civil war. Whereas Aquinas is very clear that the peace of the Church flows immediately from the bond of charity and is constituted by it (Thomas Aquinas 1953d: 2:2 §59), he is considerably more circumspect when it comes to peace in the civic and international spheres. With respect to the latter two, he suggests that peace is achieved by analogy with charity (understood as a form of communion) rather than being itself a direct instantiation of this highest religious virtue. His point is that every community, of whatever sort, requires fellow-feeling and shared identity; formal relationships of law and justice are never enough to bind people together. But the bond in question will vary according to the type of community involved: the way that members of a family identify with each other will be very different than, say, the fellow-feeling required for a national community; the inter-relations of different peoples (independent political communities) will hinge on a still-different type of bond.

CAN PEACE EXTEND ACROSS RELIGIOUS LINES OF DIVISION?

During an age of faith such as the Middle Ages, the question whether friendship (hence peace) is possible in different religious traditions was handled in contrasting ways. Few, if any, thinkers were prepared to admit that civic amity could extend very far beyond the members of the dominant faith community. Shared faith was then viewed as integral to the unity of the civil sphere, so that even theologians such as Aquinas who could differentiate peace at the two levels of the Church and state nevertheless assumed that non-Christians could not be integrated as full members of even the latter community. Restrictions were placed on interaction with them, and they were not deemed to be fit targets of civic friendship (Thomas Aquinas 1895: II–II, q. 10, a. 7–12). The attitude toward fallen-away Christians was even more severe. Individuals placed under ecclesial ban ("excommunication") risked losing their property and other civic privileges, and should they actively encourage others along the path of dissidence, they could be found guilty of apostasy or even heresy, wrongs that were treated as serious civil crimes, and could be punishable by death. A constant in medieval Christian thought, a parallel teaching existed within Islam. For instance, Ibn Rushd (1126–1198, known in the Latin West as Averroës), wrote that "heretics must be killed"; by their denial of key principles about religion they undermine the foundations of social existence (Averroës 1978: 322).

FIGURE 2.3: Statue of Averroës, Cordoba, Spain. By Marco Chiesa, Madrid, Spain - Averroes, CC BY 2.0. Source: Wikimedia, https://commons.wikimedia.org/w/index.php?curid=39377664

Jews, on the other hand, had little to say about civil punishment (as opposed to spiritual sanctions such as exclusion from the synagogue) for unbelief; living as minorities within Christian or Muslim states, they were not in a position to impose such penalties themselves.

Despite the general consensus among Christian thinkers regarding the religious foundations of society and hence the need to punish dissidence, there was a spectrum of views on the possibility of peaceful co-existence among different faith communities. On the one side there was the exclusivist position advocated by the canon lawyer Henry of Suse (1200–1271), who is better known by the sobriquet "Hostiensis" (from the town of Ostia in Italy where he served as cardinal-bishop). Hostiensis maintained that "right" (*ius*) derived ultimately from God's message as revealed in the Old (and especially) New Testaments. Having no direct access to this revelation, "infidels" (which included both pagans and Muslims) possessed no legitimate right to the lands on which they lived. Thus, Christians could legitimately use force to make these lands their own. This provided a clear rationale for the medieval crusades to recover the Holy Land from Muslims, who (it was assumed) did not have true title to lands they had expropriated (Muldoon 1979). A similar reasoning was applied two centuries later when "new" lands were discovered in the Americas and the inhabitants were dispossessed of their goods. Moreover, in the absence of any shared embrace of revelation, there could be no permanent condition of peace between Christians and these infidels. This led Hostiensis to argue that waging war against the latter was, in principle, always legitimate. He termed this kind of war *bellum Romanum* (Roman war) to emphasize its likeness to the wars, legitimate in his eyes, which ancient Rome waged against foreign peoples (thus considering Christendom as heir to the legal prerogatives of the Roman Empire). By contrast, whereas violent conflict was, as it were, the natural condition that obtained between Christians and non-believers, he viewed peace as the default (normative) condition among Christians, such that any armed conflict between them was considered illegitimate and could only happen with special justification and by permission of the emperor (these views are elucidated in his *Summa aurea*, a section on "Truce and Peace"; for a translation, see Reichberg, Syse, and Begby 2006: 161–8). Moreover, when Christians fought against each other they were bound by a more restrictive set of rules than those that would be applicable in confrontations with Muslims or other "unbelievers." This adherence to contrasting rules, one set for fellow Christians, and the other vis-à-vis the infidels, would persist during the centuries ahead.

On the other side of the spectrum, Hostiensis's contemporary Sinibaldo de Fiesco, better known as Pope Innocent IV (reigned 1243–1254), maintained that by natural right infidels were possessed of dominium; hence their ownership of property, and self-rule, must be respected. The foundation for this view of natural right was the Book of Genesis wherein it was taught that "God had subjected the world to the dominium of rational creatures for whom He made all things . . ." ("On Vows and the Fulfilling of Vows," selection translated in Reichberg, Syse, and Begby [2006]: 152–5). Innocent understood this to imply that by our very creation as rational creatures (thus prescinding from adherence to divine revelation as attested in the Scriptures) all goods are held in common and can be appropriated for our individual use as needed.

> From the beginning things belonged to anyone who occupied them, because they belonged to no one except the Lord. Therefore it was licit for anyone to occupy what was not already occupied, but it was not licit to occupy what was occupied by another, because it would be against natural law (*lege nature*), which enjoins everyone not to do unto others what one does not wish to be done to oneself.
> —Reichberg, Syse, and Begby 2006: 152–55

FIGURE 2.4: Portrait of Pope Innocent IV, writing. Detail from a manuscript of his *Apparatus in quinque libros Decretalium*, London, British Library, MS Royal 11 E II, fol. 1r. Italy, first quarter of the fourteenth century. Public domain image available from the British Library: https://www.bl.uk/catalogues/illuminatedmanuscripts/ILLUMINBig.ASP?size=big&IllID=56499

The upshot was that if the crusades to recover the Holy Land could be justified, this would have to be on a basis other than the one alleged by Hostiensis (namely that the Muslims, as unbelievers, were deprived of dominium over their lands). Innocent located this basis in the fact, evident in his eyes, that the Muslims had wrongly seized a land whose original ownership pertained to Christians. Jesus Christ had consecrated this land (hence it was *terra sancta*, a "holy land") by his birth, life, and death, such that these lands had become the "inheritance" of Christians. On the related topic of war, Innocent maintained that it cannot be waged against non-Christians simply to eradicate their condition of unbelief: "infidels should not be forced to accept the faith, since everyone's free will ought to be respected, and this conversion should [come about] only by the grace of God" (Reichberg, Syse, and Begby 2006: 154). Only some cause over and above this condition of unbelief could, in his eyes, justify such war, for instance if infidels refused "to admit preachers of the Gospel to the lands under their jurisdiction" (ibid.) or they had wrongly expropriated Christian lands, or for other unwarranted reasons they had mounted an attack on Christians.

Writing under the influence of Innocent, Thomas Aquinas similarly held that "unbelievers . . . who have never received the faith . . . are by no means to be compelled to the faith, in order that they should believe, because to believe depends on [free] will" (1895: II–II, q. 10, a. 8). The implication followed that offensive holy war, namely war to expand the boundaries of Christendom, was to be excluded. Along with his peers, Aquinas nonetheless acknowledged that it was justifiable to defend religious interests by forcible means, namely, in his words, "to impede [unbelievers] from hindering the faith of Christ" (ibid.). Similarly, in line with the received thinking of his time, he held that individuals who had withdrawn from the true faith (heretics or apostates) and encouraged others to do the same, could be compelled by "bodily compulsion" to "fulfill what they have promised [by their baptismal vows], and to hold what they at one time received" (ibid.). Although he does not say so explicitly, Aquinas would likely have agreed that an entire war could be fought in view of this purpose, as had happened in the south of France some fifty years prior, when pope Innocent III launched a crusade to repress the Cathar heresy.

Apart from commenting on these special religious rationales for waging war, Aquinas stood out from his contemporaries inasmuch as he could discuss war in abstraction from these religious reasons. His famous treatment of just war in the *Summa of theology* mentions three criteria by which any engagement in war may be deemed permissible: such a war must proceed from a legitimate authority, who resorts to force for a just cause, and does so as animated by an upright intention. The defense of faith no longer occupies center stage. Instead, the resort to force is justified by reference to the well-being of the *respublica* and the protection of the *common good*, terms of Greek and Roman origin. In approaching the question of war in this way, Aquinas proceeds from the background assumption, buttressed by the respect for nature that he inherited from Aristotle, that the nations of the world form a kind of community that has the good of our humanity as its foundation. Grace perfects nature but does not destroy it; thus Aquinas could conceive of ties of friendship that might be established across different peoples and cultures (for further elucidation, see Reichberg 2017: 20–7). These ideas would be more amply developed in the sixteenth century by Aquinas's disciple Francisco de Vitoria (Reichberg 2003). In Aquinas we accordingly find articulated a new conception of peace, one that seeks to identity a foundation for universal bonds—based on nature rather than being restricted to principles drawn from positive divine revelation—that can stretch across peoples and nations.

PARALLEL DEVELOPMENTS IN ISLAM AND JUDAISM

During the Middle Ages there appears to have been little direct sharing of ideas on war and peace across the three Abrahamic traditions. We have explored above some leading ideas on this theme within Latin Christianity, but it goes without saying that this period also witnessed important parallel discussions within Islam and Judaism.

Virtually all medieval Islamic jurists established a sharp line of division between the Muslim commonwealth, on the one hand, and the world of non-believers, on the other. Significantly, for our purposes, the first was called the "abode of peace" (*dar al-Islam*), and the other the "abode of war" (*dar al-harb*). In practice, the content that was assigned to these key concepts varied from author to author. Roughly, however, two orientations emerged. According to one, a condition of perpetual hostility existed between the adherents of Islam and members of other religions. War could rightly be waged against these infidels, following the words of the Prophet: "And fight them until there is no persecution and the religion is God's; then if they give over, there shall be no enmity save for evildoers" (Qur'an 2:193). A special status was nonetheless recognized for "peoples of the book," namely Jews, Christians, and (on some accounts) Zoroastrians, insofar as by their Scriptures they had a share in divine revelation. The hostility that would normally obtain was tempered by their commitment to monotheism, but because they failed to recognize Mohammad as God's highest prophet, they would be permitted to live on

Muslim lands, and follow their own religious law, provided that they acknowledged their subordinate status by effecting a special payment called *jizya* ("poll tax"). This teaching was summed up in the eleventh century by Shaykh Tusi (995–1068), "Master of the Clan" (*Shaykh al-Tai'fah*):

> Jihad against all infidels is obligatory for all Muslims. Unbelievers are divided into two categories. One group includes all unbelievers [in Islam]. Nothing short of accepting Islam is acceptable from them. If they refuse, they must be killed and their offspring captured and their properties confiscated. This rule does not apply to Jews, Zoroastrians, and Christians. If they pay the obligatory tax (*jizyah*) and decide to remain in their religion, fighting against them is not permissible. Otherwise, the rule that applies to infidels applies to them as well and in such a case fighting against them is obligatory (Tusi, *al-Nihayah fi mujarrad al-fiqh wa'l fatwa* (*The Ultimate Source on Principles of Jurisprudence and Legal Verdict*); passage translated in Reichberg and Syse (2014): 425–6).

In contrast to this priority given to offensive *jihad*, namely war to subjugate unbelievers and thereby to expand the boundaries of the *dar al-Islam*, another group of jurists emphasized that relations of peace with non-believers should instead take precedence. On this understanding, war cannot rightly be waged against adherents of other religions simply on grounds of their unbelief. Citing the words of the Prophet "No compulsion is there in religion" (Qur'an 2:256), these jurists held that Muslims could justifiably fight non-believers only when the latter had attacked first, according to the verse which states "And fight in the way of God with those who fight you, but aggress not" (Qur'an 2:191). On this basis, it has been argued that jihad can defensively be undertaken to impede the persecution of Muslims by non-believers, to resist their annexation of Muslim lands, or to defend Muslims when war has been imposed on them. This line of argument is explicitly developed by contemporary jurists who draw on the writings of medieval predecessors such as Ibn Taymihah (1263–1328) and Ibn Qayyim (1292–1350). It has found a particularly fertile terrain among those Shi'ite jurists who hold to the teaching that no offensive jihad can be waged without an edict of an infallible imam. Ever since the "occultation" of the Twelfth imam in 941, his seat has remained empty (so to speak), and in the absence of his authorization, no offensive warfare can henceforth be allowed. Defensive warfare remains the only religiously legitimate course of action.

Somewhat akin to the contrasting positions of Hostiensis and Aquinas (discussed above) the Islamic debate on offensive vs. defensive religious warfare has likewise given rise to attempts at nuancing the otherwise stark oppositions between the "abodes" of peace and war. As Vitoria and other Christian thinkers sought to develop Aquinas's intuitions about the natural sociability of individuals and political communities, Muslim thinkers have introduced subdivisions to the original *dar al-Islam/dar al-harb* categorization. Thus, the *dar al-Hudna* ("Abode of Calm") has been posited as the condition of infidel lands that are in a state of truce with Muslims. Under the Ottoman Empire, others similarly referred to the *dar al-'Ahd* or *dar al-Sulh* (Abode of Treaty or Peace). These designated the non-Muslim lands where Muslims could live and practice their religion freely. A recent author notes how the "existence of these legal terms and entities in fact demonstrates that Islamic understandings of relations with the non-Muslim world is not limited to war and peace alone, but that within the confines of the *Shari'ah*, a wide variety of possible relationships indeed exist" (Reichberg and Syse 2014: 432).

Within medieval Jewish thought, discussion of peace and war was oriented in a very different direction than what has been said above concerning Christianity and Islam. Not having their own commonwealth, the Jews showed little concern with explaining how they, as a politically organized people, could or could not coexist with other peoples. Lacking a state of their own, they could not exercise the attendant political power, which rendered discussion of war nearly otiose. But since war was nonetheless an important topic in the Hebrew Scriptures, it was unavoidable that the rabbis should take it up in their commentaries, if only as a purely theoretical enterprise. This being the case, their discussion of war was orientated around the distinction, which emerged from their reading of Scripture, between "obligatory" (or "commanded") wars, on the one hand, and merely "permitted" (or "optional") wars on the other.

As the name suggests "obligatory wars" were commanded by God. All adult Israelite men had a religious obligation to fight in such wars. Examples advanced included (i) the injunction to fight the Amalekites from generation to generation (Exod. 17:8–16; Deut. 25:17–19; 1 Sam. 30:1–16), (ii) and the similar injunction to forcibly subdue the Land that God had given the Israelites as an inheritance, thereby (iii) killing off the idolatrous occupants (Deut. 20:17), (iv) Joshua's war of conquest against the Seven Nations (Josh. 1–12), and more generally (v) any personal or collective defense from attack. The last-named rationale was summed up by the rabbinical principle (articulated *c*. AD 500) "If someone rises up to kill you, kill him first!" (a much-repeated saying that first appeared in the Babylonian Talmud: tractate Sanhedrin 72: a, see Afterman and Afterman 2012). These passages raised a wide set of questions and even perplexities (e.g., Who were the Amalakites, and did they even exist? Had there actually been a war against the Seven Nations or was this intended to be understood allegorically?).

Permissive wars were those ordered by the kings for their political purposes. The wars conducted by King David were usually thought of in this light. There was no religious ("halakhic") obligation to take part, and the rabbis offered many exceptions for those men who wished to abstain from such fighting. Moreover, the rabbis showed considerable skepticism vis-à-vis wars of this sort, and circumscribed them with a set of conditions that were hard to meet (e.g., an authorization of the Sanhedrin was required before the king could lead his troops into battle, and this authorization, in turn, could be handed down only if the Temple oracle, the *Urim ve Tumin*, had conveyed God's approval). "The point of [this twofold] authorization . . . was not to provide religious or divine justification . . . [for] the king's independently initiated wars, but just the opposite . . . [this] approval . . . was meant to be a constraint by which the Rabbis hoped to prevent and control kings from going to war at all" (Reichberg and Syse 2014: 15). Moreover, both functions (the Sanhedrin and the *Urim ve Tumin*) had long ceased to exist by the time medieval thinkers came to their reflections on the biblical texts that had spoken of war, For this reason, such rationales could no longer function to justify war.

Two contrasting approaches emerged. First there was the account proposed by Moses Maimonides (1135–1204). Chiefly interested in detailing the characteristics of a righteous king, Maimonides reframed ancient Israel's wars of conquest, describing them allegorically as an attack of monotheism against idolatry. This was "a battle of mind and consciousness, rather than a battle for land and resources" (Reichberg and Syse 2014: 16). War in the literal sense of one army confronting another, carried out with the expressly "divine" purpose of eradicating idolatry, he thought, could have warrant solely within the land of Israel itself (further elucidation on Maimonides may be found in Chapter Four in this volume).

Writing after Maimonides and in reaction to his views, rabbi Moses Nachmanides (1194–1270) placed the obligation to conquer and hold the Land of Israel at the heart of his comments on war. Criticizing his esteemed predecessor for having failed to posit the settling of this Land as a definite commandment, Nachmanides argued that this ordinance of God was binding on all generations, and thus should not be considered as abrogated after the destruction of the Temple in AD 70. He accordingly recognized that efforts toward its recovery, and the fighting that would be necessary to dislodge its unworthy occupants, had rightly been termed by "our sages . . . a holy war" (Reichberg and Syse 2014: 17).

CONCLUSION

After an initial reflection on the metaphysics of peace, we have concentrated on the moral, social, and political dimensions of peace, as conceptualized by Thomas Aquinas and several other medieval thinkers. This overview is by no means exhaustive but has aimed, instead, at exhibiting some of the representative tendencies. All the thinkers concerned, whether Christian, Muslim, or Jewish, shared a set of assumptions regarding the dependency of human beings upon God. All would have agreed that peace can be achieved, within its various zones, only when human beings and their communities actively subordinate themselves to God. But how this subordination should come about, what concrete steps should be taken toward its implementation, and the end-state that should be sought, was parsed out in contrasting ways, both between and within different religious traditions. How each religious community should conduct itself in relation to the others was the subject of particular disagreement; narrow and broad conceptions of peace were advanced, and in their wake, we find authors advocating for war on similarly broad and narrow grounds.

CHAPTER THREE

Peace, War, and Gender

KATRIN E. SJURSEN

In 1347, Queen Philippa of England journeyed to Calais, France to visit her husband Edward III after a long separation caused by his military campaign to seize the throne of France. Edward had recently forced the city of Calais to surrender to his months-long siege, and he was quite annoyed at the burghers who had led the resistance against him for so long. According to the chroniclers Jean le Bel and Jean Froissart, Edward had determined to kill six city representatives on the spot, but, convinced by Philippa's tears and pleas for mercy while on bended knee, he offered a pardon (and eviction from the city) instead (le Bel 1904: 166–7 [§ 81]; Froissart 1873: 62 [§312]).[1] This episode of intercession has become a hallmark of medieval women's active engagement in warfare. Yet, just a few pages before the Calais episode, the chroniclers described how Philippa had assembled an army to oppose an incursion into England undertaken by King David II of Scotland: she took him prisoner, shored up the borders between England and Scotland, and then departed for the continent to join her husband (le Bel 1904: 125–31 [§76]; Froissart 1873: 18–29 [§295–99]). As Philippa's actions demonstrate, medieval noblewomen actively participated in peacemaking and warfare in a variety of ways, despite the widespread cultural conviction of a gendered division between warfare and peace.

While the conception of warfare as masculine and peace as feminine has been well researched, the role of women in these activities, particularly in warfare, is understudied and rife with myths and misconceptions. The small handful of general articles that survey women's support roles in warfare (Truax 1999; Dubois 2004; Gilbert 2005) find only a single complementary survey of women fighting or leading troops (McLaughlin 1990). The bulk of the scholarship focuses on individual women or groups from similar regions and periods, with the crusades prompting a good deal of study (Gershenzon and Litman 1995; Edgington and Lambert 2001; Maier 2004; Hodgson 2007; H. J. Nicholson 1997 and Nicholson 2015; Mazeika 1998). Anglo-Norman and French women have garnered the most attention to date. The following essay will survey the current scholarship on the relationship of peace and war to gender, with a particular focus on correcting commonly held myths about the role women played in both.

IMPRINTING WAR-MAKING AS MASCULINE

It should come as no surprise that in the Middles Ages, as it still is today, warfare was coded as masculine. Both canon law and secular advice literature emphasized that women should not participate in warfare. Eleventh-century churchmen, such as Bonizo de Sutri, Regino of Prüm, and Burchard of Worms, based prohibitions against women exercising public authority on Paul's injunction against women speaking in church (1 Cor. 14:34–35) and on early Church condemnations found in Canon 19 of the Council of Nantes in 896 (Hay 2004). Meanwhile, in their political treatises on good rulership, the scholastic writers Ptolemy of Lucca (c. 1236–1327) and Giles of Rome (1243–1316) utilized current medical theories about biology and knowledge of animal behavior to argue against women participating in warfare (Blythe 2001). Ptolemy, for example, ingeniously argued that the exercise of weapons practice might help women to both warm and dry themselves, an obvious benefit for the notoriously cold and moist female sex, but he ultimately agreed with Giles about the mental and physical insufficiencies of women for military arts (Blythe 2001: 242–70). Like these authors, Raymond Lull, a Majorcan knight-turned-monk whose book on chivalry, written between 1263 and 1283, was extremely popular throughout the later Middle Ages, unconditionally rejected women's participation in warfare. He argued that women were not as courageous nor vigorous as men, and that females were too vain to be knights (Lull 2004: 17–18 and 58). The prevailing opinion in these genres pronounced women unfit to engage in warfare as either warriors or generals.

When turning from the proscriptive literature of law codes and secular manuals to the ostensibly more descriptive literature of chronicles, utilizing examples of real contemporary people, the scholar finds warfare's masculine nature upheld. According to the Anglo-Norman chronicler Orderic Vitalis (1075–1142), before the restless Normans ventured into southern Italy, the locals customarily paid off Saracen raiders to keep the peace. The Normans, Orderic wrote, were appalled at this practice and "chaffed the Apulians for purchasing their liberty like helpless widows instead of defending it as men should, sword in hand" (Orderic Vitalis 1969–80: vol. 2, 56–57). Chroniclers of the crusades concurred with the Normans' way of thinking. In Robert the Monk's version of Pope Urban II's call for the First Crusade, the pope declared, "neither should a woman set out under any circumstances without her husband, brother or other legitimate guarantor. That is because such pilgrims are more of a hindrance than a help, a burden rather than of any practical use" (Robert the Monk 2006: 83). Urban believed these women would participate only as defenseless pilgrims, in need of a male protector and likely a distraction to the men whose purpose was to take the Holy Land by force of arms. Warfare more rightly belonged to men.

To further underline the gender division, some chroniclers used women to shame men for failing in their masculine duties of fighting. Orderic Vitalis approvingly noted that Adela of Blois famously sent her husband, Stephen of Blois, back to the Holy Land when he returned early from the First Crusade and earned the constant criticism of their friends and neighbors (Orderic Vitalis 1969–80, 5: 325). One Anglo-Norman chronicler of the Third Crusade wrote of the shaming in more general terms:

> A great many men sent each other wool and distaff, hinting that if anyone failed to join this military undertaking, they were fit only for women's work. Brides urged their husbands and mothers incited their sons to go, their only sorrow being that they were not able to set out with them because of the weakness of their sex.
>
> —Nicholson 2005: 48

Using women to shame men into fighting did not belong only to Christian writers. A Jewish chronicle describing how participants of the First Crusade massacred the Jewish community while passing through Mainz, Germany, recounted that the Jewish women berated their men for letting the unclean Christians touch and even tear apart the holy Torah. Suitably moved to "exceeding zeal," their men fought back against the attackers (Gershenzon and Litman 1995: 77).

FIGURE 3.1: Women numbered among those who followed Peter the Hermit on Crusade. Eleventh-century manuscript miniature from France. London, British Library, Egerton MS 1500, fol. 45v. Photo by DeAgostini/Courtesy of Getty Images. Credit: DEA PICTURE LIBRARY/Contributor.

While chroniclers promoted warfare as the preserve of men, they also provided a loophole through which women could honorably wage war. To do this, chronicles coded any participant in war, male or female, as acting in a "manful" way. For example, Thietmar of Merseburg (975–1018) explained that the Byzantine empress Theophano "manfully kept guard over the reign of her son" (Bange 1955: 155). Likewise, Lambert of Wattrelos described Sybil of Anjou, Countess of Flanders, as "assuming a virile heart against the count [Baldwin IV of Hainaut]," who had dared to attack her husband's lands while she was regent. Here, Sybil's heart becomes masculine, though the writer took care to describe her as a "prudent woman," indicating that she had retained her female sex throughout her military endeavours (Lambert of Watrelos 1859: 516). Similarly, the anonymous chronicler of the lords of Amboise wrote that Elizabeth of Jaligny "manfully won her land, which had been her ancestors'" and "often committed many manly and audacious deeds" (*Gesta Ambaziensium Dominorum* 1913: 112). Note that this chronicler described Elizabeth's *actions* (winning her land and the deeds themselves) as manly. The chroniclers thus upheld the belief of war as a masculine activity, albeit one performed here, quite ably, by women.

These chroniclers' acceptance of women's participation in warfare and lordship suggests that some observers could understand the gender of an activity as separate from the sex of the participant. If this were not the case, it would have been redundant for chroniclers to use the term "manfully" when describing men who fought or ruled well.[2] Gislebert of Mons, for example, explained that "when the duke [Godfrey of Louvain] and his men advanced with arrogance and ferocity, Baldwin [VI of Hainaut] and his men resist[ed] manfully" (1904: 102). Robert of Torigny wrote that King Henry II manfully defended his territory against attacks by his brother (1884: 165–6), and Lambert of Ardres wrote that "Arnold of Ghent hurried to Audruick ... and manfully besieged the castle along with the castellan of Bourbourg and Arnold of Hames with their supporters and helpers" (1879: 588). The use of "manfully" to describe a man demonstrates that, in the medieval mindset, certain *activities* had permanent genders, which *people* of either biological sex could perform.

CODING PEACEMAKING AS FEMININE

In conjunction with imprinting warfare as masculine, medieval society described peace as the work of women. As the prolific late medieval writer Christine de Pizan put it:

> Women particularly should concern themselves with peace because men by nature are more foolhardy and headstrong, and their overwhelming desire to avenge themselves prevents them from foreseeing the resulting dangers and terrors of war. But woman by nature is more gentle and circumspect. Therefore, if she has sufficient will and wisdom she can provide the best possible means to pacify man.
>
> —1989: 86

Medieval conceptions excluded men from peacemaking, just as they prohibited women from waging war, but as in the corollary, men certainly did participate in peace and truce negotiations throughout the period.

Even at a very young age, girls could begin peacemaking as peace brides, physical symbols of peace between two polities. Evidence abounds for peace marriages throughout the Middle Ages, from the Vikings and Anglo-Saxons through the fifteenth century (McMillin 1989; Jamison 2004). Not all of these proposed agreements reached marriage, however, such as the proposed union of 140 men and women from four towns in Italy in 1306; despite the lengthy peace contract, neither the marriages nor peace resulted (Lett 2012). Much more common were single pairings between individuals of high estate, such as the unions between James II of Aragon and Blanche of Naples to end the 20-year War of the Sicilian Vespers or between Isabella of France and the future Edward II of England in 1308 to end continual disputes over control of Gascony (McMillin 1989; Lord 2002). Modern scholarship tends to ignore that, quite often, the groom also had little say in his future mate. In effect, both parties to the marriage acted as peace pledges.

Once married, women could participate more actively as peaceweavers. Sometimes this mediation took the form of personal intercession, as was the case with Philippa of Hainaut interceding on behalf of the Calais burghers, mentioned at the start of this chapter (see also Strohm 1992, Huneycutt 1995, Parsons 1995, Howell 2002, Mulder-Bakker 2003). Medieval writers viewed intercession as a positive side effect of women's weak nature that

FIGURE 3.2: The marriage between Margaret of Anjou and King Henry VI of England was arranged to signal a peace between England and France, and an end to the Hundred Years' War. From the "Talbot Shrewsbury Book," 1444–45, London, British Library, Royal MS 15 E VI. Photo by Universal History Archive/UIG courtesy of Getty Images.

lent itself toward pity (McAlpine 1997: 237–8). As Nicolas Offenstadt (2001) explains, conciliators of both sexes were always portrayed the same (falling on one's knees, weeping to express sincerity, using soft voices) and their actions were thought of as particularly feminine. Rather than viewing such deeds as inferior to the work of warfare and governance, however, peacemaking was recognized as hard work and labour. Equally important, a wife's intervention on behalf of mercy complemented a male ruler's duty to embody righteous (or royal) anger toward transgressors, allowing the male ruler to offer the softer side of mercy without diminishing his masculinity. Scholars have recently begun to recognize the complementary roles within a marriage that allowed for such smooth functioning of monarchy or rulership (Mulder-Bakker 2003; Earenfight 2007).

In addition to interceding on behalf of individuals or small groups of transgressors, women participated in truce and peace negotiations aimed at ending armed conflicts and wars. For example, King Robert of Naples and Frederick of Sicily agreed to a one-year truce in the midst of the War of the Sicilian Vespers due to the efforts of Maria of Hungary, the queen mother of Naples, and her daughter-in-law, Yolanda of Aragon (McMillin 1989: 128–9). Opportunities to act as peaceweavers abounded throughout the Middle Ages; the Hundred Years War (1337–1453) alone, ostensibly between England and France, saw efforts by Jeanne of Valois (1343–1373), wife of Charles the Bad; Isabelle of Bavaria, wife of King Charles VI of France; Yolande of Aragon, Duchess of Anjou and mother-in-law to King Charles VII of France; and Isabella of Portugal, wife of Duke Philip the Good of Burgundy; among others. These women participated in formal negotiations with representatives from all sides of the conflict, and often, papal legates. For instance, in 1345 Jeanne of Valois (1297–1353), sister of King Philip VI of France, brought together ambassadors of the French and English kings and of the Duke of Brabant to hammer out the Truce of Esplechin, an attempt to end the hostilities that formed the first part of the Hundred Years War. In the same year, Jeanne also mediated a local dispute, between a group of citizens and a magistrate within the town of Tournai, demonstrating that women's peace-weaving work was valued at all levels of society (Mulder-Bakker 2003: 254–56).

BLURRING THE LINES

Despite the firmly held conviction of a gendered division between peace and war, medieval society still recognized that women participated in warfare in a variety of ways: as victims, as instigators, as support staff, as combatants, and as generals. Women's non-combatant roles have long been acknowledged in modern scholarship and popular culture based, in large part, on the medieval proscriptions aimed at protecting women, as non-combatants, from the excesses of war. Thus, the Peace of God movement, begun in Aquitaine in 989 and spreading across Christianized Europe via localized synods, prohibited violence against women, children, merchants, and peasants (Head and Landes 1992). Similarly, during the Hundred Years War, a diarist in the employ of the Black Prince, King Edward III's eldest son, wrote that "the English king . . . issued an edict throughout the army, that . . . no old people, children or women in his [claimed] kingdom of France were to be harmed or molested; nor were they to threaten people, or do any kind of wrong on pain of life or limb" (Barber 1997: 28–9). These sentiments and accompanying threat of punishment were repeated by Edward's successors in the Hundred Years War, Richard II in 1385 and Henry V in 1419. In 1387, the French prior Honoré Bouvet opined in his chivalric manual written for the French side that women should not be imprisoned or violated (Gibbons 1996: 24).

PEACE, WAR, AND GENDER 57

Nonetheless, it became difficult to sustain such divisions between combatants and non-combatants, when "non-combatants," even women, financed wars through subsidies or personal wealth, victualled armies, transported equipment, and prayed for victory (Allmand 1971; Truax 1999; Gilbert 2005; Curry 2009). These support roles allowed the troops to focus on the business of fighting without the added distractions of logistics. During the Third Crusade, King Richard I of England arranged for one particular group of women to provide such assistance for his army when he prohibited all females except old washerwomen from accompanying them as it moved on from Acre.[3] Presumably their advanced age rendered them unable to distract Richard's troops.

FIGURE 3.3: Women besieged in a fortified town. The Swiss gentleman and poet Werner Graf von Homberg (1284–1320), at the service of Emperor Henry VII, besieges a city defended by the troops of the Anjou. From Codex Manesse (c. 1300) by Rudiger Manesse and his son Johannes. Heidelberg University Library, Cod. Pal. germ. 848, fol. 44v. Photo by Prisma/UIG/ Courtesy of Getty Images. Credit:Universal Images Group/Hulton Fine Art/Contributor.

Some women's support activities blurred the line between combatant and non-combatant, as when they acted as spies or messengers, or participated in the defense of a besieged city (Jouet 1969: 86; Dubois 2004; Curry 2009: 205).

When under attack, advised the fourth-century military manual *De Re Militari*, popular throughout the Middle Ages, townswomen should cut off their hair to provide sinewy ropes for catapults and other war engines or prise up paving stones to hurl at the enemy below (Vegetius 2004: 4.7 and 4.9, 128–30). In June 1342, Jeanne of Monfort took such advice to heart when she found herself besieged by Charles of Blois and Jeanne of Penthièvre at the castle of Hennebont; Jeanne of Montfort rallied the women and children inside the town, urging them to tear the stones from the streets, to use as ammunition against the attacking men (Le Bel 1904: 307–11 [§54]; Froissart 1867: 142–6). Other accounts record unnamed townswomen operating siege engines themselves, as in Guibert of Nogent's assertion that "the women [of Le Castillon] with equal courage hurled stones from the catapults and shattered both towers" successfully repelling those attacking their castle (1984: 206). For his part, Simon of Montfort, leading the Albigensian Crusade in southern France, ended up on the wrong side of a mangonel operated by the townswomen of Toulouse in 1218 and died from the encounter (Guillaume 1996: 205).

Several noblewomen, such as Simon's wife Alice of Montmorency, used their status as co-lords with their husbands to assemble reinforcement troops, which they then led to their husbands' outposts. According to the *Song of the Cathar Wars*, Alice led 15,000 men to relieve Simon's forces during his siege of Moissac (Guillaume 1996: 116.59). Similarly, Blanche of Castile, wife of King Louis VIII of France, went to Calais and "assembled all the people and knights that she could to send to England" to help her husband, who was at that time fighting the English on their own soil (*Histoire des ducs de Normandie et des rois d'Angleterre* 1840: 198).

In addition to providing material resources, noblewomen acted as trusted military advisors for their husbands and sons. Sometimes, chroniclers did not approve of a woman's military meddling, as with the chronicler of Vézelay, who wrote of Ida of Carinthia:

> that old Herodias, Jezabel's daughter of the seed of Amalech, Ida, mother of Count William of Nevers, enthusiastically poured the virus of hatred from her plague-bearing mouth into her son's heart. Envious of honesty, an enemy of all goodness, and a promoter of her son's cause she vigorously incited her followers to persecute the monastery of Vézelay.
>
> —Hugh of Poitiers 1992: 256

Ida and her son spent decades despoiling the chronicler's monastery, so his condemnation of Ida rests more on her political choices than on her sex. For the most part, chroniclers noted women's military advice only in passing, indicating that women often provided such counsel. For example, in the twelfth century, Elizabeth of Jaligny advised her son, Sulpice II of Amboise, during his wars with neighbors (Fanjoux 1849: 18). In 1218, Alberic of Trois-Fontaines noted that Blanche of Navarre's son Count Thibaut IV of Champagne built the castle Montéclair on his mother's advice (1874: 907). Ralph of Diceto asserted that Petronilla of Grandmesnil (1145–1212), Countess of Leicester, helped devise strategy during Henry the Young King's rebellion against his father, Henry II of England, such as urging her husband Robert III of Beaumont to meet the old king's forces despite her husband's misgivings (1876: 377). In the early thirteenth century, Violante of Hungary participated alongside her husband, James I of Aragon, acting as an interpreter in secret negotiations over the surrender of two cities; she later advised him during the Valencian revolts (McMillin 1989: 130). In the fifteenth century, the captains of two key cities in Normandy, at the time still under English control, turned over their troops to King Charles VII of France, at the urging of their wives (Gibbons 1996: 24–5). Even though these accounts always play on the personal relationships between the women and the men they advised, the chroniclers certainly note the women's involvement in military strategy.

Chroniclers in some regions oftentimes expressed approval of women's military advice. One anonymous chronicler, recounting the exploits of Matilda of Braose, a marcher lord living under the reign of King John of England, averred, "There were no arguments from her barons on her opinions; she maintained the war against the Welsh, from whom she conquered much" (*Histoire des ducs de Normandie et des rois d'Angleterre* 1840: 111). In fact, he implies that her barons' unquestioning faith in her military opinions directly resulted in extending the Welsh borders. In this way, he indicated that many men within society were confident enough in Matilda's military acumen that they put their lives at risk to follow her advice without dispute. Similarly, in 1341, when John of Montfort ascertained that he would not get a favorable answer from King Philip VI in regard to his suit for the duchy of Britanny, John turned to his wife, Jeanne. As the chroniclers report it, it was "then [that] he went, by the advice of his wife, who had well the heart of a man and a lion, through all the cities, castles and good towns that were to be rendered to him, and establish throughout good captains and so great a number of foot and mounted soldiers as he could there, and plenty of provisions" (Froissart 1867: 105; le Bel 1904: 262 [§47]).

Regardless of the definition of "combatant" and what activities women were performing, they became targets for captivity and ransom. Sometimes, the abduction of a woman led to warfare, as in the case of Dervorgilla, wife of Tiernan O'Rourke, whose abduction in 1152 led to the Norman invasion of Ireland (McAuliffe 1996: 158). Many times, captives were taken as the spoils of war, including men and women of all ranks in society. During the Hundred Years War, untitled people could pay protection money, *patis*, to avoid such capture (Wright 2000). According to Yvonne Friedman, women in the Holy Land were much more likely than men to be held as captives, but both males and females could expect their treatment to depend on their social status and rank (Friedman 1995, 2002; Seabourne 2011). Friedman has, however, found a difference in the treatment of captive women upon their return to their natal society. Whereas Muslims and Jews did not expect their captive women would remain chaste, Christian men would repudiate wives who were raped, and thus soiled, while in captivity; Christians expected their women to prefer death to rape (Friedman 2002).

Whether as passive captives or active instigators, medieval writers often imputed the inception of wars to women. Isabelle of Angoulême, the Middle Ages' answer to Helen of Troy, began a war as a preteen, when the smitten King John of England abducted her from the house of her fiancé, Hugh of Lusignan. Hugh appealed to their joint overlord, King Philip II of France, who used John's refusal to answer his summons as an excuse to mount an attack on his northern French lands in 1204. Viking literature and art provides several examples of women inciting their male relations to war, often in retaliation for wrongs done to the women (Eshelman 2000; Jochens 1986). In Book VIII of his chronicle, Orderic attributed the civil unrest in the county of Evreux to the squabbling of the wives of the two ruling brothers. Helwise started the war by urging her husband, Count William of Evreux, to requite some slurs her sister-in-law Isabel of Conches had apparently made against her. A bad war began, Orderic implied, for a bad reason: the women were concerned about silly remarks (Orderic Vitalis 1969–80, 4: 212). As Martin Aurell has noted, chroniclers could present such persuasion negatively, when women incited violence between Christians, or positively, such as when women encouraged loved ones to go on crusade (Aurell 2005). Thus, chroniclers cared more about their religious world view than condemning women for participating in a masculine activity.

Turning from inciting warfare to actively participating in warfare requires some discussion of medieval versus modern conceptions. Most modern readers want to know the degree of women's active involvement in warfare: did they don armor, wield a sword, engage in personal combat? Medieval descriptions of warring women, however, seem designed to obscure this information; chroniclers, for example, often place a noblewoman in the midst of a conflict, but without detailing her particular contribution. As Orderic related about Isabel of Conches, "in the campaigns, [she] rode armed as a knight among the knights, showing no less courage to the horsemen wearing hauberks or the retainers with spears than the maid Camilla, the glory of Italy, to her companions in arms at Turnus" (1969–80, 4: 212–14). He left it up to the reader to imagine how she might have "showed this courage." Similarly, Lambert of Ardres explained that several local barons banded together to oppose Matilda of Flanders's *chevauchée*, to the point that she "fled with a few men to her castle at Furnes and from there to Dunkirk at night, escaping with their lives" (1879: 641). She must have been present if she fled for safety, but what had she been doing personally up to the moment of escape?

By contrast, descriptions of male commanders could range from similarly vague to quite detailed. For instance, when Orderic described William the Conqueror leading the Normans into England, he enthused, "in war three horses were punctured and killed underneath him. Three times that intrepid one dismounted, the death of the carrier did not remain unavenged for long. He penetrated shields, helmets and hauberks with an angry sword and with disdain" (1969–80, 2: 174–76). Orderic's audience has no trouble picturing William swinging his sword without restraint. Just a few pages earlier, though, Orderic wrote that Harold of England "abandoned Hastings and Pevensy and other seaports opposite Normandy, which he had skillfully guarded that whole year with many ships and soldiers" (168). Clearly Harold himself could not "skillfully guard" each one of those seaports, and the chronicler's wording leaves unclear the degree of Harold's physical involvement.

Because the precise degree of a woman's active participation is so difficult to determine, scholars of medieval noblewomen and war point to the distinction made by medieval society between two types of commanders. During the high Middle Ages, kings and princes began to use specialized, or tactical, commanders to move the troops while retaining ultimate command for themselves (France 1999: 142; Verbruggen 2002: 106). In fact, in time the king need not have been present at all battles, yet he still received recognition as the head of the army (Lalou 1991: 39–41). Even noble and royal men credited by medieval authors as the commander of a particular campaign may not have truly controlled the fighting, due to their youth or incompetence (Prestwich 1999: 161–3). David Hay has pointed out that this distinction, between a supreme commander aloof from the fighting and a tactical commander in the heat of it, provided a command job that noblewomen could assume (Hay 2008: 9–12). Jean Truax took a further step back from the combat, identifying the control of the two basic resources—money and manpower—as the key qualifiers necessary for waging war. Any woman who directed funds and men in the pursuit of military goals should, in Truax's opinion, be considered a commander (Truax 1999). Since the medieval accounts do not use specific terms to signify these types of command, scholars are left sifting through vague descriptions of noblewomen's activities to define their roles.

Scholars have traditionally viewed women's active involvement in warfare as exceptional. Joan of Arc springs to mind immediately, as the divinely inspired peasant maid who led French troops to victory in the final phase of the Hundred Years War (DeVries 1999). Joan's divine connections and low social status, rather than her proclivity for picking up a sword, mark her as unique, for scholars have identified several other medieval women they have deemed exceptional for engaging in war. Aethelflaed, for instance, ruler of Mercia in the early tenth century, allied with her brother, Edward the Elder of Wessex, to defend their Anglo-Saxon territories from Danish invaders. Her efforts included building fortresses and seizing cities, before her death while besieging York (McLaughlin 1990: 118–19). The Countess Matilda of Tuscany gained fame as the fiercest of Pope Gregory VII's defenders during the Investiture Conflict between the papacy and the empire in the late eleventh century (Eads 2003; Hay 2008). The twelfth century furnished Eleanor of Aquitaine, whose alleged adulterous behavior while on the Second Crusade has attracted much attention. She also aided her sons in their rebellions against her husband, King Henry II of England, and led mercenaries against her grandson, Arthur, who attempted to claim the throne from his uncle, John (Flori 2007; Turner 2009). Successive centuries supply their own examples: among them, Jeanne of Navarre, Queen of France and wife of King Philip IV, in the thirteenth century; Countess Jeanne of Montfort in the fourteenth; and in the fifteenth century, Jacqueline of Hainaut.

FIGURE 3.4: Joan of Arc at the siege of Orléans. Manuscript miniature from Martial de Paris known as Auvergne (1420–1508), *Vigiles de Charles VII*, 1484. Paris, Bibliothèque nationale de France, MS Français 5054. Photo by DeAgostini/Courtesy of Getty Images Credit: DEA PICTURE LIBRARY/Contributor.

The problem with labeling such women as exceptional is that in recent years scholars have continued to add to the list of bellicose women. At what point do women, especially noblewomen, engaging in war cease to be deemed as exceptions to normal behavior? After all, the writer Christine de Pizan (1364–1430) advocated teaching noblewomen about warfare as they often needed to command troops and defend fortifications (Pizan 1989: 9). Given the long list of politically and militarily active women Christine included in another of her books, she was not shouting into the wind (Pizan 1998).

Current conventional wisdom on medieval nobility states that noblewomen did indeed lead men but almost always only in defensive positions, such as defending a fortification in the absence of their husbands; such thinking is incorrect.[4] Medieval chroniclers furnish numerous instances of women bringing troops to sieges, battles, and on campaigns, in other words on maneuvers that took place away from and outside the home castle. For example, Gidinild of Catalonia led a force to conquer Cervera in the early eleventh century, built a tower, and earned recognition as castellan by Countess Ermesinde of Barcelona (McLaughlin 1990: 203). Likewise, Gislebert of Mons noted that, in 1173, Countess Margaret of Hainaut "summoned an army throughout Hainaut and came to Mauberge. [Later, her husband,] the count of Hainaut ... came to Mauberge, where he found his wife the countess and her knights prepared in arms against Jacob [of Avesnes]" (1904: 113–14). Similarly, Orderic Vitalis depicted Matilda of Boulogne, wife of King Stephen of England, directing troops in the mid-twelfth century. He wrote, "the queen commanded her friends and kinsmen and dependents of Boulogne to confine the [enemy] army by sea," which they did (1969–80, 6: 520), whereas in his own account of Queen Matilda, the anonymous chronicler of the dukes of Normandy and the kings of England recounted that she did not "sit home and cry" when she learned of her husband's capture, but "she sent knights to all parts of the land" (*Histoire des ducs de Normandie et des rois d'Angleterre* 1840: 78). All these women engaged in warfare beyond a single "home" fortification.

Descriptions of later medieval women leading troops follow the same pattern as that laid out for the eleventh- and twelfth-century women. Blanche of Castile assembled an army to counter the noble uprising aimed at replacing her son Louis IX on the throne in 1226. According to the Minstrel of Reims, the rebellion soon disbanded due to Blanche's position on the moral high ground, though the rebels most likely found her leadership of a large army very persuasive (1876: 180–1). At the turn of the century, Jeanne of Navarre, married to King Philip IV of France, brought troops to her own county of Champagne to stop the attempted usurpation by her cousin, the count of Bar (Desnouelles 1855: 184–5).[5] These ladies led troops on campaign across the countryside, much as did Philippa of Hainaut, mentioned at the start of this chapter, when defending England against Scottish invasion. A chance survival of a fifteenth-century letter by Jeanne of France, Duchess of Brittany, allows a glimpse of the strategic thinking of one woman commander. Jeanne's husband, Duke John V, had been kidnapped by a rival claimant to the duchy of Brittany, and in response, Jeanne called together a convocation of knights, churchmen, and peers of the duchy. The chronicle written later that century recounts only that she called the council and that it was decided therein to put a popular lord in charge of the search for the missing duke (Le Baud 1907–22: 454). The letter, however, dated from a few days after the council, reveals Jeanne's involvement in directing offensive maneuvers. The duchess wrote to the forces besieging one of the kidnappers' fortresses and ordered them to destroy the place once it fell to the siege (Morice 1744: 1019).

Another commonplace amongst modern scholarship is that medieval noblewomen participated in warfare only temporarily and in a pinch, when male kin were unavailable.

There do exist many examples of women defending counties while their husbands were absent, on campaign or at court perhaps, but medieval chronicles recount equally many instances of noblewomen working in conjunction with their husbands to achieve military goals. For example, Emma, countess of Norfolk (*c.* 1059–96) joined her husband, Ralph of Gael, Earl of Norfolk, when he rebelled against William the Conqueror in 1075. Emma held Norwich castle from the king's forces for three months before obtaining favorable terms of surrender and retiring to Brittany (Douglas 1999; Williams 1997: 63). The couple then departed on crusade together, where they both died (Hodgson 2007: 116). Similarly, in 1095, Matilda de l'Aigle (newly married to Robert of Mowbray, Earl of Northumberland) found herself defending her husband's castle against King William Rufus. Matilda surrendered when William threatened to blind her husband, whom the king had recently captured trying to sneak into a nearby castle. The husbands of both Emma and Matilda deliberately chose their wives to defend their castles and lead the accompanying garrisons; the women did not suddenly and unexpectedly find themselves besieged, for their husbands chose to rebel in their home territory. There were plenty of able male commanders available whom the husbands could have chosen to lead the defenses, indeed Earl Robert entrusted care of his castle to both Matilda and his kinsman, Morel, but the men took care to appoint their wives instead of (in Emma's case) or alongside a male commander (in Matilda's case). The earls viewed their wives as able partners in the military defense of the patrimony (John of Worcester 1998: 76–9; Barlow 1983: 346–59).

Chronicles provide many other cases of noble women acting in tandem with their husbands. For example, Eleanor of Provence recruited mercenaries in the Low Countries, France, and Savoy (her own counties and beyond) to help her husband, King Henry III of England, against the revolt of Simon of Montfort in the 1260s (Dunn 2000: 146–7). In 1315, Aodh (Hugh) O'Donnell, King of Tirconnell in Ireland, ransacked Carbury after "being advised thereto by his wife . . . she herself, with all her gallowglasses and men of the Clan Murtagh that she could obtain, marched against the churches of Drumcliff and plundered many of its clergy" (McAuliffe 1996: 159). Wives acted as more than just temporary placeholders for absent husbands, stepping in temporarily during unexpected moments of crisis. Instead, the cases reviewed here reveal a pattern of noblemen viewing their wives as capable partners, whose participation in warfare increased the chance of success in their military goals.

Carl von Clausewitz, who died in 1831 but is still considered one of the foremost western scholars of warfare, defined warfare as much more than mere battles. "War," he wrote, "is not merely an act of policy but a true political instrument, a continuation of political intercourse, carried on with other means. What remains peculiar to war is simply the peculiar nature of its means" (*On War* 1.1.24, edited in Clausewitz 1984: 87). As later military historians have pointed out, the reverse is also true: diplomacy is often warfare carried out by other means. Since medieval women, particularly noblewomen, were deemed especially suited to the art of peace, it makes sense that they should also participate in warfare, as the alternative method for achieving a common goal. Despite the medieval gendering of war-making as masculine and peacemaking as feminine, medieval women did participate in both activities in a variety of ways.

CHAPTER FOUR

Peace, Pacifism, and Religion: A Universal Longing Unfulfilled

ANNE MARIE WOLF

In the nineteenth book of his *City of God* (*De civitate Dei*), St Augustine of Hippo (354–430) argued that all creation longs for peace, in accord with a universal order the Creator implanted in all things. For humans, according to Augustine, peace is true happiness and the ultimate goal of life, a state in which all virtues would find their fulfillment. Life's anxieties and temptations only serve to intensify our yearning for peace, which all mortal beings desire above all else. For him, peace was linked to eternal life—not exactly equivalent to that, but an essential descriptor of the type of life that would follow earthly life. This promise of true happiness and eternal life was the great challenge he made to pagan philosophy, which could not bring its adherents to such a worthy end (Barrow 1950: 218–20 [lb. XIX, ch. 10–12]).

Writing in the early fifth century, in the midst of incursions by Germanic tribes into Italy and even the capture of Rome itself, Augustine also had a fair amount to say about varieties of peace short of the fullest, ultimate, peace to be found in eternal life. He explained that even inanimate objects show an orderly process at work in nature (such as the process of decay), and this order is a manifestation of the peace undergirding all of creation. He discussed the peace of the body, which consists of the correct ordering of its parts and the overall well-being of the person, since the body is not separate from the mind and the soul. On earth, a well-lived life brings the blessings of peace. Peace implies law, order, and fellowship with other human beings. Indeed, those undertaking wars, even as the aggressors, declare that their aim is the peace that will follow, which Augustine considered further proof of his point that all creation longs for peace. The order of the universe assigns each member a place in the workings of creation, so there is a peace of the lower aspects of human life, proceeding up to the ordering (and therefore peace) of higher aspects, and these higher aspects of peace depend upon the lower ones (Barrow 1950: 220–26 [lb. XIX, ch. 12–13]).

Students of the medieval Christian tradition would be hard pressed to name an author with more influence on European intellectual developments in the Middle Ages than Augustine. They would be equally challenged, if prompted, to identify a Christian thinker from those centuries who thought more deeply or systematically about the nature of peace. For many, the Middle Ages are more likely to conjure images of the Crusades or violence—often against Jews—than serious thinking about peace (Moore 2007). Most medieval writers who concerned themselves with peace took a less comprehensive approach than Augustine had, focusing on a specific aspect of peace or a particular conflict. Nonetheless, their discussions of peace sometimes were quite bold and exceeded the levels of tolerance toward "others" conventionally credited to people from that era (Laursen and Nederman 1998; Nederman 2000; Muldoon 2001). This essay will focus on religious approaches to peace, leaving aside practical strategies employed in conflict resolution (e.g., customs governing treaty negotiations) or rejections of violence by those either indifferent to religious ideology or driven by more mundane concerns than religion, such as neighbors sharing a field or merchants more alarmed at the prospect of disrupted trade than at the spread or strengthening of Muslim rule. Our concern will be with those whose promotion of peace and objection to violence was rooted in religion. What resources from religious traditions did people mine as they thought about violence and peace?

By the end of late antiquity and the early years of the medieval centuries, all three of these monotheistic religious communities had competing and ambivalent strains within them regarding the proper place of peace and violence. Jews were the heirs of the rabbinic tradition, which formed in the first two centuries C.E. and greatly influenced the trajectory of Jewish thought and life in the European Middle Ages. Although it is not accurate to speak of a unified rabbinic tradition, in general rabbinic Judaism placed more emphasis on peace and peacemaking than biblical Judaism had (Eisen 2011: 68–71). For Christians, the Gospels urged the forgiveness of enemies, and Christ had promised to send his Spirit to be with them to the end of time. Peace was one of the gifts of the Holy Spirit, listed by Paul in his letter to the Galatians. Muslims, for their part, honored a Prophet who was widely acclaimed, even before his revelations began, to be a skilled arbitrator of disputes (Funk and Said 2009: 148), and the Qur'ān placed a strong emphasis on forgiveness (*maghfira*) and peacemaking within the emerging community (Funk and Said 2009: 150). Indeed, one of God's "most beautiful names" was Al-Salam, literally "The Peace" or "The Author of Peace, Safety, and Security." In its fullest sense, then, peace belonged to God alone (Funk and Said 2009: 61).

Yet Christian forces had waged offensive wars, some in the name of converting others to Christianity, and neither the officially Christian Late Roman Empire nor its successor kingdoms proved to be demonstrably inclined toward peace. Not all that long after the Prophet's death in 632, disputes over leadership of the Muslim community (*umma*) culminated in bloodshed, and the borders of the Dar al-Islam, the territory under Muslim rule, often spread through military expansion. Although Jews were not in possession of political and military power, Jewish scholars grappled with what to make of biblical stories describing the conquest and annihilation of the Canaanites and the Amalekites, in which the Israelites were directed by God to destroy these people and even their livestock, as part of the chosenness of the Israelites and the promise of the land to them. In the early rabbinic period, commentators struggled to explain this slaughter at God's urging, and their unease continued in the writings of medieval Jewish thinkers (Sagi 1994: 328–9; Eisen 2011: 89–92). Thus despite strong enjoinders to seek peace, all three traditions had experienced the ravages of violence and had plenty of reason to reflect on peace as a goal. All three had to come to terms with the ambivalence of their traditions embracing violence at some point, despite their ideals supporting peace and justice.

This essay will take soundings from representative sources, often iconic but some anonymous, from within these three traditions to illuminate two areas of interest: the nature and purpose of peace and the possibility of peace with people outside of one's own religion. Concerning the nature and purpose of peace, our first consideration here, witnesses from different quarters of medieval society produced a variety of answers to fundamental questions, a variety that some modern readers might find surprising. Was peace only the absence of overt conflict, or was it something more abstract? Was it necessarily a spiritual thing or was it a worldly one produced by human efforts or perhaps given by God, but as a distinctly worldly blessing? Was it a goal in itself or merely the foundation necessary for something else? With what other features of human life and conduct was it most closely associated?

THE NATURE OF INTERNAL PEACE: CHRISTIANITY

For all of Augustine's lofty and comprehensive thoughts about peace as a good associated with the ultimate happiness and fulfillment of human beings, later Christian thinkers' discussions about the nature and purpose of peace were often driven by more limited concerns. As early as 697, Adomnán, the abbot at the Irish monastery of Iona, convened a gathering that produced the *Law of the Innocents* (*Lex Innocentium*), signed by ninety-one chieftains and clerics and guaranteeing clergy, women, and children protection from violence, including from war and physical assault. It also declared Church property off limits for attacks (O'Loughlin 2001: 9; another translation is in Márkus 2008). Although not exactly an exploration of the nature of peace, this was one of the early attempts by Church leaders to restrain violence. In the late tenth century a movement began in Aquitaine, Burgundy, and Languedoc in which local clergy would issue proclamations declaring that noncombatants (especially peasants and clergy) must not be subject to violence, and those who violated this rule would be excommunicated. Known as the "Peace of God," this practice spread to other places in Europe and was most common in the eleventh century. The Peace of God movement eventually gave way to the "Truce of God," which prohibited all fighting, but only on certain days of religious significance (Head and Landes 1992: 1–6; Gergen 2002). In the Later Middle Ages, well after the Peace and Truce of God had become less commonly invoked, the concept of leaders ensuring peace remained an ideal and still held weight. Many sermons and mirrors of princes reminded rulers and aspirants that ensuring peace was one of the central duties of the good prince, and popes promoted their role as brokers of peace. Invoking the language of the "peace of God" also helped sovereigns to assert their legitimacy (Offenstadt 2002: 63–5).

In the Later Middle Ages, discussions of peace appeared in the course of disputes surrounding the relative power of the monarchy or empire and the papacy. One of the best known writers to venture into this controversy was Dante Alighieri (1265–1321), whose views on the matter are most developed in his *On Monarchy* (*De monarchia*). He argued that a single, universal emperor would be best able to ensure peace, since there would be no separate kingdoms to fight against each other. Equating the Holy Roman Empire with the original Roman Empire, he noted that it existed prior to the Church, so clearly it was inappropriate to view the pope as the source of this authority. Instead, a universal and secular ruler he posited could achieve peace through the usual political means, and this peace would provide the conditions for the Church to carry out its ministry. The Church depended on the success of the temporal ruler, and peace itself was valuable primarily because it afforded the Church this ability to function (Colish 1997: 338–9; edition in Cassell 2004).

Dante's contemporary, philosopher and physician Marsilius of Padua (1275/80–1342), was another author whose work on peace was really a stance in the dispute over the Church's authority. He also placed the responsibility for peace on the secular government, although his primary metaphor and context was the city rather than the empire. As presented in his *Defensor Pacis* (*Defender of the Peace*), his ideal city was based on the principles of rationality rather than any biblical or religious notions of ethics, and he was careful to stipulate that building and maintaining such a rational city was a role shared by everyone, not entrusted to an intellectual elite. The Church figured even less into his thinking about the source of peace than in it did in Dante's work. For Marsilius, who also invoked the image of the body in his discussion of society, the clergy existed as merely one more part of the body, just like those exercising the various trades. A city rationally organized would produce peace, and peace was valuable not because it provided the conditions necessary for the Church's ministry, as Dante posited, but because it allowed the arts and sciences to flourish (Strefling 2010: 155–6; edition in Brett 2005). Marsilius avoided any reference to any supernatural qualities of peace or the need to learn about peace or its prerequisites from the Bible or any religious authority.

In some cases, peace was invested with more powerful religious language, and the arrival of peace even called a miracle. After the Treaty of Auxerre (1412) ended a civil war between the Armagnacs and the Burgundians, several contemporary authors described it as a miraculous event. One of them, Enguerrand de Monstrelet, even noted that "the people" saw it that way (Douët-d'Arcq 1857–62: 295). In a sermon, Jean Gerson, the esteemed chancellor of the University of Paris, referred to a peace achieved at Pontoise as something of a miracle (*velud pro miraculo manifesto*) (Bellaguet 1839–1855: 136–8). Sometimes the chroniclers recorded that negotiations toward peace were marked by meteorological events like especially violent storms, which drove the parties to a hastier resolution of conflict because they took those signs as a divine warning. Other texts presented such events as a manifestation of the devil's displeasure at the fact that people were seeking peace. The peace makers could rest assured, though, since God was accompanying them. Further evidence of the link medieval writers made between peace and divine intervention is found in numerous saints' lives and exempla lauding peacemaking as a holy and virtuous endeavor (Offenstadt 2002: 67–70).

For the chroniclers and the envoys sent to negotiate with their adversaries, peace might have been the cessation of armed conflict. For philosophers like Marsilius of Padua and politically involved poets such as Dante, peace might have prompted reflection on the political realities they advocated. But for medieval theologians, peace was emphatically a spiritual reality, as it had been for Augustine. In his *Summa Theologiae*, Thomas Aquinas (b. *c.* 1225 in southern Italy, then part of the Kingdom of Sicily) situated his treatment of just war in the *Summa Theologiae* (II–II, q. 40) under the heading of charity or love (*dilectio*) (Reichberg 2011: 468–9). He cited joy, peace, and mercy as the effects flowing from the virtue of charity. He distinguished between "perfect peace," which reigns in heaven and is therefore not susceptible to harm through human vice, and "imperfect peace," which describes the condition of the Church in this world. According to Aquinas, this imperfect peace is built on belief, so its main threat is schism (Reichberg 2011: 472–4).

Although initially (*Summa Theologiae* II–II, prologue to q. 34) he named only discord and schism as sins against peace in his discussion (Reichberg 2011: 469), as he expanded his thoughts in subsequent questions, he ultimately gave four modes of conflict (ecclesial, instrastate, interstate, and substate) and identified their respective types of peace, along with additional sins against each type. As Gregory Reichberg has emphasized, Aquinas was the only medieval writer to have classified war and other forms of violence as sins against peace. Other thinkers usually treated war and violence as questions of justice, unravelling the circumstances in which war was just or unjust. It was possible for Aquinas to present war and violence as sins against peace because he also considered temporal peace (*pax reipublicae*) as a good in itself and peace among nations as a normative condition (*Summa Theologiae* II–II q. 123, a. 5, discussed in Reichberg 2011: 477–9) and, as already noted, peace itself as an effect of the exercise of the virtue of love. We will consider other aspects of Thomas Aquinas' boldly unconventional approach to peace later, when we consider whether medieval thinkers could accommodate a concept of peace with those outside their own religion communities. Although his treatment of this subject departed from the standard one that had preceded him, he shared with other theologians, at least, the strong belief that peace was fundamentally a spiritual reality.

THE NATURE OF INTERNAL PEACE: JUDAISM

Medieval Jewish thinking also associated peace with spiritual developments. Medieval Judaism was deeply influenced by the rabbinic tradition, which emerged as the dominant version of Judaism after the Romans crushed two rebellions, destroyed the Temple in Jerusalem, and drove many Jews out of Palestine. The rabbis were scholars whose main concern was biblical interpretation, with the use of oral traditions and creative readings of these ancient texts. They developed a new way of practicing Judaism that did not depend on the now-destroyed Temple, on Jewish sovereignty, or even occupation of a specific land. Their understanding enabled Jews to weather the devastation and yet retain some cohesiveness as a community. The rabbis' message was that these events had happened due to their sins, but if they carefully observed the commandments (other than those requiring Temple sacrifice), they would rebuild their relationship with God. Eventually, God would reward their faithfulness to the law by sending a messiah, who would return them to their land and restore the Temple (Eisen 2011: 65–66). It is important to note that the discouragement of armed rebellion did not preclude aggressive verbal attacks against Christianity and the behavior of Christians. A rich polemical literature developed despite the rejection of outright violence (Chazan 2010: 246; see also Chazan 2004).

Although the rabbis did not speak with one voice, the main contours of their perspectives on war and peace are clear. Rabbinic Judaism served to diminish the impulse toward violence by dampening Jews' anger at the violence of the Romans and the motivation for revenge. It assigned responsibility for the destruction to Jews' own failure to obey God's commands. The remedy for the situation was not to be found in staging a successful attack on the Romans, but in repentance. Furthermore, the redemption that would come with the messianic age would be due to God's initiative, not human actions. In the rabbinic texts, Israel's defeat of its enemies was nothing like the problematic conquest of the Canaanites or Amalekites in the Bible; the rabbis never taught that Israel's enemies would be wiped out. And in the meantime, they urged, Jews should patiently accept their status and devote themselves to repairing their relationship with God through obedience to divine laws (Eisen 2011: 84–5). Medieval Judaism would reiterate this instruction to wait patiently for God to redeem the people and mute any inclinations to foster speculation on the time frame or to actively bring about this redemption (Caputo 2008: 132–5). In Spain, the eleventh-century poet and philosopher Judah Halevi even wrote that the Jews' vulnerability and subjugation was actually a sign of their chosenness, since of all the monotheistic faiths, they alone could truly embrace the virtue of humility (Eisen 2011: 87).

Medieval Jewish exegetes remained troubled over the biblical stories of the conquests of the Canaanites and Amalekites, whom God ordered the Israelites to destroy. Thirteenth-century commentator Nahmanides suggested that the Amalekites were punished so harshly in the narratives because they were rebelling against God himself. When they heard about God's miracles in saving the Israelites, all the other nations trembled with fear, but not Amalek. Other medieval sources interpreted this conquest as symbolic, with Amalek representing some aspect of evil. In this interpretation, God commanded Israel to destroy evil, not to annihilate a people (Eisen 2011: 92). Some rabbinic sources in the Middle Ages argued that the imperative to fight against the Amalekites no longer applied, either because they did not exist or because the struggle was to be postponed until the messianic era.

The most influential Jewish scholar of the Middle Ages was Moses Maimonides (1135–1204), who was born in Córdoba, Spain, a city in the part of Iberia under Muslim rule, and died in Egypt. He was among those who viewed the fight against Amalek as symbolic, with Amalek representing idolatry and the rejection of God's unity. According to this view, the struggle was an intellectual war against error. Some modern scholars have even suggested that the idolaters Maimonides had in mind were Christians of his day. Indeed, medieval Jewish writers frequently identified Christians with Amalek. Whether or not he was associating the two, it is clear that his interpretation of the imperative to annihilate the Amalekites was designed to discourage acts of violence and instead rally his coreligionists to vigorous intellectual endeavors (Eisen 2011: 117).

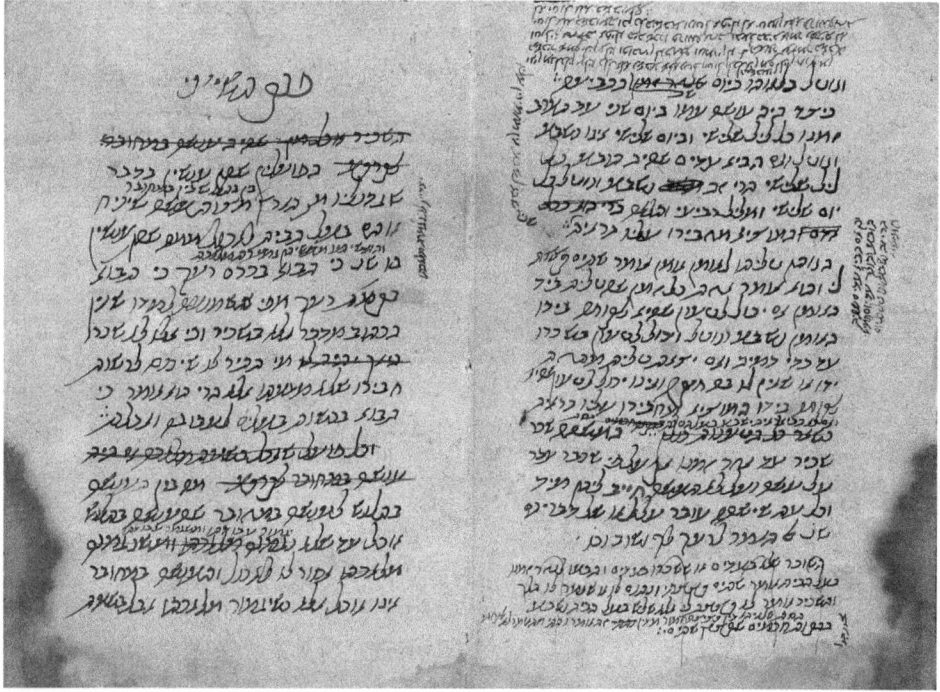

FIGURE 4.1: Maimonides' draft of his legal code, *Mishneh Torah* (from the Cairo Genizah), in his own hand, Sephardic script, written in Egypt *c*. 1180. Oxford, Bodleian Library, MS. Heb. d. 32. Photo by VCG Wilson/Corbis, Courtesy of Getty Images.

According to Maimonides the whole purpose of peace was to allow the study of God's law without distractions. In several works he discusses the messianic era as one in which peace will reign because the world will be infused with the knowledge of God. War is inconsistent with that intellectual perfection or its pursuit, so in Maimonides' ideal society there is no war. Neither would there be any interest in Jews holding power over other peoples, or even in the conventional attractions of a life of ease and pleasure. His readers received clear guidance on what the messianic era would involve:

> The sages and the prophets did not long for the days of the Messiah that Israel might exercise dominion over the world, nor rule over the Gentiles, nor be exalted by the nations, nor eat and drink and rejoice, but that they be free to devote themselves to the Torah and its wisdom, with no one to oppress or disturb them.
> —Eisen 2011: 118; Maimonides *Mishnah Torah* Melakhim 12:4

This view of peace primarily as the precondition for knowledge of God and study of the divine law parallels that of Dante (peace as allowing the Church to minister) more than that of Augustine or Aquinas, who saw peace as a goal in itself.

THE NATURE OF INTERNAL PEACE: ISLAM

For the Muslims living within or close to European societies, including in Iberia and southern Italy (the respective homelands of Maimonides and Aquinas) peace was also fundamentally a spiritual matter. The most important sources for the Islamic tradition are the Qur'ān and the hadith, or sayings of the Prophet. The word "Islam" itself meant submission to God, and it was understood that this submission, by following God's guidance, would bring peace to the individual as well as to the surrounding community (Funk and Said 2009: 61). Like Augustine, the Qur'ān taught that human beings, deep down, yearn for peace. According to the Qur'ān, original human condition (*fitra*) is good and the natural state of humans one of harmony with each other (Funk and Said 2009: 62; see Qur'ān 30:30 and for more on this theological concept, Gobillot 2000). This revered book strongly argues against unnecessary conflict and issues a stinging rebuke to those who, through their selfish pursuits, court destruction and inflict violence (*fitna*) on others. It even warns about the dangers of too zealously fighting injustice or promoting rights, since such zeal could easily spin out of control (Funk and Said 2009: 64; Qur'ān 5:33).

However, the study of peace in Muslim societies in the Middle Ages takes a different turn than in the other circles we have considered. In Islam, the connection between justice and peace was stronger than in medieval Christianity or Judaism. The primary religious field of study in Islam was not theology or philosophy, but law (Esposito 1998: 74). Certainly Islamic thinkers believed there was a difference between the peace that was a basic condition of the soul and paradise and the peace that was possible in this world, which was more fragile (Funk and Said 2009: 107). This distinction they shared with their counterparts in the other two faiths. However, their Sharia, or body of law (literally "the road to the watering hole") (Esposito 1998: 78), was an important expression of Muslims' notions of peace, and it had no parallel in the other two religions. Sharia served both a religious and a political purpose and was meant to facilitate a harmonious social order. The desired social order involved just relationships between individuals, between Muslims and God, and ultimately between people and the rest of creation (Funk and Said 2009: 64–5). Since it was the yearning of all people and the natural state of things, peace would be maintained if the roots of violence were discouraged or thwarted. Sharia challenged disrupters of the peace such as selfishness and greed, racism, tribalism, and economic exploitation (Funk and Said 2009: 122). It included laws about the proper behavior of sovereigns and the resolution of disputes, including standards of evidence (Funk and Said 2009: 64–5). Sharia built a strong social ethic supporting peace through equity and fairness and the provision of basic human needs.

Sharia and its study were promoted in four main legal schools of thought by scholars traveling throughout the Muslim world and in contact with other legal scholars. It was not produced by any given ruler or constrained by the boundaries of a specific polity, although rulers sometimes served as patrons for legal schools. Sovereigns appointed judges, who would seek out the most applicable laws in a case, sometimes favoring one school of thought over others, but the development of the law itself was not under the direct purview of the rulers or the judges. Sharia's main sources were the Qur'ān and the hadith tradition, although judges also considered local tradition. Matters of justice were evaluated in the context of the ideal of a peaceful society in accord with the vision of right living revealed to the Prophet and developed in his own words and actions which followed this revelation, in the early days of the *umma*, or Muslim community (Esposito 1998: 74–88).

Over time, grievance courts arose, initially as a way for caliphs to provide a check on the power of senior officials accused of wrong doing, whose status might have intimidated the judges. Gradually, there were two parallel court systems in most places: Sharia for matters related to family law and religious endowments, and grievance courts for criminal law, taxation issues, and commercial activities, especially as communities faced issues not covered in Sharia. In deference to the status of Sharia, though, governments deliberately avoided using the term "laws," instead issuing "ordinances," and these were not to be contrary to laws that were part of Sharia (Esposito 1998: 86–7). Although ordinances were specific to an area, Sharia remained the backbone of Islamic society and transcended national, ethnic, and social class differences. Both an ethical and a legal code, it presented a blueprint for a well-ordered society where members were at peace with each other and with God. In this conception, peace was more the goal in itself rather than, as with Dante and Maimonides, the precursor to the advancement of spiritual goals. The difference between this approach to peace and that advanced by Augustine and Aquinas, who also considered peace a goal in itself, is that in Islam, day-to-day justice was more closely linked to that goal.

PEACE BETWEEN PEOPLE OF DIFFERENT FAITH

In all three traditions, people most readily envisioned and contemplated peace within a given society, among members of a common religion, rather than between people or nations with different faiths. It could be argued that the idea of a Christian commonwealth helped to define European civilization. Even people on different sides of an armed conflict, or holding opposing views about the proper powers of the pope and emperor, held this in common (Colish 1997: 336). The situation was similar in the Muslim world. Sharia and the local ordinances were intended to structure life within the *umma*, and there was a strong sense of solidarity with other Muslims. Even after the age of unified caliphates, an ideal of political unity persisted (Funk and Said 2009: 85). The rabbinic tradition left Jews, too, with a strong sense of community identity, one not dependent on a shared territory. Because medieval Jews never lived in a land they governed, they had no choice but to make peace with non-Jews. However, this did not mean that they entertained no thoughts of violence or superiority to other peoples. The messianic period Maimonides envisioned would be peaceful, but it would be ushered in by a heroic warrior who would defeat Israel's enemies. Not a few Jewish philosophers maintained the superiority of Jews over non-Jews, especially in the fifteenth and sixteenth centuries (Eisen 2011: 125–26). For the most part, when people thought of peace, they thought of an end to strife within their own communities or of the peace that would come beyond earthly life. For some, it was inconceivable that peace was possible, or even desirable, with members of other faith traditions. And yet within all three of these religious communities, despite a strong pull to contemplate peace only internally to that community, some conceived of a more expansive horizon for peace, even with members of other faiths.

IN ISLAM

This broadened view of peace is most apparent in Islam, seemingly due to the confluence of teachings found in central texts and the practical fact that lands under Muslim rule were home to many non-Muslims. If Jews by necessity had to accustom themselves to being in a minority religion and hence to living in peace with non-Jewish neighbors, Muslims mainly lived the converse situation of governing in a society that included a significant percentage of non-Muslims. But policy makers in the *umma* could find more than practical necessity to support their plans for productive coexistence with the non-Muslims in their midst. Several passages in the Qur'ān express an openness to human diversity or pluralism (Funk and Said 2009: 125 and 152).[1] In addition, early Islamic jurisprudence produced norms for conflict between Muslim and non-Muslim states, but also legal categories for lands with which Muslim states enjoyed peace. Beyond the stark *dar al-Islam* and *dar al-harb* ("land of Islam" and "land of war"), jurists also created the *dar al-sulh* or *dar al-ahd* (both meaning "land of treaty/truce") and the *dar al-aman* ("land of security"). In the twelfth century, the Persian scholar Fakhr al-Din al-Razi proposed an alternative distinction to the land of Islam/war dichotomy: *dar al-ijaba* ("land of Islamic practice") and *dar al-dawa* ("land of invitation"). Although Islam, like all world religions, included some practitioners whose interpretations of its teachings were intolerant of other religions, the continued existence of sizable Christian and Jewish minorities living under Muslim rule for the entire medieval period and into the modern one demonstrates clearly that these voices were not the norm (Funk and Said 2009: 124–5).

By the ninth century, in the early Abbasid period (750–1258), the mystical tradition of Sufism had become a widespread movement across the Muslim world, creating a major impetus toward universalism by emphasizing the divine presence in all of creation. In broad strokes, Sufism was similar to the contemplative traditions in Christianity and Judaism, or the early Christian desert fathers and mothers, but in the Muslim world this movement was much more widespread. Although it was not without its critics and detractors, Sufism built far-flung social networks along trade routes, infused spirituality into craft guilds, and influenced some of the finest minds in the Islamic tradition. According to the Sufi path of God, the entire created world expresses God's being and action. It is based on the theological concept of *tawhid*, which did not originate with the Sufis, but certainly received more emphasis through that movement. This principle held that God was one, but also that all creation was saturated with the presence of God and depended completely on this foundation in God. Those seeking God needed to allow God's love for all creation to infuse every aspect of their lives, both internal and external. This is a spiritual ethos that promoted deep, personal intimacy with God and love for all humanity, and it certainly promoted peaceful relations, even loving ones, with non-Muslims. Perhaps best known to modern western readers through the poetry of Jalaluddin Rumi (thirteenth century) and Shamsuddin Hafiz (fourteenth century), Sufism was a vital part of the cultural landscape of the Muslim world (Funk and Said 2009: 206–12; see also Murata and Chittick 2004: 246–7, 262–4, 304–9).

IN JUDAISM

In the Jewish community, religious thinkers accepted the reality of non-conflictual relations with the majority Christians or Muslims, and in general, the rabbinic and medieval writers counseled against violence and urged their co-religionists to wait patiently for God's actions to bring in the messianic age. However, this did not mean that they uniformly subscribed to ideas that warmly embraced non-Jews. One of the common views found in medieval Judaism, sometimes called the "essentialist" position, was that God had given Jews superior souls. This idea had its roots in the rabbinic period and was further elaborated by Judah Halevi in the eleventh century and accepted by most Kabbalists, practitioners of a Jewish mysticism that arose in thirteenth-century Spain (Eisen 2011: 115). Still, even this view fell short of advocating violence against those with inferior souls.

Another dominant approach found among medieval Jewish thinkers was considerably more universalist and was certainly capable of accommodating the idea of peace with non-Jews. Philosopher, mathematician, and scientist Abraham bar Hiyya (eleventh and twelfth century, Barcelona and Narbonne) taught that in the messianic era, God would transform human nature and make everyone, all nations and religions, adopt the principle of loving every person as oneself. A major characteristic of the messianic age, then, would be the fellowship of all human beings (Eisen 2011: 120–1; Wigoder 1970, sec. 4). In the final sections of his *Mishneh Torah*, Maimonides advanced a position that Christianity and Islam were part of God's plan because they prepared the world for the messianic age. When it arrived, non-Jews would accept the truth of Judaism because they would finally recognize that it contained the highest truth. Modern scholars disagree over whether Maimonides thought non-Jews would actually convert to Judaism or adhere to a universal religion through which they would worship the God of Israel but not become Jews (Eisen 2011: 117–17).[2] Regardless, he accorded Christians and Muslims at least a significant role in the story of the world's redemption (although, in some places, his attitude toward Christians and Muslims was harsher; see Eisen 2011: 124). Maimonides' vision of the messianic age, in which peace would reign and create the necessary freedom from distraction that people would need to study God's law and the world would be filled with the knowledge of God (Eisen 2011: 118), could certainly accommodate those who would have recognized their previous waywardness at the beginning of this era, and accepted the truth of Judaism.

Maimonides was not among those who saw Jews as having a superior soul, and he seems not to have recognized any essential difference between Jews and non-Jews. He believed that the mastery of wisdom and knowledge, about the world and about God, led to intellectual perfection, and that it was through intellectual perfection that humans draw close to God. Non-Jews who diligently developed their intellects would attain closeness to God, the same as would a studious Jew (Eisen 2011: 115). As Robert Eisen has observed, this leaves Jews and non-Jews only hypothetically equal, since Jews actually had the Torah to help them achieve this intellectual perfection (2011: 122). Still, Maimonides highlighted the importance of a peaceful society so that the intellectually gifted could pursue knowledge. Nothing in his thought seems to have precluded intellectually inclined non-Jews from enjoying or deserving the fruits of that peace. In addition, although he was most concerned with peaceful relationships between people and groups within a society, it seems that his approach was consistent with an ideal of peace between societies, too. War and violence would be just as inimical to anyone's pursuit of knowledge, and for him, all pursuit of knowledge was a means of drawing closer to God (Eisen 2011: 118).

IN CHRISTIANITY

Undoubtedly, some humility and caution are in order when offering observations about these three traditions' approaches to such a vast topic as peace. Nonetheless, some preliminary observations emerge. Of the three groups, medieval Christians seem to have had the most problems envisioning peace with members of other religions, at least when this question is looked at through the lens of religious approaches rather than pragmatic ones adopted by traders and neighbors. It is most evident when looking at the ideas of Christian religious writers about peace with the Muslims, who had states and armies that could challenge Christian Europe's power. The Gospels and the epistles were full of teachings and actions directing people to love their enemies, forgive others, and cherish peace. But what held sway in most intellectual and religious circles was not the Gospels, but some amalgamation of custom, various types of secular law, canon law, decrees from religious leaders, and the like. Most Christians who weighed in on the subject of peace envisioned it only within the Christian commonwealth. This is true even of a figure like Francis of Assisi, who has nonetheless since entered the popular imagination as a strong voice for peace. Francis, like many mendicants who followed him, strove for peace within the fractious Italian city states. In 1219, he famously approached the Egyptian sultan, Malik al-Kâmil, with a goal of presenting the case for Christianity, arguing against a battle Christians had engaged in against the city of Damietta. But scholars now point out that his argument was not against crusading in general, but against going to battle on a certain day. He was supportive of the crusading initiative (Michetti 2005; Powell 2007; Hoose 2010; and, for an excellent study of how Francis's encounter with the sultan has been memorialized, Tolan 2009). Francis and the other Mendicant friars were intensely interested in peace in troubled cities, but this interest did not extend to Muslim nations.

Although they were never the dominant or mainstream voices, other Christians in Europe were more open. Thomas Aquinas, whom we considered earlier for his notions of peace as an effect of love and war as a sin against love, is an intriguing case for considering whether Christians could conceive of peace with non-Christians, particularly Muslims. Although Aquinas never directly took up the question of whether peace could occur between Christian and non-Christian polities, several choices and connections that he made in his writings suggest that his thought was expansive enough to accommodate such a vision of relations between polities not sharing the same religion. One example occurs in his discussion of a passage in Aristotle's *Nicomachean Ethics*, book 8. As Gregory Reichberg explains, Aristotle had written that all polities are bound together by friendship. Aquinas commented on this idea in his *Sententia libri Ethicorum* and would certainly have noticed how Aristotle connected friendship with the related idea of concord (see Chapter Two in this volume). For Aquinas, charity was the highest form of friendship, and the theme of concord, referenced by Aristotle, would have led him to recall Augustine's association of concord with peace.[3] Interestingly, in the course of commenting on Aristotle's text, which the Greek philosopher had intended to refer to relationships within a given polity (a city-state such as Athens), Aquinas quietly added that "political friendship" also occurred between polities. It seems unlikely that he extended this political friendship beyond a given polity simply because he was thinking of the unity of all Christians. He made clear distinctions between peace in the supernatural sphere and peace in the temporal sphere, and nothing in this text refers to a common faith (Reichberg 2011: 475–7 and 2017: 24). As Reichberg suggests, it is quite possible that Aquinas was positing an innovative idea: that the various nations of the world formed a natural community based on ties of friendship and concord (2011: 477 and 2017: 25). His addition of a reference to friendship between polities would not have been careless or accidental. Moreover, in his commentary on the *Sentences* of Peter Lombard (*Scriptum super Sententiis*, IV, d. 24, q. 3, a. 2, q. 3), written as a young man, he had used the phrase *communitas totius mundi* (community of the whole world) (Reichberg 2011: 478 n. 28). War, including war against non-Christian polities, would violate a natural state of peace among nations (Reichberg 2011: 479). Whereas canon lawyers like Hostiensis wrote of a state of perpetual hostility between Christian and Muslim polities in their discussions of when war was justified, Aquinas remained conspicuously silent on the matter (Reichberg 2011: 484; 2017: 31). Where Hostiensis considered friendship among nations only possible when the nations were Christian, Aquinas adopted no such restriction (Reichberg 2017: 31). Even though he did not energetically push for an idea of a community of nations, his thought definitely could have accommodated that, and even appears to have been leaning toward conceptions of international community that would develop more fully centuries later (see Chapter Two in this volume).

There is some evidence of this notion among the general populace, albeit without the sophisticated scaffolding for it that Aquinas offered. The Crusades offered ample opportunity for the religiously inclined to reflect on violence against non-members, and some questioned the crusading impulse. Most of the objections arose from disillusionment after defeat, as after the disastrous (for Christians) losses at Damascus in the Second Crusade (1147–49) (Siberry 1985: 190–92). More intriguing is the indirect evidence from as early as the twelfth century that some voices of dissent were based on principle rather than merely on wariness about another defeat. We know little about the people dissenting on principle because they are known only through references in texts promoting crusade. Around 1130, Hugh of Payns mentioned such anonymous objectors as he addressed his Templar knights:

> We have heard, brothers, that some of you have been troubled by people of lesser wisdom, as if your profession, I say—that life to which you have dedicated yourselves, of taking up arms against the enemies of faith and of peace for the defense of Christendom—is illicit or pernicious, that is, that it is a sin or an impediment to reaching a higher goal.[4]

He assured them that they fought for justice, that the Devil urged men to embrace humility and surrender their arms, and that any lack of worldly praise for their efforts would be redressed later. This leaves us yearning for more information on those "people of lesser wisdom" who were troubling the new knights with thoughts that their goal of taking up arms against Muslims might be sinful.

Similarly, Bernard of Clairvaux's *In Praise of the New Knighthood* (*De laude novae militae*), an apologetic work requested by the founder of the Templars, emphasized that if there were another means of ending the Muslims' oppression of the faithful, it would have been adopted. He argued that, alas, there was no other way, so it was better to kill

FIGURE 4.2: Knight of the Order of Knights Templar during the battle of al-Bocquee or Buqaia (Lebanon) in 1163, against the Saracen Nur ad-Din, fresco in the Chapel of the Templars, Cressac sur Charente. France, late twelfth century. Photo by DeAgostini/Courtesy Getty Images.

them than to allow the evil to spread. He distinguished between a worldly knight and one who fought to defend fellow Christians, stressing that there was no crime in killing a Muslim and that a knight who died in such a fight took his place among the martyrs (Siberry 1985: 209–10). Yet it is striking that this work was requested and that Bernard thought it necessary to defend the enterprise of crusading.

Writing not about the Crusades per se, although with the Crusades as a context for his work, twelfth-century Italian monk and canon lawyer Gratian discussed the use of force in Causa XXIII of his *Decretum*, in a discussion of the just war. Before refuting them each in turn, he listed the main arguments of pacifists. These were scriptural, such as Christ's encouragement to be patient and turn the other cheek (Mt. 5:39; Lk. 6:29) or his warning to Peter that "those who live by the sword die by the sword" (Mt. 26:52). Had Gratian actually heard people challenging the crusades, or violence in general, based on these texts, or was he trying to be thorough in anticipating possible objections to his main point that war, for a just cause, was not prohibited? Even if the answer is the latter, it shows that it had occurred to at least him that a case could be made against violence and war, and it was necessary to make the case for war or armed defense of the Church.

In the thirteenth century, James of Vitry felt compelled, in sermons to the military orders, to decry those who "falsely assert that [they] are not allowed to take up the physical sword or fight bodily against the church's enemies" and told listeners that if Christians had not risen up against these enemies in the past, the entire Church would by

FIGURE 4.3: A knight, probably a crusader, in a gesture of homage. Manuscript illustration, England, early thirteenth century. London, British Library, MS Royal 2 A XII ("The Westminster Psalter"), fol. 220r. Public Domain image available from the British Library: https://www.bl.uk/catalogues/illuminatedmanuscripts/ILLUMINBig.ASP?size=big&IllID=38924.

then have met its demise at the hands of Saracens and heretics. He called the arguments against crusading the machinations of the devil and, like Gratian, cited texts asserting that it was right to use violence to challenge violence or redress injuries. He joined Hugh of Payns and Bernard in insisting that knights in the military orders had received the material sword so that they might protect the Church and even called it the duty of all Christians to do so (Siberry 1985: 211–12).

What is significant in all of these examples is that, even at the height of the crusading era, those participating were facing opposition from others in society, enough to require reassurances from the apologists for crusade that it was morally acceptable to participate. That opposition to crusade on principle, rather than on likely success, came from anonymous people whom the aspiring crusaders encountered in their daily lives.

In the Later Middle Ages, these anonymous voices of opposition were joined by some who were more prominent. One of these was Juan Alfonso de Segovia (*c*. 1390–1458), more commonly known as Juan de Segovia, a Castilian theologian and professor at Salamanca who became one of the Council of Basel's most active participants. While he was still living in Iberia, a portion of which was under the rule of the Muslim Nasrid dynasty, he approached two Muslims who were visiting Castile to discuss theology with them. These encounters in the 1430s left a lasting impression on him. Decades later he described them in letters and treatises that he sent to leading figures he had known at Basel, including Jean Germain, Nicholas of Cusa, and Juan de Cervantes, the archbishop of Seville. In all these works, all the more remarkable because he wrote them in the aftermath of the Ottoman conquest of Constantinople in 1453, he argued that war was not the answer and that Christians should instead seek peace with Muslim nations (Wolf 2014: 2–8).

Juan de Segovia was a theologian and would have been trained in scholastic theology. Yet in presenting his arguments for peace, he reached for support most often from the Bible. Had Christ not taught his followers to love their enemies and do good to those who hate them? Had Paul not told the early Christians that there were no divisions between Gentile and Jew, servant and free? So why not welcome the Saracens into the Christian fold and have no divisions with them? Did Christ not say that God made the sun to rise over the good and the bad equally? Segovia wrote that peace was the buried treasure in the Gospel parable, so precious that the farmer sold his land to buy it. Christ had bestowed peace on his followers, the peace of the Spirit, which he promised would be with them even to the end of time. For Segovia, that made valuing peace an essential requirement of the Christian faith. If Saracens were waging war on Christians (as they certainly did in 1453), should Christians not take their cue from Christ, whose response to his enemies was not to wage war, but to accept death on the cross? (Wolf 2014: 157–9). Although there is no way of knowing what arguments those earlier, nameless, critics of crusade were presenting that made the apologists' responses necessary, those arguments might well have referenced some of these same teachings and passages.

Segovia even had an idea of how a peace delegation to a Muslim leader might work. He thought it should be small and unarmed, so that it would be allowed to travel through the Muslim lands to reach the leader. It should be composed of people theologically trained enough to explain the truths of Christianity clearly, and should include people of high rank, so that it would be taken seriously. Mostly, he seems to have believed that such an endeavor could not possibly fail since, after all, Christ had left his peace with the Church and promised to be with his followers until the end of time, so they would be fulfilling his command by seeking peace. But he also wrote that even if results were not immediate, Christians should pursue this method rather than resorting to war. He even noted that it had taken Christianity centuries to be accepted in the Roman Empire, so Christians should be prepared for this to take time (Wolf 2014: 176–80).

The Spanish theologian sometimes employed the, by-then familiar, anti-Muslim tropes that were circulating in the Middle Ages, such as that Muslims were especially lascivious and prone to violence. However, such language is rare in his lengthy works on how Christians should enter into dialogue with Muslims, and may have been a specific rhetorical move to capture the ear of his fellow Christians, rather than reflecting his attitude toward Muslims. In his later years, he worked side-by-side with a Muslim jurist and scholar from Castile, Yça Gidelli, whom he recruited, with much effort, to travel to Aiton in the French Alps to help him produce a new translation of the Qur'ān. The two produced a trilingual edition of the Qur'ān (Arabic, Latin, Castilian). He praised Gidelli's qualifications and showed genuine excitement at what he was learning from his collaborator about the Arabic language and about how Muslims understood the Qur'ān. They even maintained a correspondence after Gidelli returned home. If he had been spiteful or their interactions charged with hostility, it seems likely that Gidelli would have left before the work was finished and would not have bothered writing to his tormenter (Wolf 2014: 187–91).

Juan de Segovia's goal was to achieve the conversion of the Muslims by peaceful means. One of his correspondents, the German bishop Nicholas of Cusa (also known as

Cusanus), a friend of his from their days at the Council of Basel, shared this goal but went even further. In his *De pace fidei*, Cusanus presented a dialogue involving seventeen different participants, including Muslims, from various parts of the world. This was a fictional dialogue, in which one member is the Logos, not the actual dialogue Segovia had proposed involving a delegation of Christians to a Muslim land. Still, it is striking that the entire affair ends (§68) with the King of Kings (who had convened the gathering in the first place) calling for everyone to lead their nations in "unity of true worship" and "come together in Jerusalem as to a common center and accept one faith in the name of all and thereupon establish an everlasting peace so that in peace the Creator of all, blessed forever, will be praised" (Wolf 2014: 140; edition in Hopkins 1994; see also Izbicki 1991). Segovia never went so far as to suggest that there could be one faith that everyone in the world embraced, and Nicholas of Cusa did not everywhere present such an open-minded approach to other religions (Wolf 2014: 140–1). Nevertheless, Cusanus welcomed and praised Segovia's proposals and the two men are often considered examples of a moment of greater openness toward Islam in the Later Middle Ages (see, e.g., Biechler 1991 and Álvarez Gómez 1999). Unfortunately, their ideas failed to gain momentum among their contemporaries.

Popular notions about the Middle Ages often emphasize violence and intolerance toward religious "others," but clearly all three of the major monotheistic religions produced serious thoughts about peace during this period. One tentative conclusion from this study is that the ability to conceive of peace with those not of one's own religion appears to have been more mainstream and consistent among Muslim and Jewish religious thinkers than among their Christian counterparts. This is not without irony, since the very foundation of Christianity was the life and teachings of Christ, who even prayed on the cross for forgiveness for those who mocked and crucified him. It makes sense when we realize that the practical realities either of living as a religious minority or ruling a land that was home to many such minorities created its own exigencies. Even though the Gospel's calls for forgiveness and peace did not dominate in policies or thinking about peace, they nevertheless provided powerful support to thinkers such as Juan de Segovia (and quite possibly to a number of anonymous "people of lesser wisdom") who were raising religious objections to crusading. Another general observation is that seeing peace as the normative condition of humanity seemed to facilitate a broadened approach to the subject in interesting ways. Scholars have devoted significant attention to medieval warfare and violence. More study of medieval approaches to peace is in order.

CHAPTER FIVE

Representations of Peace: Heavenly Dreams, Earthly Needs

WALTER SIMONS

Like the culture from which it arose, the peace which medieval people imagined or represented in texts and images drew on a diverse heritage, of Judeo-Christian, Greco-Roman, and Germanic or Celtic origins. No single image of peace imposed itself, not because peace was of only fleeting concern but rather because the constituent parts of what we now call "medieval society" never fully crystalized into a homogenous civilization that could forge such a consensus. While symbolic expressions of peace—whether by Christian, Jewish, and Muslim intellectuals or by simple artisans—largely built on dominant religious concepts, those images evolved over time and were subject to multiple influences. Of course, the social realities of the medieval age and the vagaries of preservation since then affected the range of peace images available for study today. The vast majority of material and textual remains from the era reflect the interests of the religious and aristocratic powers that financed them, and relatively few artifacts or sources tell us how the majority of the people—rural peasants and working-class inhabitants of cities—imagined peace, peace practices, and the benefits of peace. Yet, a careful study of ritual and social history allows for a few assumptions about popular ideals, which sometimes deviated from elite attitudes or spoke to other concerns. This chapter will concentrate on the most influential themes in the medieval representation of peace, paying close attention to their cultural roots but also to ways in which they might be interpreted differently by various groups in secular and religious life.

THE LEGACY OF ROME

The ancient Roman tradition of representing peace as a woman lived on in Christian allegories of the Middle Ages, starting with the influential *Psychomachia* ("The Battle, or Conflict of the Soul") by Prudentius (348 AD–after 405), an imperial official and Christian poet active in northern Spain. An epic narrative, solely populated by allegorical characters, *Psychomachia* depicts the internal struggles of the human soul, long seduced by vices but ultimately victorious over evil thanks to its Christian virtues (Prudentius 1966). The poem consists of seven episodes, each devoted to a battle that pits "new" against "old." Faith and Hope fight old pagan cults and decadent morals, only to see Lust (*Luxuria*) casting its alluring spells and Avarice sowing terror, until Good Works (*Operatio*) crushes the opposition, paving the way for Peace, momentarily threatened by Discord, then reinstated with the help of Faith. The final scenes of the poem see the erection of a temple of Wisdom, symbolizing the God-given reign of perfection. Although no illustrated manuscript of the poem has survived from the first 400 years after its creation, no fewer than sixteen exist from the ninth through thirteenth centuries, suggesting a rather wide popularity in intellectual milieus of the latter era. Some of them display an iconographic program probably based on a fifth-century archetype, placing the illustrations close to the poet's lifetime. The artist responsible for the original program would have been guided by the poem's textual descriptions of battle (evoked in hair-raising detail) but also by the classical figurative language preserved, for instance, on Roman triumphal columns (Katzenellebogen 1989: 1–13). In Additional Manuscript 24199 of the British Library, of c. 1000 AD, Peace (*Pax*) appears in stylized Roman garb, ordering the dispersion of the oppressors, Suffering (*Labor*), Fear (*Metus*), and Deceit (*Fraus*). She is indistinguishable from the other female characters except, perhaps, for her lack of bloodthirstiness, since virtually all other allegorized virtues relish in the gory deaths of their opponents (see also Nugent 2000).

Medieval culture loved allegory, and Prudentius's poem spawned a panoply of allegorical tales on the theme of the Christian vices and virtues, from the central Middle Ages into the early modern period. However, further exploration of Peace's role in this tradition soon ran into obstacles. For one thing, the Christian virtues were traditionally imagined as seven in number: prudence, justice, fortitude, and temperance ranked as the

FIGURE 5.1: Pax overseeing the flight of *Labor* (suffering), *Metus* (fear), and *Fraus* (deceit), in a manuscript of Prudentius, *Psychomachia*, about 1000 AD. London, British Library, Add. MS 24199, fol. 29r. Public domain image available from The British Library: http://www.bl.uk/manuscripts/Viewer.aspx?ref=add_ms_24199_f029r

FIGURE 5.2: "The Good Tree" (*Ecclesia*), displaying the fruits of the Spirit, including Peace (*Pax*) at bottom left. Autograph manuscript by Lambert of St Omer, early twelfth century. Ghent, Belgium, University Library, MS 16, fol. 231v. Photo by Art Media/Print Collector/Getty Images.

four "cardinal virtues," while faith, hope, and charity counted as the three "theological virtues." Peace might thus result from the exercise of virtues (for Prudentius, peace was the "Whole work of virtue"; 1966: 176) or, more broadly, from conversion to a more perfect Christian life, but it was rarely imagined as a virtue in itself.

So we find Peace in Lambert of St Omer's *Liber Floridus*, a twelfth-century manuscript "encyclopedia," as one of many—and not nearly as the most important—of the "fruits of the Good Tree" (Mt. 7:7–20), following the Apostle Paul's description of the fruit[s] of the Spirit as "Charity, joy, peace, patience, benignity, goodness, longanimity, mildness, faith, modesty, continence, chastity" (Gal. 5:22–23). Additionally, for Christians of the Middle Ages, any personification of Peace that likened her to a goddess in the Roman mode held uncomfortable associations with classical idolatry. One might, as did Robert Grosseteste (d. 1253) in a hat tip to the Talmud, identify peace as "God's daughter" along with the three more traditional virtues of mercy, truth, and justice. Grosseteste placed them as four "sisters of Christ" next to God in the governance of the divine kingdom (Grosseteste 1918; Newman 2003: 2, 23). But that fit did not come easily, and few followed Grosseteste's suggestion in later centuries.

CHRISTIAN IMAGERY: PEACE IN THE CELESTIAL JERUSALEM

Medieval authors wishing to hone more closely to the Christian tradition when reflecting on peace turned to the liturgy and its plethora of literary images based on the Bible, Jewish customs, and early Christian exegesis. Calls and praises of peace rang through the celebration of Mass and divine office in both the western (Latin), and eastern (Greek Orthodox) rites. Occupying a central place in daily routines, the language of those images reflected terms derived from common life in antiquity that became solidified and were thus preserved until the twenty-first century. Bishops saluted the congregation with the phrase "Peace to you," or "Peace be with you" (*Pax vobis, pax vobiscum* in Latin), echoing Hebrew and Arabic greetings still conventional today. Church officials of lower rank like ordinary parish priests replaced it by "The Lord be with you," which became the phrase used in modern Catholic celebrations, but the original peace greeting was maintained in the Greek Orthodox rite.

The sixth-century antiphon *Da pacem, Domine, in diebus nostris* (incorporating elements from 2 Kgs 20:19, 2 Chron. 20:12, and Ps. 122:6, each with distinctly martial flavors), incorporated during the Reformation in the Book of Common Prayer, gave us the English phrase "peace in our time":

> Give peace in our time, o Lord, because there is no one else who fights for us, but only you, our God.
> Versicle: Let there be peace within your walls
> Response: And abundance within your towers
> (*Breviarium Parisiense* 1680: 34; my translation).

In several rites of the early medieval West, the celebrant ended Mass with the words "Go in peace" (*Ite in pace*); the dismissal formula in Catholic and Lutheran usage is now "Go, dismissal is made/mass has ended" (*Ite missa est*; Chambers 1877: 417).

As suggestive as those pleas for peace might appear on their own, they should be understood within the context of the whole liturgy, oriented toward a precise goal: the ordered worship of God in preparation for the life to come, made manifest in the image

FIGURE 5.3: Antiphon for Peace (*Da pacem, Domine, in diebus nostris*) in a Book of Hours, Use of Sarum ("The Taymouth Hours"), second quarter of the fourteenth century. London, British Library, MS Yates Thompson 13, fol. 88r. Public domain image available from the British Library: http://www.bl.uk/catalogues/illuminatedmanuscripts/ILLUMINBig.ASP?size=big&IllID=29108

of the celestial Jerusalem, or, as the Book of Revelation put it, "the holy city, the new Jerusalem, coming down out of heaven from God" (Rev. 21:2). Imbued with the rhetoric of the Hebrew Psalms and prophets, the liturgy of medieval Christians looked backwards at Jewish laments over the loss of Jerusalem and forward toward the end days of the New Jerusalem, the heavenly city. Christian iconography usually visualized it in the form of a fortified city of abundance, mirroring the language of the antiphon, versicle, and response cited above.

That "vision of peace" (Ezek. 13:16), came into sharp focus at particular moments in the liturgical calendar, mainly in the weeks around Easter commemorating Christ's death and resurrection, and in Advent (the four weeks before Christmas), dedicated to Christ's birth and his second coming at the end of time. These periods of intensified eschatological sentiment encouraged the faithful to consider enduring peace after death and the virtues that would render it possible. In his *Commentary on the Divine Office*, the Benedictine monk Rupert of Deutz (d. about 1129) explained the liturgy of Easter Week as an hexameron in which every day stood for one of the beatitudes from Christ's Sermon on the Mount. The office of Saturday after Easter signified the seventh beatitude, "Blessed

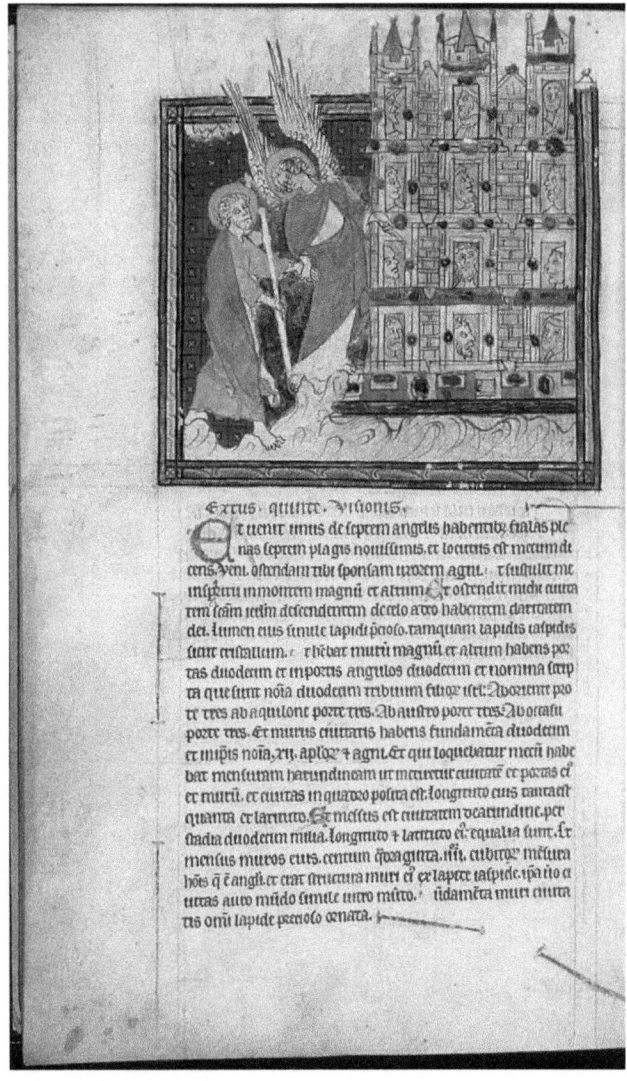

FIGURE 5.4: The Heavenly Jerusalem in the Book of Revelation. Manuscript illumination in "The Abingdon Apocalypse," third quarter of the thirteenth century. London, British Library, Add. MS 42555, fol. 79v. Public Domain image available from the British Library: http://www.bl.uk/catalogues/illuminatedmanuscripts/ILLUMINBig.ASP?size=big&IllID=46926

are the peacemakers for they shall be called the children of God" (Mt. 5:9; Rupert von Deutz 1999, 3: 1062–139).

A similar logic informed manuscript illustrations (and engravings based on them) of St Augustine's *City of God* in the French translation of 1375 by Raoul de Presles. Augustine (354–430) had contrasted the trajectory of the eternal City of God (the community of the elect, prepared by the work of the Church on earth), to the City or world of Humankind, inherently flawed and destined for perdition at the end of time. Late medieval illustrations of *La cité de Dieu* show the City of God as the celestial Jerusalem, a walled city populated by the saints (already in heaven, even though the Last Judgment is still to come), while the seven virtues, personified by haloed female figures, guide newcomers to the heavenly gate. In the bottom half of the image, vice and virtue compete in the earthly city of humankind, divided in seven segments that show sinners engaged in vices while God-fearing humans practice the corresponding virtues. The crazy jumble of pairs (of lust and chastity, gluttony and moderation, avarice and generosity, laziness and diligence, anger

FIGURE 5.5: Augustine, *City of God*, after a fifteenth-century engraving: saintly order in the heavenly community of God is contrasted with the terrestrial world of humankind below, in which vice and virtue compete. Photo by Universal History Archive/Getty Images.

and patience, envy and charity, pride and humility) is cheered by demons performing a satanic choral dance along the walls of the doomed city.

Literary works depicting a peaceful New Jerusalem at the end of time matched the visual arts quite closely. A popular example of the genre is Guillaume de Deguileville's *Pilgrimage of Human Life*, written in French in 1331. Guillaume, a Cistercian monk at Chaalis in northern France, starts the allegorical poem with a vision that "concerns the mighty and the humble, without exception. I have put it all in French," he explains,

> So that laymen can understand it. Everyone can learn from it which path to take and which to leave and abandon. This is something very necessary to those who are pilgrims in this wild world . . . As I was sleeping, I dreamed I was a pilgrim eager to go to the city of Jerusalem. I saw the city from afar in a mirror that seemed to me large beyond measure. The city was richly decorated both inside and out. The streets and lanes were paved with gold. The foundation was set up high, the masonry was made of living stones (see 1 Pet. 2:4–5 and Eph. 3:18–22), and a high wall enclosed it on all sides. It had many houses, squares, and mansions. Inside, all was gladness and joy without sorrow. To be brief, all those within it had, in general, more of all good things than they could ever think of or ask for.

After completing the external description of the New Jerusalem, based on Rev. 21:10–21, Guillaume goes on to detail the presence of saints (with Augustine "sitting high up on the battlements"), of Church officials who carried out the work of the City of God on earth, and of the poor—for "the one who does not lie has said that the rich cannot enter there any more than a camel can pass through the eye of a needle," in a free adaptation of Mt. 19:24. Captivated, Guillaume declares himself "inspired to go there as a pilgrim . . . It seemed to me that I would find great peace if I could be within its walls" (Guillaume de Deguileville 1992: 3–5). In the 12,000 lines of verse that follow, Guillaume spells out how to reach that destination: through the sacraments of the Church and good works, namely by the practice of the virtues and avoidance of vice.

The image of the human individual as a pilgrim to the New Jerusalem, where peace awaits the elect, proved powerful in the late medieval imagination. It was doubtless a source of inspiration for Hieronymus Bosch (c. 1450–1516), who left two, possibly three, original paintings on the enigmatic theme of *The Wayfarer*, depicting a poor, anguished traveler fleeing a world of vice and mayhem.

Celestial Jerusalem formed a spiritual counterpart to the terrestrial, material Garden of Eden, itself a product of an ancient, cross-cultural tradition that also shaped paradise in the Epic of Gilgamesh or the Greco-Roman fantasies of a Golden Age. Whereas the opening pages of the Jewish-Christian Bible set the scene for Adam and Eve's paradise, we must wait for the last book of the Christian New Testament, Revelation (or Apocalypse), to encounter any substantial treatment of the Celestial Jerusalem. Its description of the "holy city" fulfills the prophesy contained in the Jewish Bible of a perfect union between God and his people, symbolizing a new covenant that replaces or supplants the old. There is a clear tension between the concept of Celestial Jerusalem and the earthly Jerusalem "of the Jews," and although the one was often associated with the other—especially during the crusades, when the capture of the historical city by Christians and its subsequent loss to Muslims were invariably interpreted as stages in an eschatological scheme (Gaposchkin 2017)—Christian theology left no doubt that the "new" Jerusalem came down from heaven, demonstrating its superiority over the material city of the same name. Except for the short period during the twelfth century when Christians dominated

FIGURE 5.6: Scenes from Guillaume de Deguileville, *The Pilgrimage of Human Life*: the image on the top right represents Chastity following Voluntary Poverty to the Celestial Jerusalem, where they will enjoy heavenly peace. Manuscript of 1393, Paris, Bibliothèque nationale de France, Ms. franç. 823, fol. 88r. Photo by Art Media/Print Collector/Getty Images.

Jerusalem, artistic and literary representations of the Celestial Jerusalem in the Christian world did not resemble the Jewish city (Kühnel 1987). They formed highly symbolic, stylized expressions of an ideal community in the Christian perspective. Moreover, they were intended to represent a state rather than a place. Listing the qualities of the souls in heaven, St. Anselm (d. 1109) wrote of beauty, agility, strength, health, joy, and, of course, a serene perpetuity; bodies would endure no pain or hunger, and there would be comfort of all possible kinds (Fortin 2008). However, only souls (reunited with their bodies) in union with God would enjoy that serenity.

The theological underpinnings of the Celestial Jerusalem described above may help to explain the particularities—and limitations, from the modern perspective—of the concept of peace it expressed. That peace was exclusively transcendental and otherworldly,

FIGURE 5.7: Human life as an earthly pilgrimage to heavenly existence: Hieronymus Bosch (c. 1450–1516), *The Wayfarer* or *Peddler*, Madrid, Museo del Prado. Photo by Fine Art Images/Heritage Images/Getty Images.

applicable solely to the Celestial Jerusalem, a community ruled by perfect order, and to the individual being who dwelled there, content in its union with God. None of this was possible or even comparable to anything on earth; in fact, the human mind was scarcely able to comprehend it. Paul had declared celestial peace "surpassing all understanding" (Phil. 4:7). Not only humans, but even creatures of pure intellect, the angels, could not understand it, according to Gregory of Nyssa (335–94) (Pelikan 1993: 52). Hence the tendency, in medieval portrayals of the New Jerusalem, to limit visualization to the bare outlines provided by the Book of Revelation, and to imagine human figures in it as organized according to the structures of the Church, the most perfect one attainable this side of heaven, if we believe Gregory of Nazianze (329–90) (Pelikan 1993: 150).

We may now also understand how easily the language of peace modulated through the Christian liturgy might cease to refer, in certain circumstances, to human interaction or take on a distinctly martial flavor. As in the case of the antiphon *Da pacem, Domine, in diebus nostris*, analyzed above, the peace intimated by the vision of a New Jerusalem was one between God and his people. All those who were perceived as threats to it thus became his enemies and given the eschatological context that always hovered over the celestial city the stakes could rise quickly. In the very same pages on the liturgy of Easter Saturday that lauded "the peacemakers" of the beatitudes, Rupert of Deutz launched an attack on the Jews, the great "enemies" of Christ. The shift from celebration of peace to aggressive denunciation is swift: "peacemakers," he writes, "are all those who, after accepting the peace that exists between them and God, will not tolerate anything that offends God. They will try to live a life in peace with everyone, following Paul's advice, "If it be possible, as much as in you, have peace with all men [Rom. 12:18] . . . But that begs the question: what is the role of the Church in peace-making?"

Rupert's answer is significant because it once again demonstrates that, in the Christian mind, the imagery of the New Jerusalem carried with it a need to usurp the concept of God's covenant from the Jews. Rupert appeals to the contrast, sketched in 1 Pet. 2:8, between the "living stones" (the apostles and the clergy as their successors) who follow in Christ's footsteps and make up the basis of the Celestial Jerusalem, and Christ as the "stone of stumbling and rock of scandal" for those who disobey his message. He concludes that "the [Jews'] stumbling and offense are evidently in opposition to the peace" (Rupert von Deutz 1999, 3: 1117–20). Rupert's call for peace then morphs into an assault on Jews sustained throughout the *Commentary*'s Book XII, covering the twenty-three Sundays

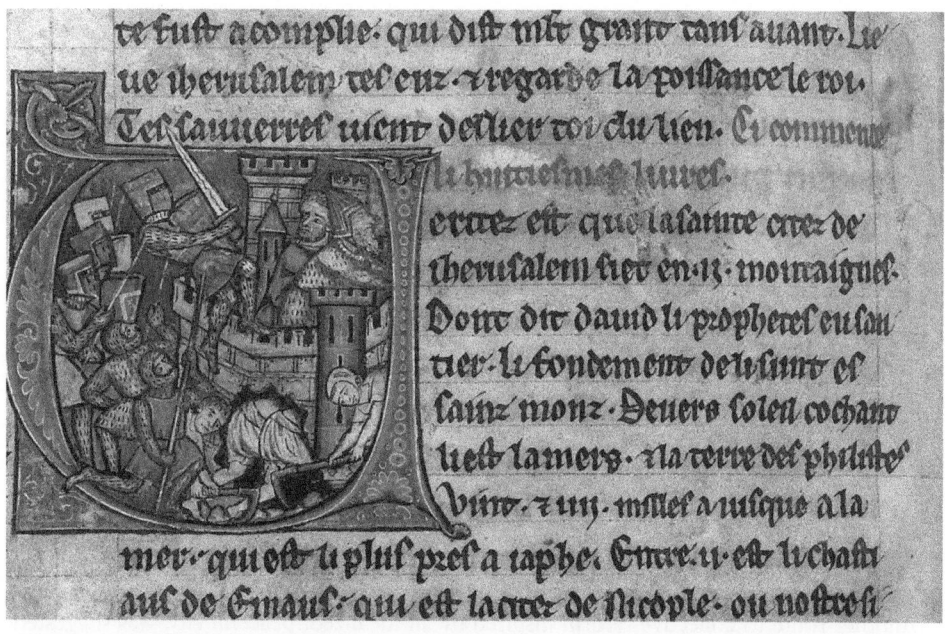

FIGURE 5.8: Crusaders besieging Jerusalem. Detail of a historiated initial, William of Tyre, *Histoire d'Outremer*, British Library, MS Yates Thompson 12, fol. 40v. Northern France (Picardy?), 1232–61. Public domain image available from the British Library: https://www.bl.uk/catalogues/illuminatedmanuscripts/ILLUMINBig.ASP?size=big&IllID=56614.

after Pentecost, which, in Rupert's interpretation of the Divine Office, tell the story from the Jewish refusal to join the conversion of the Gentiles, down to the (expected) conversion of all Jews in the end days. Written in 1109–20, when the memory of crusader violence was fresh in the minds of the Jewish community in the Rhineland, the *Commentary* must have sounded like a distinct threat. In his later works, John Van Engen has argued, Rupert developed an even fiercer rhetoric that blamed Jews for Christ's death and accused them of "curs[ing] Christ in their synagogues." While Rupert did not believe Jews deserved to be killed, he recommended heavier taxation and stricter secular control over their lives (Van Engen 1983: 241–8; see also Schmitt 2010: 130–44).

The same eschatological narrative virtually demanded that invocations of the peaceful kingdom in crusader liturgy implied a call to arms, sometimes explicitly so, as in the hymn *Jerusalem laetare*, where those who wish "to capture the heavens" are made to "gird [themselves] with arrows" (*Analecta Hymnica* 1886–1922, 45b: 76–8, nr. 95). In ceremonies to take up the cross, in celebrations of victory after the conquest of Jerusalem during the First Crusade (1096–99), and in lamentations over crusader losses in the next centuries, the Christian liturgy developed multiple rituals which transformed prayer—that most peaceful of human activities—into a "spiritual weapon" (Gaposchkin 2017).

PEACE ON EARTH

In sum, representations of the most perfect peace possible, that enjoyed in the heavenly Jerusalem, tended to encourage an individual response that sought personal salvation through moral correction, or a collective response through militant action against perceived enemies of the faith. A collective response that would improve interpersonal relations on earth through societal reform seemed rather futile to intellectuals who shared St. Augustine's conviction that human society was inherently flawed.

Yet, there were at least three exceptions to the general skepticism about social change. The first is provided by a specific strand of apocalyptic theory, chiliasm (or millenarianism), which inspired in some a hope that God might redeem society collectively in the form of an imminent millennium on earth, before the end of times. These fantasies, with deep roots in Jewish and Roman culture, sometimes assigned qualities of heavenly bliss to the terrestrial realm, including a reign of peace and prosperity for all the elect. The north-African writer Lactantius (d. about 317), for instance, a teacher of Latin rhetoric who converted to Christianity, described the rule on earth that God thus will establish as "that quiet, tranquil and peaceful age that the poets call 'Golden'." He seamlessly merged the old Roman belief of a lost Golden Age with the Christian vision of a holy city, built "in the middle of the earth" and lasting 1,000 years, until the last battle between God and Satan (McGinn 1979: 22, 72–80). Millenarianism became a powerful force during the central and late Middle Ages, spawning several popular movements and a substantial, though only partially preserved, literature. While those texts usually concentrate on the revolutionary violence required to "purge the world" rather than on the peaceful millennium that will follow it, they affected popular thought, disseminating ideas about a more just world and an alternative social order (Cohn 1970).[1]

Another route to collective reform inspired by an idealized, peaceful city, was suggested in a most indirect manner (i.e., by quasi-utopian vistas of life in far-away lands) as in the legend of "Prester John," an imaginary Christian ruler in the east, circulating from the twelfth century onwards, or in the fictional travel account of "Sir John Mandeville" (mid-fourteenth century). Translated into multiple languages for middle-to-upper-class readers eager to expand their knowledge of the world, these stories described model societies in which social, political, or religious discord was unknown, offering a moral critique of western European society in an attractive package. The *Travels of Sir John Mandeville* is particularly noteworthy for its equable, even positive, portrayal of the Muslim world, its praise for the Great Khan of the Mongols, who allows all kinds of religions to flourish in his lands, and its appreciation of people in the East who are without strife, leading "by natural instinct . . . a commendable life," a topos inherited from the ancient Alexander Romances (*The Travels of Sir John Mandeville* 2005: 178; see also *Prester John* 2015; Bejczy 1994). The "religious tolerance" of such tales, however, is often more theoretical than real or practical (Heng 2018: 349–416), and it does not extend to the Jews, the only people in this remarkable book whom "Mandeville" condemns as evil. Here again, eschatological concerns account for the virulent anti-Semitism, aggravated by the conviction—increasingly shared by Christian thinkers of the Late Middle Ages—that conversion of the Jews in the end times was not assured.

A third collective response to the model of the ideal peaceful city came to the fore in the thirteenth century: it advocated active engagement with the values exemplified by the model to promote a more just and peaceful world. The most prominent example is found in the work of Dante Alighieri (1265–1321), particularly in the *Divine Comedy*. Although Dante did not formally develop the third and last part of the *Commedia* based on the Celestial Jerusalem (the structure is inspired by classical cosmography and by the pseudo-Dionysius), Christian doctrine evidently governs the voyage through Paradise in multiple ways. In fact, Dante's theology in the *Commedia* is profoundly traditional and orthodox. We should not be surprised, then, that he claims one loses all powers of expression in the face of God. The joy of heaven consists in losing the self in God: "his will is our peace" (*Paradiso* iii.85). But that famous phrase, often cited, is only part of a larger consideration of the values that engender peace. As Piccarda, the sister of a close friend, explains to Dante:

> Brother, our will is quieted by virtue
> Of charity, that makes us wish alone
> For what we have, nor gives us thirst for more.
> If to be more exalted we aspired,
> Discordant would our aspirations be
> Unto the will of Him who here secludes us;
> Which thou shalt see finds no place in these circles,
> If being in charity is needful here,
> And if thou lookest well into its nature,
> Nay, 't is essential to this blest existence
> To keep itself within the will divine,
> Whereby our very wishes are made one;
> So that, as we are station above station
> Throughout this realm, to all the realm 't is pleasing,
> As to the King, who makes his will our will.
> And his will is our peace; this is the sea,
> To which is moving onward whatsoever
> It doth create, and all that nature makes.
> —Paradiso iii.70–87, Dante 1870: 13–14; Montemaggi 2015: 196

Peace (*paca*) is the very reason why God made humans: it is the "final" purpose of human creation and it comes from being "in charity" with God, but also with other human beings, and with the perfect order of heaven. The lesson, then, that we should draw from the vision of perfection, is to pursue the love and will we recognize as the purpose of our being. The procedure Dante suggests is not unlike the one Guillaume de Deguileville encourages his readers to observe in the *The Pilgrimage of Human Life*, and indeed, like the protagonist of the latter work, Dante meets personifications of the cardinal and theological virtues who guide him on his journey. But rather than limiting oneself to the practice of those conventional virtues for personal salvation, Dante's message emphasizes the societal dimensions of such virtues in the form of justice: human accord with God's will implies rendering to each his or her due on earth. Dante confirms that lesson in his *Monarchia*, which not only explicitly links justice and peace but also argues that the prime goal of the ruler is to secure just relationships, not only between governed and subjects, but also also between individuals: if that goal is met, justice gains peace, freeing individuals to pursue virtue (*Monarchia* I, iv and III, xvi, 11; Dante 1995: 12–13 and 147).[2]

THE WORLD OF RITUAL: THE KISS

Few medieval people, if any, would have argued that peace is a natural state; it must be *made*. As several contributions in this volume show, peacemaking involved performative acts that initiated, symbolized, or memorialized being at peace. That could be done in a variety of ways, depending on the conditions: gestures of subjugation, an exchange of gifts, the swearing of an oath, a communal meal—all of these served, and many are recorded in writing or images. One form of symbolic action, however, stands out for its universality and intuitive power: the kiss.

The practice of embracing and kissing, to enact and represent peace, existed in both religious and secular customs of medieval Europe. The Kiss of Peace was—and to some extent still is—a formal part of the Christian Mass. Early followers of Christ adopted the ritual to signify the bond of charity that should rule among them, following Peter's injunction to "greet one another with the kiss of love" (1 Pet. 5:14). Paul felt the need to emphasize its sacred significance by calling it a "holy kiss" (1 Cor. 16:20), perhaps because it met with some unease. Translating from the original Greek, the medieval Latin Bible used the same formula, *in osculo sancto* ("with a holy kiss"), in both passages (*Biblia* 1994: 1789 and 1869). It was customary in Mediterranean and Middle-Eastern cultures for relatives and close friends to exchange kisses upon meeting, but Christian ritual extended the practice to strangers coming together for worship. Historian L. Edward Phillips called the early Christian kiss of peace a "counter-cultural family bond," reflecting the Christian inclination to imagine such gatherings as an alternative family, created by the Holy Spirit (1996: 36; see also Petkov 2003: 13). By the fourth century it was incorporated in the ceremony of Mass as part of the offertory, in response to Christ's words: "If you are offering your gift on the altar and remember that your brother has a complaint against you, leave your gift on the altar and go first and be reconciled with your brother and then come and offer your gift" (Mt. 5:23–24); evidently, it was understood to cast off feelings of grievance and to enact reconciliation. Around 400, the Kiss of Peace found its final place in Mass just before the Eucharistic prayer, when the priest says the "Peace be with you" (*Pax vobiscum*). Augustine explained:

> After this is said: "peace be with you"; and Christians kiss one another with a holy kiss. It is the sign of peace; as the lips make it known so let it be in our minds. That is to say, as your lips approach the lips of your brother let not your heart withdraw from his.
> —Sermon CCXXVII, 4, in Augustin d'Hippon 1966: 240;
> transl. Perella 1969: 24

Since Christ was the "peace" that came with *Pax vobiscum* to the communicants soon to be assembled, moving the ritual to just before communion made sense. Augustine's testimony confirms that, like the kiss between relatives and close friends, the Kiss of Peace was, in his day, still made from mouth to mouth. Apparently that level of intimacy became difficult to maintain as congregations grew, and it caused discomfort when genders were not segregated during Mass (such separation became customary only gradually). By the thirteenth century in the western, Latin Church, the priest used a small tablet of wood or precious metal (the *pax*, or *pax*-board), usually ornamented with an image of Christ, for the faithful to kiss; that ritual often served as a substitute for lay communion. Eventually a physical embrace became the preserve of the clergy, exchanged solely between clerics who co-officiated, for instance between priest and deacon, at high Mass. Even though lay people may not have participated actively in the "kiss" by the sixteenth century, they were familiar with the symbolism of that part of Mass, since primers explained it at some length (Bossy 1983: 53–8; compare the more nuanced view in Rubin 1991: 73–4).

There is considerable debate about how and when the "Kiss of Peace" became customary in secular rites of reconciliation; we also do not know if the latter are older than written records suggest (Petkov 2003; Jansen 2018: 165).[3] In cities of late medieval Italy, formal ceremonies to establish peace between feuding families or to redress crimes certainly included a kiss, exchanged by protagonists in the dispute, to seal the agreement. The textual and visual discourse surrounding those civil procedures bathed in a religious aura that emphasized the penitential aspects of peacemaking, and images commemorating such pacts often feature "an angel of peace," a celestial mediator, overseeing the act. Katherine Jansen has recently argued that "the angel's presence impacts a sacrality to the scene, elevating the civic transaction of peacemaking above the mundane world and into the transcendent state of holy peace that human beings can reach only through an act of repentance" (Jansen 2018: 21).[4] These civil procedures existed also in cities north of the Alps, for instance in the densely urbanized regions of the Low Countries. Although the ritual elements of those ceremonies have not yet been examined in much detail, some evidence links the northern customs with Germanic and proto-feudal notions of bonding; indeed, the peace concluded between the parties virtually created a new kinship between the feuding clans (Van Caenegem 1954: 280–7; Petkov 2003: 105–7). Yet, here, too, religious penance played a role: so-called expiatory pilgrimages were commonly adopted as acts of atonement. Here, too, a kiss of peace performed and completed the pact. In late medieval Ghent, the procedure was called a *zoendinc*, evidently in recognition of the central role played by the *zoen*, a middle-Dutch term that meant "reconciliation or pact" but also "kiss" (Van Caenegem 1954: 280–323).

Sacral and profane forces evoked by the kiss of peace would thus jointly compel warring clans towards making peace and honoring agreements. Yet, that was not always possible. In a famous feud involving two prominent lineages of Ghent, the Borluuts and van Sint-Baafs, the clans were formally reconciled by a *zoen* some time before 1294. Bad blood continued to fester, however, to the extent that, when the two families found themselves attending the same funeral Mass in January 1296, ancient feelings of hatred and revenge boiled over at the very moment of the Mass when a spirit of peace was supposed to unite them: after the offertory, members of the Sint-Baafs clan left the church, armed themselves at home, and returned to attack the Borluuts as they were leaving. The revived feud was settled in 1306 through a pact that prescribed twenty-seven pilgrimages on both sides (Blockmans 1935).

FIGURE 5.9: Judas' kiss. Giotto, fresco, Arena chapel of Padua, Italy, 1304–05. Photo by Antonio Quattrone/Archivio Quattrone/Mondadori Portfolio via Getty Images.

For those who might contemplate performing the peacemaking ritual under false pretenses, another image of a kiss loomed large: the Kiss of Judas. The *Constitutions of the Apostles* (II.vii), from the fourth century, already understood it as a warning against approaching the liturgical kiss of peace dishonestly: "Let no one have any quarrel against another: let no one come to it in hypocrisy. Then let the men give the men, and the women give the women, the Lord's kiss. But let no one do it with a deceit, as Judas betrayed the Lord with a kiss" (transl. Perella 1969: 28).

By identifying Christ for his captors with a kiss, the sacred sign of love, kinship, and peace, Judas was guilty of utter betrayal, one that has, throughout the centuries, epitomized the violation of honor, indeed perversion itself, from which there was no escape; only suicide, the ultimate sin, remained. Ambrose of Milan (337–397) called Judas "a species of monstrosity" and his kiss a "bestial conjunction of lips" (Mormando 1999a: 186). When Giotto painted the scene of Judas' betrayal on the triumphal arch of Padua's Arena chapel, around 1305, contemporaries no doubt fully grasped its horror and terrifying consequences.

AN URBAN VISION: AMBROGIO LORENZETTI'S *PEACE AND WAR*

Our final image of peace, the most famous from the medieval period, is also one of the most enigmatic. It is part of a series of frescoes painted in 1338 by Ambrogio Lorenzetti (1290–1348) on the walls of the Palazzo Pubblico of Siena, Italy. Although later scholarship often called the scenes "Allegories of Good and Bad Government," medieval descriptions speak of them as "images of peace and war" (Dessi 2007). Both titles are apt insofar as they allude to a fundamental linkage, throughout the program, of peace and good government: peace and prosperity issue from good government; conversely, war and disaster follow from bad government. Few (art) historians will now venture interpretations that go beyond that rather elementary observation, as so much in the work is still the subject of dispute. Over the centuries, the frescoes have received several overpaintings, additions, and restorations, some of them contested, while one wall of the hall (on the western side) bears large lacunae because of water damage. Opinions differ about the precise meaning of several figures, how exactly they relate to one another, and whether they convey a particular political theory.

The room in which the paintings are found, now called the Hall of Peace, or Hall of the Nine (*Nove*), formed the meeting place of *li signori Nove*, the nine-member citizen-committee who governed the city-state of Siena from 1287 to 1355 and commissioned the frescoes. These occupy the western, northern, and eastern walls of the room, which lack windows. The west wall is dominated by a horrible creature representing "Bad Government" or "Tyranny," inspired by three vices (Avarice, Pride, and Vainglory?) and assisted by six figures that (probably) stand for Cruelty, Treason, Fraud, Furor, Division, and War. They oversee the effects of tyranny's rule, spread by fear soaring over discrete scenes of mayhem: murder, robbery, a soldier's killing of a woman, while Justice lies bound and helpless on the ground. Desolation strikes the barren countryside; a city is devastated by plunder.

The contrast with the opposite, eastern side of the room could not be greater. The scene on this wall (sometimes called "Good Government"; "the Virtues of Good Government" would be better) has two focal points. On the left side, three female figures placed on a vertical axis face the viewer. Identifications are sometimes controversial, but it is possible to think of them as Justice, seated on a throne between scales held up by Wisdom above her; directly under her, foregrounded but smaller than Justice, sits Concord, handing out braided cords to men who march in orderly files toward the right, where they arrive at the feet of a group of seated figures who form the second, horizontal axis.

An old man sitting on a throne (the city of Siena?) towers over everyone else; seated on a bench on his left are Magnanimity (?), Temperance, and Justice (again), with Faith, Hope, and Charity depicted in the sky above them; on the old man's right side are (from right to left) Prudence, Fortitude, and Peace, the most radiant figure of all. Clothed in a white diaphanous robe, she reclines contently, holding an olive branch and crown (ancient biblical and Roman symbols of peace), with armor buried under her pillow.

Peace seems to be lost in thought but she is looking up and to the right, toward the scenes on the northern wall (painted perhaps somewhat later, between 1338 and

FIGURE 5.10: Ambrogio Lorenzetti, *Peace and War*. Detail: Virtues of Good Government. Fresco in Siena, Italy, Palazzo Pubblico, 1338. Photo by VCG Wilson/Corbis via Getty Images.

FIGURE 5.11: Ambrogio Lorenzetti, *Peace and War*. Detail: Peace. Fresco in Siena, Italy, Palazzo Pubblico, 1338. Photo by DeAgostini/Getty Images.

Ambrogio's death of the plague in 1348), where the effects of virtuous rule can be admired in all their splendor: a city, secure within its walls, basks in bright sunlight, with people dancing in the streets, others engaged in the crafts and commerce of a thriving medieval center; at the foot of the walls a magnificent landscape unfolds, rich in vineyards, bountiful harvests, with farmers working the land while travelers make their way safely into the distance.

No doubt much of this goes back to old conventions: the galleries of personified virtues opposing similarly traditional series of vices, for instance; the image of the fortified city; or the signs of abundance among the effects of peace. Like Dante and other theoreticians of politics in the thirteenth and fourteenth centuries, the scenes emphasize the central role of justice, meted out fairly and swiftly. The association of peace and justice is quite old, and for medieval people, it would have been rooted in the Psalmist's portrayal of divine providence, when "justice and peace have kissed" (Ps. 85 [84]: 11).

Still, it is worth noting that at the Hall of Peace in Siena, that traditional pairing is given new vigor in a particular environment: that of the city state or urban community. The work was not commissioned by a monarch or other ruler, but by a republican form of government. Although reverence is paid—naturally—to divine support, the program's outlook is supremely inner-worldly, even secular. Scholars now hesitate to identify

FIGURE 5.12: Ambrogio Lorenzetti, *Peace and War*. Detail: Effects of Good Government. Fresco in Siena, Italy, Palazzo Pubblico, 1338. Photo by DeAgostini/Getty Images.

concrete references to Aristotelian conceptions of good government channeled through the Christian, scholastic, lens of Thomas Aquinas. That is too narrow a view, ignoring the actual traditions of government in cities around 1300. Instead, we might read the frescoes in tandem with written sources generated by urban centers in Italy and elsewhere (see e.g., Boone 2010), celebrating the common good, internal justice, orderly existence, respect for craftsmanship, and dreams of boundless productivity. These ideals welcomed Aristotelian political theory, rediscovered in the late thirteenth century, but they were formed on a wider platform than university doctrine, and shaped by urban institutions and the medieval urban experience itself (Skinner 1986 and 1999; Boucheron 2005; Dessi 2007; Kumhera 2017: 12–14; Jansen 2018). As such, the frescoes are unique, testifying to a specific era in cultural history, when that medieval city community, rather than divine authority, the monarch, or the emperor, made peace.

CHAPTER SIX

Peace Movements: Peace in the Communes

JAMES A. PALMER

When we think about peace movements today, our tendency is to emphasize the popular character, whether actual or aspirational, of collective public demonstrations aimed at preventing or decrying armed conflicts between states. The medieval age did not know peace movements in this sense (Heyn 1997). Despite the apparent participation of everyday people in various manifestations of the Peace of God movement, for example (Head and Landes 1992, Koziol 2018), it is, in fact, difficult to know what the average person thought about peace, which ideas might have energized them to coalesce into something we might recognize as a movement, and how they promoted and preserved peace in their own communities. The voices we tend to hear are most often those of the great and learned: counts and kings, popes and prelates. Meanwhile, the overwhelming majority of Europe's population was rural, not particularly well educated or inclined to the production of written records. Their voices, speaking on the matter of peace, are generally silent.

Over the course of the eleventh century, however, a new phenomenon began to appear in much of Europe that would change this: the town. By 1100, these urban societies, though usually still modest in size, were well-established economic centers (Nicholas 2003). As towns proliferated and urban populations grew throughout Latin Christendom, the denizens of the towns began experimenting with new kinds of community, new modes of governance, and new expressions of what their inhabitants believed a rightly ordered world to be. Though their societies were novel in many ways, the fundamental attitudes of townsfolk were not so different from those of their age. In a world marked by feudal relations and a sense of masculine, martial honor, engagement in violent disputes was often natural and even obligatory. Private feuds were, across much of Europe, one of the main structural elements of social life (Bisson 2009; Brunner 1992; Miller 1990). Such values were not alien to urban elites. It is clear that for many of the laity, urban and otherwise, peace was often conceived not in absolute terms but rather in the sense of limiting or managing violence, so that enmity and reconciliation necessarily became two equally natural sides of the same coin (Hyams 2003). We know this because the medieval towns have left various kinds of evidence, increasing in volume with each passing century, which attest to values and practices relating to peace that were espoused by people who were neither secular lords nor erudite ecclesiastics. The polycentric organization of towns, which were essentially societies made up of smaller societies, meant that conflict was inevitable and not necessarily seen as a source of problematic disorder. When conflict did become a problem, or when it behooved particular actors to claim that it had, the towns gave rise to a variety of means by which conflict could be controlled (Lantschner 2015). These took various forms, from pious peacemaking movements to legislative programs.

Towns appeared in much of Europe but few places were more marked by urban culture than Italy and the Low Countries. In both areas, towns and cities established new practices of peace sustained by collective and private institutions that were typical of urban life and emerged along with it. In what follows, this essay will concentrate on Italy, which not only generated the richest surviving evidence but was also the only site to develop popular "movements" in support of peace. There were many reasons for this: among them an ancient past rooted in urban life, an enduring tradition of lay literacy, and a particular propensity for the instrumentalization of writing in matters both public and private. In addition to being an important site of medieval urban life, Italy was also home to several examples of what can fruitfully be understood as medieval peace movements, despite their marked difference from what is now generally meant by that term. Famous examples include the Alleluia of 1233, the flagellant movements of 1260 and 1310, and processions like that headed by Venturino da Bergamo in 1335 or undertaken by the Bianchi of 1399. During each of these instances, waves of religious enthusiasm swept large parts of Italy, inspiring people to congregate in great celebrations of peace and harmony, and sometimes to leave their towns and spread their devotion, their numbers swelling with each new community. Italian peace movements, then, were primarily movements within and between urban centers.

If we are to understand medieval Italy's peace movements we need to consider them in terms of urban life and a culture of peace derived from the Christian theology and piety that played a prominent role within it. Medieval Italy, like the rest of Europe, was the heir to a rich tradition of early Christian thought that to a certain extent privileged the clergy as agents of peace. The novel realities of urban life, however, inflected these ideas and practices both in terms of the role of the laity and the practical goals of peacemaking. During the medieval period, the urban laity would play an increasingly prominent and active role in the pursuit of peace, fundamentally shaping the nature and desired outcomes of peace movements along these lines. Ultimately, religious expressions of peace and pacification, associated with preaching, penance, and pilgrimage, were but one aspect of a wider culture of pacification that, as the Italian case makes clear, also included the political parties and ideologies of the towns.

PEACE AND THE COMMUNE TO THE EARLY THIRTEENTH CENTURY

Medieval notions of peace understood it as early Christian thinkers had: the product of a correspondence between the order of things and the will of God, imagined in its ideal form as the peace of the Kingdom of God or an idealized heavenly Jerusalem. However, they inflected these understandings with the ideas and practices of subsequent centuries. Classically, though the ideal result striven for was social, its achievement depended on the correct orientation of individual human hearts in relation to God's will. For this reason, in a world understood to be tainted by sin, the conversion of human hearts and the repentance of that sin was a *sine qua non* in any effort to achieve a tranquil, rightly ordered, society. Perhaps the most important source of these ideas was Augustine of

Hippo, the fifth-century bishop most famous for penning *The City of God*. As Augustine's ideas were the product of a late Roman world wherein Christian ecclesiastical authority and secular governance often went hand in hand, they provided a rich reservoir of inspiration for both clergy and laity with an interest in working to create and sustain the ideal Christian community. To this late antique inheritance, the Middle Ages added a crucial element: the notion that, in addition to repentance, penance was required to reorientate sinful hearts and set them on the path to peace (Hamilton 2001; Meens 2014). First emerging as a practice in the early medieval period, penance was, from the eleventh century onwards, a necessary element in the creation of both inward and outward peace. Such peace was therefore understood as something that had to be actively produced and reproduced. By the early thirteenth century, at least, a precise means of making peace was emerging in Italy and elsewhere. In part because it boiled down to the making of a binding agreement, the process emerged from contract law but was ritualized in a way that incorporated clear religious symbolism. Most commonly, the exchange of the kiss of peace was used to seal the agreement. The kiss thus signaled the formal conversion of warring parties from a relationship of enmity to one of concord, in accordance with the divine will, certainly, but also with a kind of social morality according to which the parties were effectively disciplined (Jansen 2018; Petkov 2003). The emergence of practices like this in the towns of both Italy and the Low Countries, as well as in other areas of Europe, suggests a widespread peace impulse from at least the late twelfth and early thirteenth centuries. The chronology of this development is significant because it corresponds with the emergence of new forms of urban life.

Between roughly 1050 and 1150, urban life in Italy came to be characterized by a single organizing idea, that of the commune (Wickham 2015). Though often urban, communes were not the same as towns. Instead, a commune was a sworn association, an idea of union and an agreement to act for the general good in specific ways. The founders of urban communes were generally affluent, often members of the feudal aristocracy, and frequently bound by ties of obligation to their city's bishop, who was generally the main governing authority prior to the communal age (Coleman 2013). The communes did not emerge in conjunction with anything we might describe as a peace movement. Rather, they arose in a period of, and in part due to, conflict between German emperors, the papacy, and Italian communities caught up in their disputes. The Peace of Constance, in 1183, marked Emperor Frederick Barbarossa's formal acknowledgment, at the behest of an alliance of communes known as the Lombard League, that their polities had the right to elect their own officials and enact their own laws. Most communes had some kind of assembly of citizens, rotating magistracies with brief terms of office, and *de facto*, and later *de jure* autonomy. All these important developments in secular governance should not distract us, however, from the religious character of communal life.

Although most Italian communes arose during a process in which the local laity took over the reins of governance from the bishop, the communes themselves were at no point purely secular institutions. Not only did communal governments emerge from those of bishops, but the civic culture of the communes also emerged from ideas and practices of association that first appeared in a pious context. The heart of the commune was its cathedral, the "mother church" in which locals were baptized and the community was thereby continuously renewed. The liturgical pattern of the year, with its many feasts, provided a kind of rhythm that was etched into urban life through regular processions and other pious practices (Thompson 2005). Although rooted to an extent in the memory of ancient republicanism, the very legitimacy of communal regimes was, by the early thirteenth century, increasingly based on their self-presentation as societies marked by good governance and order that was productive of peace and justice. Although there cannot be said to be a single homogenous communal ideology that all such polities shared, these ideas were common and are perhaps best captured in a series of allegorical frescoes produced by Ambrogio Lorenzetti in Siena during the 1330s. The ideal of good government emphasized justice, peace, and prosperity. Clearly then, the notion of peace, as both a desideratum and a marker of political legitimacy, was central to Italian urban culture. In theory, a medieval town was a species of Christian community, the social world enclosed within its walls a microcosm of the broader order of things. Certain earthly cities, like Jerusalem or Rome, were particularly marked by such ideas (Lilley 2009).

Ideal models are ever-distant from lived realities, however, and medieval urban life was famous not only for its novelty but also for the moral quandaries it provoked. In the

FIGURE 6.1: St Francis' exorcism of the city of Arezzo's demons leads to the resumption of agricultural labor and commerce, as demonstrated by the merchant and farmer emerging from the gates. Giotto, The Exorcism of Arezzo, *c.* 1297–99, Upper Basilica of S. Francesco, Assisi. Photo by Montadori Portfolio/Getty Images.

towns, both the concentration of wealth in the hands of a few and the disturbing contrast of poverty were starkly visible. Concern with such injustices led to reform movements like those of the Waldensians and the new mendicant orders (Franciscans, Dominicans, and others), which pursued justice by eschewing wealth in favor of an apostolic life of voluntary poverty (Little 1978). This concern was perhaps the dominant moral question of urban life in the twelfth century and remained an important aspect of Italian urban lay piety well into the thirteenth. Furthermore, we know that members of the laity understood economic inequity to be a fundamental cause of conflict. Diagnosing and treating this problem was something in which they assigned to themselves an active role, along with

FIGURE 6.2: The diversity both of a preacher's audience and the mode of their engagement with him can be seen in this detail from a fresco by Andrea di Bonaiuto, St. Peter of Verona preaching, 1365–67, Spanish Chapel, Santa Maria Novella, Florence. Photo courtesy DEA/S. VANINI/Getty images.

the clergy (Powell 1992). However, by the early thirteenth century, we see in Italy a steady shift of emphasis away from economy injustice and toward the problem of violence. The centering of violence as both a social and a political problem rendered Italy ripe for its first great peace movement.

THE ALLELUIA OF 1233

By the end of the twelfth century it had become clear that no matter how short their terms, executive officials drawn from within the commune were too thoroughly implicated in local tensions to be able to govern in a disinterested manner. This problem led to the creation of a new office, the *podestà*, a supreme executive official not native to the city and thus ostensibly free from personal interest in its various disputes. The frequency and scale of conflict within the communes, which the *podestà* was expected to manage, is important to acknowledge if we are to appreciate the place of peace and peace movements in Italian communal life. As urban populations grew, the powerful lineages of the traditional feudal elite increasingly clashed with affluent newcomers, whose families were of humbler and more recent origin, over access to political office and questions of honor and social distinction. Escalating conflict between these two groups would lead to a widespread emphasis on the importance of peace and concord and to a growing interest in various political, legal, and penitential means of achieving those ends. In particular, the newer, less aristocratic members of the communal political class, commonly referred to as the *popolo*, were increasingly critical of the disruptive and disorderly violence of the old elites. Although, in reality, all parties were prone to violence, the *popolo* used this critique to wrest control of communal governments from their rivals and establish what are known as "popular" governments. Violent factional conflict between the *popolo* and their rivals was a constant and escalating problem, and it is in this context that the first great peace movement of communal Italy was born.

That movement, the Alleluia of 1233, was inspired and led by mendicant preachers (Thompson 1992). The mendicants, however, had risen to popularity largely because of their ability to draw support from Italy's middle- and upper-class urban residents, and their ideas must be understood as having emerged in part from a dialogue with those groups (Powell 2008). Preaching, by both clergy and laity, was an important medium for the communication of ideas as well as a common source of entertainment. Some preaching was done by locals but itinerant preachers, again both lay and ecclesiastic, were a familiar phenomenon.

In 1233, Franciscans and Dominicans, perhaps inspired by the example of successful lay preachers, sparked the wave of devotion known as the Alleluia, primarily in Lombardy and the Emilia-Romagna. The Alleluia was a short-lived phenomenon, ramping up in the spring of 1233 and ending sometime in the fall of the same year. But it was also an important sign of things to come insofar as the marriage of communal politics and an evolving ideology of peace were concerned. Not only did the preachers oversee the reconciliation of violent disputes in large numbers, but they were also so popular that communes entrusted them with the task of revising their legal statutes as part of a broad program of social reform. Some, like Gerard of Modena, rose to prominence and remained in a single city (Parma in Gerard's case). Others, like John of Vicenza, operated on a very large scale, spreading the devotion to Bologna, Verona, Padua, and Treviso, among other places, effecting the reconciliation of regional disputes as well as local ones. In all cases, the preachers promoted one another's efforts from the pulpit, building momentum for the movement and creating a sense of social transformation on a large scale. This coordination served to further strengthen a movement already fueled by the preachers' personal charisma, miracle working, and the spread of news by word of mouth. This coordinated effort was impressive, but we might still wonder how it was that communal governments so easily handed over the reins of power to the preachers of the Alleluia.

At the heart of the program promulgated by the Alleluia preachers was the conceptual union of peace and justice, expressed through preaching, acts of public peacemaking, and statutory reforms. The Alleluia preachers rose to popularity by critiquing the social ills of usurious money-lending and violent conflict, and they leveraged that popularity to achieve astonishing things. By publicly converting the hearts of those involved in feuds and factional violence, the preachers created a reputation for being miraculously successful social reformers. It was for this reason that they were trusted both as arbiters of disputes and legislators. In many cases, they undertook measures aimed at adjusting statutory norms to reduce the likelihood, or at least the scope, of future conflicts. The means by which they did these things are revelatory of the relationship between the program of the preachers and the legal and social contexts in which they worked. When the preachers of the Alleluia arbitrated conflicts and helped bring about peace agreements between the involved parties, they did so in an entirely standard way, familiar to the laity because it emerged not primarily from ecclesiastical norms but rather from notarial documentary practice. The process of peacemaking, including the endowment of an arbiter with the power to arbitrate and rule, the arbiter's production of a formal ruling, and the production of a contractual document formalizing the terms of the peace and penalties for breaking it, was already attested in the manuals that guided notarial practice. By the second half of the century, the exchange of the kiss of peace as the formal seal of this process was also standard (Petkov 2003: 83–4; Thompson 1992: 24).

The novelty here was simply the number of disputes resolved in this way at one time and the fact that one man, the preacher, was entrusted with them all. Though it may seem shocking that communal governments were willing to hand over power to mediate their conflicts and revise their laws, this too was a familiar mechanism, bearing obvious similarities to the function of a *podestà*. In addition to reconciling warring parties, the preachers legislated on ecclesiastical and moral matters, but primarily on matters pertaining to peace and justice. Above all, they sought to ease the tensions that led to violent conflict by focusing on reconciliation rather than punishment, and offering amnesty to those living in exile due to political disputes or unresolved criminal infractions. Mercy was a common element here, offered to nearly all, with the primary exception being those who knowingly acted to break an established peace.

The Alleluia, though remarkable for its thorough intervention in communal life and the scale on which it operated, was a short-lived movement. The whole thing lasted only about ten months. In most cases, preachers ran afoul of the limits of their power of persuasion. When large-scale efforts at peacemaking began to struggle, those opposed to the social and legal reformation the preachers were advocating became more openly skeptical. Some preachers, such as John of Vicenza, began to resort not to personal charisma and miracles but to open coercion to achieve their ends, something made possible by the crowds of followers they drew. By so doing, they came to increasingly resemble the various secular powers among whom they ostensibly acted as mediators and reformers. For these and other reasons, the time of tranquility and peace created by the Alleluia inevitably came to an end, eroded by waning enthusiasm and ongoing political and social tension. Despite its brevity, however, the Alleluia had significant long-term implications. Preachers guided by the model its proponents set would enjoy fame and influence into the fifteenth century and even beyond. Perhaps even more significantly, the association of peace and justice with

FIGURE 6.3: The Kiss of Peace. Two men end a feud and seal the peace with a kiss. Michael Lupi de Çandiu, 1297–1305, Spain, Getty Museum Ms. Ludwig XIV 6, fol. 230r (detail). Digital image courtesy of the Getty's Open Content Program. Source: http://www.getty.edu/art/collection/objects/4558/unknown-michael-lupi-de-candiu-initial-n-two-men-shaking-hands-and-kissing-spanish-about-1290-1310/?dz=0.5000,0.7642,0.37

good governance, a union of politics and pious ideals that had always been present to some extent in the notion of the commune, was cemented. As part of this, the merging of ostensibly private efforts to end formally private conflicts with the statutory regime and juridical apparatus of the state highlighted the entanglement of private and public violence and the peacemaking efforts that responded to both. All this would continue to be characteristic of communal political life until the end of Italy's communal era.

THE FLAGELLANTS OF 1260

Only a generation or so after the Alleluia, what was perhaps the most iconic movement of peace and penance in the Middle Ages was born in central Italy. In April of 1260, as their city was shifting from the abstinence of Lent to the jubilation of Easter, the people of Perugia embraced a novel religious movement that would prove far more popular and influential than they expected (Dickson 1989; Vallerani 2005). The movement, led initially by a local lay penitent named Rainiero Faisani, was characterized by processions in which large groups, stripped to the waist, would whip their shoulders, going so far as to draw blood by scourging the very spot where the cross had rested on the shoulder of Christ. Moved by fear of an angry God, they chanted litanies that repeatedly called out for peace and mercy. By so doing, the flagellants were merging a traditional form of individual penance with the public and collective practice of procession. This was relatively novel, as was the movement's transition by no later than September to a fully itinerant phase, which turned local urban processions into collective acts of penitential and evangelical pilgrimage. The movement traveled to Rome, securing the release of prisoners there, as well as to Bologna and many other north-central Italian communes before crossing the Alps and spreading northwest to at least Strasbourg and northeast as far as Poland. Once it crossed the Alps, the movement, though it sustained a collective quality due in part to its success in northern urban centers, began to draw suspicious eyes from lay and ecclesiastical elites and took on an increasingly anti-clerical and perhaps heterodox tenor. But the flagellant movement did not begin this way. In Italy, it was consistently characterized by collaboration between the laity and local Church leaders, as well as by a profound emphasis on pacification (Dickson 1989). It was, in short, the opposite of a suspicious, heterodox movement characterized by hysterical or ungovernable religious enthusiasm (compare Cohn 1970).

No individual aspect of the flagellant movement was particularly shocking. The novelty of the movement lay, rather, in its pairing of modes of piety not normally linked, as well as in subtle shifts in the relationship between the laity and the Church. Flagellation was a longstanding form of penance in monastic communities. Lay embrace of it seems to have predated 1260, particularly among lay penitents who embraced a culture of penance associated with Francis of Assisi and adopted by the flagellant movement's early leader, Faisani (Meersseman 1962; Dickson 1989). Processions that included formal litanies were also a familiar phenomenon, as was the idea of a penitential pilgrimage, into which the Perugian movement eventually evolved. Though the flagellant movement began among the laity, the Perugians sought the leadership and guidance of their bishop from the very beginning, and the Italian instantiations of this movement were consistent in the inclusion of ecclesiastics in their traditional role as spiritual authorities and guides. The famous Franciscan chronicler, Salimbene di Adam, who was both participant in and chronicler of the movement, testifies to this (Baird, Baglivi, and Kane 1986). The novelty of the flagellants was twofold. First, they rendered public and collective a penitential culture and praxis that had theretofore been individual in character. The conversion of the individual soul via penance was now being effected at the level of the general community, preparing the way to peace in this collective way just as it did for individuals. In the wake of the initial enthusiasm, which, though intense, was relatively brief, confraternal organizations of *disciplinati* sprang up all over Italy, imitating many of the flagellant movement's collective modes of piety. Second, unlike their predecessors in the Alleluia, the flagellants were stirred to act by lay pious fervor alone, rather than by the inspiration of mendicant preaching. The clergy were welcome, but they were not the source of the movement. In part because of the latter, we misunderstand this movement if we assume it to have been solely a religious phenomenon, even one that is collective and potent.

The inception of the flagellant movement in Perugia corresponded with the Easter season and thus leveraged a moment of heightened religious fervor, but it also coincided with the unfolding of political events of great significance (Vallerani 2005). In 1256, the *popolo* of Perugia had taken control of the commune. On April 5, 1260, this new government issued the *Ordinamenta Populi*, a clear expression of the new popular regime's anti-magnate program and its association with a broader communal ideology of peace. The *Ordinamenta* forbade bearing arms, aiding political exiles, or swearing oaths of vassalage, all blows against the old elite presented as a program of general pacification. It is unsurprising, then, that when the popular government approved the practices of the flagellants, it did so in part due to the explicit utility it saw in the movement's emphasis on peace. In a move indicative of emerging trends in Italy's culture of peace, the *Ordinamenta* presented the popular commune not only as the keeper of the peace, but also as its enforcer, capable of legally coercing warring parties into accepting peace. This noteworthy move was linked with a clearly stated end goal of perpetual peace, a concept that made attaining the ideal of the heavenly Jerusalem—a goal with unmistakably apocalyptic overtones—the explicit aim of the commune. These measures were, of course, political and largely symbolic. The popular regime knew that the violence of their elite political rivals was perhaps the greatest threat to their government and everyone knew, in Perugia as elsewhere, that absolute peace was unachievable prior to the coming of the kingdom of God. But the measures taken by Perugia's government, and explicitly linked by it to the flagellant movement, had real and lasting effects. All over Italy, we see popular governments taking similar measures. Florence's Ordinances of Justice, themselves part of an anti-magnate political program, are the most famous example (Lansing 1991; Najemy 2006). Everywhere, popular regimes were empowering their new executives, like the Alleluia preachers before them, and the *podestà* before that, to act as peacemakers endowed with the power to legally coerce and enforce peace. The resonance between political pacification programs and pious emphasis on penance and peace, which had now evolved into a kind of social penance aimed at the creation of communal concord (Jansen 2018), resulted in an increasing tendency of lay elites to take an active hand in instigating and guiding Italy's urban peace movements.

THE POLITICS AND PIETY OF PEACE AMONG THE LATE-MEDIEVAL LAITY

Beginning in the early fourteenth century, a new instigator and mediator of peace began to appear on the Italian scene. This was neither a charismatic mendicant preacher nor a civic official performing duties of pacification. It was an angel. The figure of the angel of peace began to appear in monumental art early in the fourteenth century and continued to be a major element until the century's end (Jansen 2018: 192–203). Peace movements, whether pious or political, had always been led by either ecclesiastical or secular elites, often outsiders entrusted to reform a violent community. The image of the angel fulfilling this role suggests that the question of leadership, or perhaps of ownership over the process of peace, was increasingly marked by ambiguity. It would be too much to suggest that the angel of peace was deployed in an intentional manner, occupying the traditional leadership role a charismatic preacher or a *podestà* might have done in the past, so that leadership of Italy's peace movements, both pious and political, could be more readily diffused amongst the laity. Yet during the fourteenth century it became clear that the latter was, in fact, precisely what was happening. In both the politics and the piety of peace, the laity were increasingly to taking a controlling role.

Politically, the fourteenth century was a transformative period for Italy. Throughout the communal Italian world, popular regimes were being challenged and eventually supplanted by governments led by individual strongmen and their descendants, commonly referred to as *signori*. In addition to such political changes, Italy faced the same challenges that confronted all of Europe over the course of the fourteenth century: climate change and famine, an increase in the scale and frequency of warfare, and epidemic disease (most famously the Black Death). With the various horsemen of the apocalypse so evidently present, it is not shocking to learn that many interpreted these various crises as signs of God's wrath and the approach of the end times. Where God's wrath was plain, the necessary response was clear: penance and, with it, peacemaking. Small wonder, then, that in 1310 a new flagellant movement appeared in the Piedmont and processed from place to place crying out for mercy (Jansen 2018: 44–6). This new flagellant movement had no founder but another, which appeared in 1335 and whose participants were known as the *Columbini* (little doves), was led by a charismatic Dominican named Venturino da Bergamo. Venturino's movement began in Bergamo and processed southward toward Rome, crying out for peace, mercy, and penance, and reconciling enemies who then joined the movement as they went. Venturino and his followers seem to have been well received until they reached their destination. Once in Rome, however, Venturino ran afoul of a populace that was at first interested, but then increasingly skeptical. Eventually, the Dominican was forced to flee the city and his movement evaporated. Venturino himself was censured but then eventually rehabilitated by the papacy (Jansen 2018: 46–8). Political pacification programs continued to evoke the by-now traditional association of good governance of the commune with justice and peace, but not without hitches (Gennaro 1975). In Florence it was necessary to repeatedly renew the commune's allegiance to that city's own version of popular anti-magnate legislation, the Ordinances of Justice. In Rome, the city came briefly under the control of a charismatic demagogue, Cola di Rienzo, who declared himself Tribune of Justice and Peace. Cola would attempt to reform Rome's laws and government, emphasizing justice and peace in a manner reminiscent of previous movements like the Alleluia, but powerfully inflected as well by both the memory of classical antiquity and an urgent apocalypticism characteristic of his own age. Cola's government was fleeting. Romans, in time, became as skeptical about him as they had been of Venturino. Like Venturino he was forced to flee, returning to power in the 1350s only to die at the hands of a Roman mob (Musto 2003).

It would be easy to read the skepticism of the Romans about both Venturino and Cola di Rienzo as a sign of changing times, perhaps of growing skepticism about ideologies of peace similar to that which had brought the Alleluia of 1233 to a close. However, this is not actually what the evidence suggests. The Romans were not skeptical about ideologies of peace or about acts of pious peacemaking. In fact, the initial success of both Venturino and Cola indicate precisely the opposite. Skepticism was directed not at the fundamental ideas and practices their respective movements embraced, but rather at the leadership of those movements. Fourteenth-century Romans were enthusiastic participants in standard forms of peacemaking; some among them even embraced a highly ritualized form of the standard notarial process that evoked both the importance of peace in the community and the association of that peace and its maintenance with confession, penance, and forgiveness. Significantly, this did not require clerical participation nor did it depend on communal institutions or appear in the city's statutes (unlike more standard peacemaking practices, which did). Instead, peacemaking in Rome had become something participated in and shaped by a broad stratum of the city's lay political society (Palmer 2014). In their ultimate rejection of Venturino and Cola, the Romans, like the Italian laity more generally, were laying claim to the task of discerning the difference between real peace and false peacemaking. This was not a sign of declining enthusiasm for peace, but rather of a growing sense of ownership on the part of ever more lay people over pious peace movements and political pacification processes alike.

This subtle shift in Italy's culture of peace produced both an increasingly refined institutionalization of peace and important changes in the explicit goals of peacemaking. The consistent imbrication of peace and politics during the thirteenth and fourteenth centuries may seem to indicate that the political culture of this long period was characterized by an effort, both pious and pragmatic, to eliminate violence from society. In reality, however, few if any pursued this goal, which was, after all, only attainable in the heavenly Jerusalem. The reality is that the practice of feuding and vendetta included all levels of society. Instead of an apocalyptic, and quixotic, effort to eliminate violence entirely, we witness the redrawing of lines between legitimate and illegitimate violence and, concomitantly, the steady refinement of a model of infra-judicial justice which involved both the courts and various extra-judicial members who operated hand-in-hand (Sbriccoli 1997; Sbriccoli 1998; Vallerani 2012). We have seen that in matters of practice, as in matters of piety, peace and concord were understood as something that had to be actively made and remade. This remained the consensus view in late medieval Italy and elsewhere (McRee 1994). Success in this arena was the marker not only of divine justice but also of good governance in an earthly sense. Like the reforms of earlier peace movements, this goal was codified in the statutes of urban governments throughout Italy during the later Middle Ages and, also like those earlier phenomena, they attest to the necessary collaboration of elites and the important institutions they controlled with broader political societies and the practices of peace within which they were fluent. The line between the private violence of the feud and the public violence of politics had always been largely illusory and the same was true of that between private peacemaking and public judicial processes. The courts, like the mendicant reformers of the early thirteenth century, favored reconciliation over all else. The making of private peace was encouraged by reduction of criminal penalties and amnesty from criminal bans that meant exile. Peacemaking, like violence, was practiced across all levels of society and encompassed in both public institutions such as the courts and so-called private practices alike (Kumhera 2017).

The great peace movements of the thirteenth century and those that followed in the fourteenth placed the emphasis on social transformations, classic conversion narratives writ large. Those transformations, however astonishing, never lasted, nor could they in what was understood as a fallen human world. What the evolving piety and practice of peace among the laity of the Italian communes reveals are two crucial developments: a continuously evolving sense of justice or right order which was to be managed and maintained by lay institutions on one hand and, on the other, an effort not to utterly eliminate violence but rather to set limits and regulate it (Zorzi 2009) in what might be termed a moral economy of violence, both pious and civic, carefully delineating between the forgivable and the unforgivable, the licit and the illicit. The result is the emergence of a just economy of violence that was managed first by governing elites and later, as the age of the communes came to an end, by administrative experts. This is perhaps most vividly demonstrated in the ritualized peacemaking of late medieval Rome. In it, the language of penance and piety merged with well-established documentary practice to limit the extent of violence and evoke an image of concord and right order, a process overseen by a communal elite that was rapidly evolving into an administrative rather than a ruling class (Palmer 2019). Developments such as these mark both the culmination of medieval Italy's history of peace movements and the end of the world that had given rise to them.

ITALY'S LAST MEDIEVAL PEACE MOVEMENT: THE BIANCHI OF 1399

In the summer of 1399, somewhere in the mountains of Liguria, another penitential peace movement began. Its origins are uncertain: we know only that it was associated with miracles both of healing and peacemaking, that it began in the countryside, and that its participants were representative of society, including men and women, clergy and laity, elites and commoners. Hoping to prevent the wrath of an angry God, members of the movement dressed all in white and processed through the countryside calling for mercy and peace. They soon came to be named for the color of their garb, the Bianchi. Accompanied at first, it seems, by the clergy of the settlements from whence they came, they were received with some wariness by the governing authority of Genoa, their reception perhaps aided by the presence among them of members of the rural aristocracy. Once inside Genoa, the reins of the movement were taken up by the city's bishop, transforming it into something about which the Genoese no longer had any reservations. A city marked, like so many, by private conflicts among its great families soon became the site of extensive peacemaking. Before long, the movement surged forth again, much as

FIGURE 6.4: A Bianchi procession in 1401, depicted in a fresco, Church of S. Maria Assunta in Vallo di Nera, Italy. Photo courtesy of Zeri Photo Archive, Fondazione Federico Zeri.

the flagellants had in the late thirteenth century, with different groups headed in different directions: toward Lombardy and the Visconti-dominated Po river valley, into the Emilia-Romagna, south into Tuscany, and eventually to Rome. The Bianchi movement clearly had great appeal, gaining new adherents not only as it moved from town to town but also as it passed through the countryside.

The Bianchi were entirely typical in some respects but atypical in others. A devotional song associated with the movement declared "a new light has dawned/new grace and new life/a new dress and new habit," yet ultimately very little about the movement was innovative. They sang hymns of praise, especially to the Virgin. They produced a host of fairly generic miracles: the sick were healed, the lame walked, prostitutes married, and, of course, enduring enmities were pacified. The significance of the movement is not its novelty but rather the insight it offers into what has been termed the "popular orthodoxy" of the age (Bornstein 1994). Yet the Bianchi were unusual too. Unlike other processional movements, like Venturino's for example, the Bianchi had no leadership: no charismatic preacher led the way. Yet the movement was famous for its good order and discipline. Everywhere it went the local clergy, especially bishops, simply stepped into a managerial role, again like the earlier flagellant movements, overseeing pious processions inside and outside their cities until the Bianchi moved on again. No two cities had exactly the same experience.

Significantly, the precise nature of the movement evolved with each new town, as conditions on the ground shaped responses to the arrival of the Bianchi as well as the impact their presence continued to have, if any, after they were gone (Giraudo 2013). Like the Genoese initially had been, some governments were wary of the Bianchi. The pope feared that their arrival would spark instability in Rome. The ruling council of Lucca attempted to prevent the Bianchi from entering the city altogether and, when that failed, tried to limit citizen participation in the movement, in which effort they also failed. Ultimately, the popular response to the Bianchi was everywhere impossible to stifle and challenging to manage. Some towns welcomed them with open arms as a result, perhaps encouraged by the movement's reputation for good order. In Padua, the somewhat beleaguered Francesco Novello, whose regime had been weakened by conflict with foreign enemies, saw a chance to win back some of his people's goodwill by embracing the Bianchi. In the end, their arrival was inevitably political not only because of theoretical connection between the idea of peace and good governance, political legitimacy and justice, but also because of the kinds of pious acts that the movement encouraged: the ending of local feuds, forgiveness of debts, release of prisoners and repatriation of exiles. Whether directly inspired by the Bianchi or not, some governments, like that of Perugia, officially embraced the policing of citizen morality in the wake of the movement (Bornstein 1994: 176–7).

By the end of 1399, the Bianchi movement had come to an end. In the north, its momentum was stifled due to Giangaleazzo Visconti's efforts to prevent the spread of plague in his domain. In the Romagna it seems simply to have run out of steam once it reached the coast. In the south, the powerful allure of Rome drew the Bianchi in and then made it hard to go further; the city that was, after all, one of Latin Christendom's primary spiritual centers, was perhaps simply too natural a stopping point. Either way, the movement ended and with it the great Italian peace movements of the Middle Ages. The fifteenth century saw examples that bore a superficial resemblance to them, but were really distinct phenomena. Manfredi da Vercelli's early fifteenth-century movement, for example, was characterized more by apocalyptic enthusiasm than by peacemaking

(Bornstein 1994: 39–40). It remains, then, only to explain why Italy's peace movements came to an end. This requires us to contemplate the end of the polities in which they had emerged and between which they had spread, for with the late medieval period the age of Italy's communes also came to a close.

THE IDEAL CITY: NASCENT STATES AND RELIGIOUS IDEALS IN FIFTEENTH-CENTURY ITALY

It might be said that the communes began to come to an end at the very height of their development. In the very same era that saw popular regimes cementing their power in places like Perugia and Florence, individual rulers, known as *signori*, began to supplant the executive officers and governing councils of the communes. In places like Piacenza, this change came as early as the late thirteenth century. Milan similarly came under Visconti dominion early (Dean 2004). In other places, the commune seems to have lingered on in some form for much longer. In Rome, official dominion was handed to the papacy only in 1398 (Palmer 2019) and in Florence the city continued to claim communal status into the early Medici period (Najemy 2006). Yet, Florence is the most famous example of a city in which the mask of communalism only scarcely concealed a reality of rigid oligarchy, rule by closed political elite who would continue to govern even after their city's political regime made the decisive shift to one-man rule (Jones 2010). By the mid-fifteenth century, most of Italy was dominated by a handful of great powers: Venice, Milan, Florence, Rome, and Naples. The practice of peace continued both to reflect its conceptual linkage with penance and evince an ongoing refinement in terms of its legal and processual development (Jansen 2018; Kumhera 2017). Peacemaking had long been associated with good government in much of Europe (Benham 2010). By the late medieval period, emerging states were keen to crack down on the enduring role of feuding and private violence as a key social institution, and to shift the site of disputes rooted in personal enmity from the streets to the courts (Smail 2001). Italy's nascent territorial states were no different, and they turned the refined institutions of peacemaking they inherited from their communal predecessors to this end. However, in addition to absorbing the communal Italy's institutions of peace, these budding territorial states, with their ever more centralized and refined models of governance, developed a different relationship to the questions of moral order that had undergirded Italy's pious peace movements and political pacification programs. Keeping the peace did not cease to be one of the aims of government, rather it became one in an ever-more capacious effort on the part of paternalistic states to impose moral discipline on both public and private life. We see this in the rise of sumptuary laws and the policing of sexuality, for example.

First and foremost, the story told here of Italy's peace movements has been, in many respects, a story about the laity. However, like the thirteenth-century peace movements and their efforts at miraculous social conversion, this new moral disciplining effort found important supporters among the preachers of the mendicant orders. Throughout the late medieval period, mendicant preachers continued to be important promulgators of social ideals and reform (Paton 1982). The most famous of these was Bernardino of Siena, a Franciscan who advocated a wide-ranging program of moral reform, focused on threats to social cohesion ranging from witchcraft, heresy, and sodomy to factional violence and vendetta (Mormando 1999b). The capaciousness of Bernardino's sense of social sin in many ways reflected the similarly wide-ranging efforts at moral disciplining undertaken by late medieval states. For him, as for them, the ideal of peace and peacemaking was an integral part of this program. Yet in his advocacy of peace and peacemaking, despite his grand public example of ritual peacemaking in Siena in 1427, Bernardino was fundamentally conservative and responsive to the reality of his lay audience's expectations. Though Bernardino's rhetoric hearkened back to a grand vision of peace akin to that of Francis of Assisi and the Alleluia preachers of the thirteenth century, his actual practice reflected standard modes of peacemaking and all the pragmatic compromises inherent to the late medieval laity's understanding of peace (Polecritti 2000). No matter how lofty the theological bases of religious peacemaking might have been, they could not be separated from the more pragmatic and actually achievable goal of good order in earthly communities that had primarily guided lay participation in, and eventual guidance of, medieval Italy's peace movements.

But if Franciscan preachers remained important promulgators of peace ideals, it must be noted that the Franciscans and their political and social reform projects underwent a fundamental transformation in the fifteenth century with the emergence of the Observant movement (Mixson and Roest 2015). One of the strengths of Bernardino of Siena was his ability to simultaneously present himself as an outsider calling for dramatic reform and as one of the people who made up his audience. This was a talent also characterized by the Observant movement (Polecritti 2000: 101–2). In many ways, this movement embraced models of social and political reform that were both more global and more incremental than had been the vision of the Alleluia preachers of the thirteenth century. We see an effort to produce the ideal urban society, one rooted in economic justice and Christian purity. Unlike the Alleluia preachers, who had largely codified existing peacemaking practice, the Observants produced real novelties aimed not at peace but economic justice. The most famous of these, the *Monte di Pietà*, was a moneylending institution aimed at helping the poor while also driving Jewish moneylenders out of the credit market as part of a program of "purification" (Muzzarelli 2015). Despite this capacious vision of the ideal society, reform was actually undertaken in an incremental way. In economic terms, this is exemplified in specific innovations like the *Monte*. But more generally it was rooted in education in a manner similar to the reform vision of the Italian humanists (Delcorno 2015). Particularly in its emphasis on the education of children, this program can be seen to be approaching the creation of an ideal Christian community as a long game, rather than one rooted in miraculous social conversion. In an Italy increasingly dominated by a small number of ever-more centralized states, the Observants were ideal allies. They were great supporters of strong government and not inclined to make trouble for governing authorities (Polecritti 2000: 102).

From beginning to end, the history of Italy's pious peace movements was inextricable from the efforts of urban governments to signal their own legitimacy by means of an effort to achieve a rightly ordered community, the justice of which would be rewarded by peace and prosperity. The later thirteenth century marked a shift from economic justice to an emphasis on peace, resulting in a lay piety and a political culture that inflected Christian ideas about peace with the lived reality of late medieval urban life. This development transformed early peace movements, instigated and guided by the clergy, into a lay program of peace that manifested itself in pious movement as well as political reform, which were, in practice, simply two aspects of a broader effort. Italy's late medieval peace movements were marked by a lay orthodoxy that avoided unusual modes of piety or explicit anticlericalism but which also allowed the laity to lay claim to the right to discern which peace movements, charismatic leaders, and examples of peace politics

FIGURE 6.5: San Bernardino of Siena, preaching in the Campo, Siena. By Sano di Pietro (1406–1481). Photo by Universal History Archive/Getty Images.

were acceptable and the right to put an end to those that were not. With the waning of the communal world and its replacement by centralizing territorial states, this lay program took on a more global aspect, one also reflected in the programs of mendicant reformers. This effort at reform of a broader moral and social order marks a continuity of sorts with earlier medieval peace movements, but it also marks their end. Urban communities that were themselves experimental and transformative had embraced a model of reform that sought peace and concord through social penance and dramatic moments of conversion. The adaptation of institutional refinements produced by peace movements within medieval Italy's urban communities to suit the needs of early modern states marks the beginning of a new era and thus the end of this particular story.

CHAPTER SEVEN

Peace, Security, and Deterrence

JENNY BENHAM

INTRODUCTION

In the modern world, when we think about how to achieve peace and security and how to prevent or deter future conflict, the role of the United Nations as a facilitator and international law as a controller of this process is likely to be central to our thoughts. The Middle Ages did not, of course, have a United Nations, nor anything that purported to be international law (Fisch 2012: 27–32). However, the issue of the practicalities of peace and conflict resolution is not a new one to the modern world. In fact, how medieval people resolved conflict at a time when wars and violence were more pervasive both between and within polities than today and in a period before fully-fledged nation states, international institutions, and law, has acquired an intriguing relevance in an age of globalization, asymmetrical warfare, terrorism, and heightened religious tensions. This is because these trends have resulted in lessening the importance of the nation-state as a dominant factor in war and in securing peace, and in the proliferation of non-state actors involved in both conflict and conflict resolution. Furthermore, conflicts now are frequently not between states but rather expand across states, thereby blurring the lines between war and civil war, and violence has become harder to categorize into that carried out during war or peace or between that which is political or criminal. In short, there are many analogies in the contexts of war and violence between medieval and contemporary times but not necessarily in the context of peace, security, and deterrence.[1] Or rather, that is how medieval peace-making efforts are portrayed and perceived by non-medieval scholars and the general public alike.

This chapter attempts to give an overview of the rules and practices that guided efforts to secure and maintain peace in the medieval period and prevented conflict and violence. It will highlight the difficulties of differentiating between guarantors for peace, deterrents to war and incentives to violence; examine the role of consensus and collective action; and clarify the practicalities behind fostering good relations. In particular, the chapter aims to outline the connections between law, institutions, and diplomatic practice in the Middle Ages, and concludes by returning to the question of international law and the scholarly search for points of similarity and contrast with contemporary trends.

FIGURE 7.1: Emperor Louis the Pious treating for peace, and the sack of a town. Manuscript miniature from Paris, France, 1332–50. London, British Library, MS Royal 16 G VI fol. 212v. Public domain image available from the British Library: https://www.bl.uk/catalogues/illuminatedmanuscripts/ILLUMIN.ASP?Size=mid&IllID=43988.

PEACE, SECURITY, AND THE DISPLACEMENT OF PEOPLE

One of the most consistent threats to peace and security across the whole of the medieval period, or at least the one political entities were most worried about in an international context, was the displacement of people. This could, of course, come in many forms but here, the focus will be on just two aspects: firstly, the expulsion of those deemed to have committed some form of reprehensible act; and, secondly the repeated migrations and movements of peoples, perceived as attacks on or invasions of existing entities.

The expulsion of individuals who had committed reprehensible acts was one of the ways in which medieval rulers dealt with law and order. As an alternative to corporal punishment, such as mutilation or death, expulsion from a political entity—whether we view this as a city, region, or kingdom—was reserved for the most serious offences; those which could not be atoned for with compensation. Across the medieval West, these "unemendable crimes" tended to include arson; counterfeiting (coins or documents); thefts (recurring or above a certain amount); poisoning; killing in certain spaces (e.g., at the assembly); flight from accusations of an "unemendable crime"; and treacherous or disloyal behaviour (e.g., plotting against a king's life, or fleeing the army). It is also evident that two of these offences—flight and treachery—dominated as the cause of expulsion. However, while expulsion was intended to ensure law and order on a domestic level, it could become a threat to peace and security on an "international" level. Primarily this was because, once expelled, such individuals often committed further reprehensible acts and/or engaged in conflict against the entity from whence they had come. This phenomenon, similar to the modern crime-conflict nexus, is described well in the thirteenth-century Norwegian didactic text known as the *King's Mirror*: "But those who had to flee because of their evil conduct and lawbreaking soon begin to show hostility toward the lord whose subjects they formerly were and to rouse as much enmity as they can between him and the one to whom they have come. They take revenge for their exile by carrying murder, rapine and plundering into the kingdom" (Larson 1917: 199). As a consequence of this, it is hardly surprising to find that one of the foremost purposes of concluding treaties between rulers, or narratives describing the conclusion of treaties, was to ensure that those who had been expelled from one political entity did not find shelter in another. There are numerous examples within treaties about participants not harboring the enemies of the other. In fact, this is the most commonly recurring phrase in treaties across the whole of the medieval period (Benham 2013a: 491–2; Ganshof 1967: 37). Some treaties outline the mechanisms for dealing with such individuals. For instance, the Treaty of Falaise of 1174, whereby William the Lion, king of Scots, agreed to do homage to the English king following his defeat and capture at the battle of Alnwick, sets out that any fugitive for a serious crime should be captured by the king of Scots or his men, if possible, and handed over to the English king, his justices, or bailiffs. The English king similarly agreed that his bailiffs would deliver any fugitive found on his land to the men of the Scottish king (*Gesta regis Henrici secundi* 1867, 1: 97; *Chronica Rogeri de Houedene* 1869–70, 2: 80–1). This evidence tallies with that found in domestic laws from several kingdoms, which suggests that officials kept records of those expelled (Stubbs 1921: 172; Holmbäck and Wessén 1933). Similarly, a document of 1194 setting out the terms of the Scottish king's safe conduct to the court of the English king, outlines how the king of Scots had the right to bring with him "any fugitives who wish to clear themselves of felony" (Stones 1965: 21). Other evidence indicates that returning such individuals was sometimes a sensitive issue in diplomacy, which consequently might involve a third party, usually the Church, as a mediator (Whitelock 2004: 847).

Preventing those expelled from one political entity entering another is also an aspect of displacement of people more broadly. We know, for instance, that some of the Viking leaders who raided the western kingdoms in the ninth to the eleventh centuries had suffered this particular fate, even though the wider Scandinavian, Slav, and Muslim expansions cannot be explained through this factor alone. Our primary sources from this period are replete with references to the chaos caused by this expansion, in the form of raiding of, but also settlements in, existing political entities, though we should be wary of wholly believing these ecclesiastical authors, who often described events as apocalyptic by applying Christian moral and providential frameworks to their narratives. Rulers employed a variety of methods for dealing with this problem, including paying tribute to make raiders go away, issuing laws to regulate trade with these people or to fortify towns and bridges, and using elaborate ceremonies of sponsorship at baptism to convert any non-Christians and thereby deter them from attacking other Christians (examples are found in *Alfred the Great* 1983: 101; Hill 2013: 125–6, 128–9, 152–3; Abels 1991 and 2008; Nelson 1987). One of the most common ways to deal with the threat of raids or invasions was to use military force. A large number of agreements from the medieval period detail the employment of foreign raiders and their military men, who were provisioned or paid in return for defending the ruler, his people, and territory "against all enemies," including other raiders (Benham 2013a: 491; Bowlus 2008: 194–5). Such treaties for mercenaries became more widely used the further into the medieval period we proceed but they also lost some of their connection to displacement, with the main suppliers of mercenaries in the later period being Switzerland and the Italian city states (France 2008). From the twelfth century onwards, the mercenaries themselves became seen as a problem to peace and security, as they often resorted to plunder when not employed, and hence became the targets for legislation as well as condemnation from the Church (Appelt 1985–90, 3: 47; c. 27 of the Third Lateran Council of 1179, in *Decrees of the Ecumenical Councils* 1990,

1: 224–5, is an example). Exactly how efficient a deterrence or provider of security the use of mercenaries was is not entirely clear, but, if nothing else, their continued use by rulers indicates that they must have filled some measure of these functions.

Using military force to deal with raids could also be communal endeavours and bear the hallmarks of counter piracy. For instance, in the twelfth century the Danish historian, Saxo Grammaticus, describes a counter-piracy enterprise that began because of the inability of kings to deal with the problem of Slav raids:

> On account of the incessant raids from the buccaneers at that period, a pirating venture was started ... under the leadership of Vedeman, which observed the following customs and procedures: if any vessels looked more suitable for privateering, these men had the power to commandeer them without the owner's consent, provided they later gave him as rent an eighth of any booty they won ... Frequently they clashed with adversaries, yet in every encounter they gained an easy and virtually bloodless victory. Spoils were shared equally, in such a way that the helmsman accepted the same amount as an ordinary rower.
>
> —Fisher and Friis-Jensen 2015, 2: 1024–5

The idea of the enterprise was clearly that keeping raiders occupied in their own lands prevented raids on neighboring lands, and had the added benefit of acquiring wealth at the same time. According to Saxo, this enterprise began in the city of Roskilde but soon spread to every area of mainland Denmark and the endeavors continued until peace had been restored "to our country" (Fisher and Friis-Jensen 2015, 2: 1026–7). One thing that is interesting about this particular enterprise is that, unlike the use of mercenaries, it was seemingly sanctioned by the Church, and Saxo recounts how those involved received absolution and remission of sins before undertaking any journeys. One could speculate that this was because these Slav raiders were non-Christians and hence the endeavor took on a similar characteristic to a crusade. Religious sentiments aside, it is clear that from the thirteenth century onwards, these communal efforts to rid prominent trade routes of pirates and other raiders became enshrined in the statutes of the Hanseatic League, with each town promising to contribute towards the destruction of such threats to peace and security on the seas (Thatcher and McNeal 1905: 320–4).

From the evidence presented here, it is clear that displacement of people was as thorny an issue in the medieval period as it is today. It is, nevertheless, a useful issue for thinking about how to achieve peace, security, and deterrence, primarily because the main conflict drivers of the medieval period—land, jurisdiction, and resources—converge and are reflected in displacement. It was also an issue that operated at several levels—local, regional, and international—and, as such, required several, overlapping, solutions that could be executed and implemented at each of the different levels. Some of these measures were intended to deter, while others dealt with the effects of the measures taken or were intended to restore peace and order. Others, yet again, became part of the problem for which they had been devised.

ARBITRATION

One of the most common ways to resolve conflict, secure peace, and deter future violence was, and continues to be, arbitration. Its frequent and sustained use as a method to settle disputes at lower levels of society during the entire course of the medieval period and across most geographical areas has often been acknowledged by scholars (Andersen 2013:

123–36, 165–80; White 1978). In an international context, however, historians have seen arbitration primarily as a late-medieval phenomenon, pointing towards its use by, amongst others, the towns of the Hanseatic League to settle any differences that arose between them with regard to trade (Born 2015; Wubs-Mrozewicz 2017). Nonetheless, international arbitration was considerably more common throughout the whole of the medieval period than historians have often thought and it usually operated in two main ways; either by bringing two disputing parties together to effect an agreement or by allowing certain issues within an agreement to be settled by a panel of members from the contracting parties. The latter was by far the most common, chiefly because it was a useful tool by which warring parties could effect an agreement, while at the same time, bypassing particularly thorny issues by referring them to a panel. One of the best examples of this can be seen with the Treaty of Ivry, concluded between the English king, Henry II, and the French king, Louis VII, in 1177. This treaty, which was preceded by a dispute over the marriage between Henry's son Richard and Louis's daughter Alice and the lands and rights that would come with it, completely ignored the issue of the dispute—the proposed marriage—and asserted that the disputed rights and claims were to be settled through the arbitration of six men from either side (Benham 2013b: 221–2). Arbitration panels within agreements were thus commonly devised to deal with smaller disputes that might arise between two populations who had frequent and continuous interaction. Often, their main function was to determine levels of compensation for damages, or to ensure that such damages were paid or that other infringements of the terms were dealt with (Appelt 1985–90, 1: 207–8; Duby 1990: 217).

Arbitration intended to bring two disputing parties together to effect an agreement could follow two distinct routes: either the disputing parties themselves could appoint a set number of men on each side who would investigate, negotiate, and mediate the terms of the treaty, or a third party could be enlisted to make a decision in the dispute. An example of the first route can be found with the Treaty of Verdun, agreed in August 843, which divided the Frankish Empire into three kingdoms among the surviving sons of the Emperor Louis the Pious, the son and successor of Charlemagne. The issues at stake centered not only on the division of the realm but also on the reparation of damages suffered during the war. Contemporaries report that a commission of the leading men from each side was chosen to investigate the parts that each brother should have in the division with the intention to make it as fair as possible (*Nithard's Histories* 1972: book 4, chs. 1–6; Nelson 1991: 54; Reuter 1992: 21). That the division was hard fought is evidenced by the length of time it took for it to be negotiated: a full year.

Enlisting a third party to settle a dispute could be an equally long process. In the autumn of 990, Pope John XV sent the papal legate Leo to arbitrate in the dispute between the English king, Æthelred II, and the Norman duke, Richard I. The agreement was eventually finalized almost six months later on 1 March 991 (Whitelock 2004: 894–5). In comparison to most instances of papal arbitration, however, that of 990–91 was relatively short and possibly more successful. Theoretically, the papal court was the arbiter supreme in the Middle Ages: through the universality of Church law, the rulings of the court applied to all Christians, and furthermore, it had compulsory jurisdiction (Ullmann 1976: 362). Practically, however, the distance from Rome to the various corners of Europe often meant that negotiations were long and drawn out, and the death and defeat of one party could halt any arbitration. Furthermore, in an international context, the pope himself was frequently involved in European diplomacy and this could hinder, delay, or bias any final judgment. Hence, referring a dispute to the papacy for arbitration seems to have been a common delaying tactic—a way to continue the dispute by other means—even though the papacy's ability to muster condemnation and shame, as well as the more practical measures of excommunication and interdict to compel parties to adhere to decisions, must have been of some deterrence to continuing disputes (Benham 2011: 186).

The papacy was not the only option for involving a third party to resolve a dispute. One of the best-documented third-party arbitrations from the medieval period is that between the kings of Castile and Navarre of 1177. To submit their long-standing territorial dispute to arbitration, the two kings concluded a seven-year agreement to cease all hostilities and preserve the status quo; it seems obvious from this that the parties knew that arbitration could be a long process. The kings then sent a large embassy to their preferred third party, Henry II of England, who eventually found in favor of the king of Castile but suggested restitution on both sides (*Gesta regis Henrici secundi* 1867, 1: 143–54; Warner 1891: 218). The arbitration of 1177 is interesting for many reasons and gives historians significant insight into the processes for resolving conflict. For instance, it is clear that both the written word and oral testimony were of importance when hearing the case. Furthermore, the two sides turned up at Henry's court prepared with champions, in case he should decide to settle the dispute by a wager of battle. The documents presented in the case also indicate that should Henry refuse to take on the arbitration, the embassy was next to approach the king of France. What is evident from all of this is that the process of arbitration, as presented through the chronicle narratives and the various documents contained within them, shows that there were plenty of parallels with the practices of dispute resolution at lower levels of society (White 1978; White 1995; Geary 1986).

Arbitration in the medieval period was one of the most successful and powerful ways to restore peace and security, and to deter future conflict and further violence. The prime reason for this is that arbitration often involved different levels of society and drew upon the social, cultural, and economic bonds linking the various levels, thereby both engaging and incentivizing everyone in a community in keeping the peace. Arbitration hence shows the importance and function of consensus in resolving conflict and restoring peace. A ruler could not restore peace without involving his supporters, both lay and ecclesiastical, in negotiating and executing the terms of any agreement, in the same way that he could not, by himself, engage in a conflict.

GUARANTORS AND DETERRENTS OF PEACE AND SECURITY

Restoring and securing peace was a complex process which reflected the complexity of medieval society itself. Enforcing that process, ensuring that the peace was maintained and deterring future aggression, was tricky and required not only solutions on multiple levels but also collective agreement, confirmation, and the guaranteeing of peace.

Agreements in the medieval period were usually guaranteed by oaths, sworn on the Gospels or relics, that were an appeal to God and the shared Christian concept that oath-breakers would suffer divine retribution because perjury was a mortal sin. Common phrases in treaties such as "so help us God and these Holy Gospels and the relics of the Saints" bear witness to the clear connection to Christianity (*Chronica Rogeri de Houedene* 1869–70, 3: 64). Oaths were thus intended to deter through fear of what might happen to one's soul in the afterlife (Benham 2011: 150). However, oaths were also an appeal to

FIGURE 7.2: King John I of England does homage to King Philip Augustus of France. Detail of a manuscript miniature from Paris, France, 1332–50. London, British Library, MS Royal 16 G VI fol. 362v. Public domain image available from the British Library: https://www.bl.uk/catalogues/illuminatedmanuscripts/ILLUMINBig.ASP?size=big&IllID=43708

honour; a cultural concept which in the Middle Ages was closely linked to masculinity and shame, and which, like the religious aspect of oaths, carried obligations and consequences that were protected in law. Guaranteeing treaties with oaths thus went beyond deterrence through fear of the afterlife by hitting right at the heart of an individual's present life in which dishonor and shame could result in loss of status or exclusion from, or isolation within, the community. The appeal to both honor and religion—to linking one's present and future life to past acts—further explains the oath as a cross-cultural phenomenon, and there are many examples from this period of agreements between Christians and non-Christians which were guaranteed by different kinds of oaths. Most frequently, chroniclers describe how non-Christians clashed their weapons together or swore on other objects, such as rings (Whitelock 2004: 194; *Heinrici Chronicon Lyvonie* 1874: 281), and it is evident that rulers had a pragmatic approach in allowing each party to swear oaths according to their own laws and customs (Moravsik and Jenkins 1962: 56).

To achieve maximum effect and, like arbitration, to engage different sections of society in keeping the peace, treaties frequently involved the swearing of oaths not only by the contracting parties, usually rulers, but also their supporters or kinsmen. This created a complicated web of obligations, creating deterrence that was not only individual but also communal. The importance of the oath to agreements and its function as a deterrence further explains why many treaties are preserved as oaths (e.g., the oaths of Strasbourg (842) and Treaty of Melfi (1059) (*Nithard's Histories* 1972: book 3, ch. 5; Norwich 1967:128–9), or contain oaths either within the treaty itself (e.g., the Treaty of Bonn (921) (*Capitularia regum Francorum* 1835: 567–8)) or as an additional but separate record to it (e.g., Treaty of Porto Venere (1149) (Imperiale di Santangelo 1936: 244–7)).

Creating both individual and communal obligations was key to other ways of enforcing agreements and preventing future conflicts. Hostages and sureties relied on these obligations even though they worked in slightly different ways. Adam Kosto has outlined how hostages were a third-party guarantor of an agreement, and were subject to loss of physical liberty (2012: 9). In the earlier Middle Ages, we primarily meet hostages in dealings with non-Christians or in agreements that detailed conquest or submission of

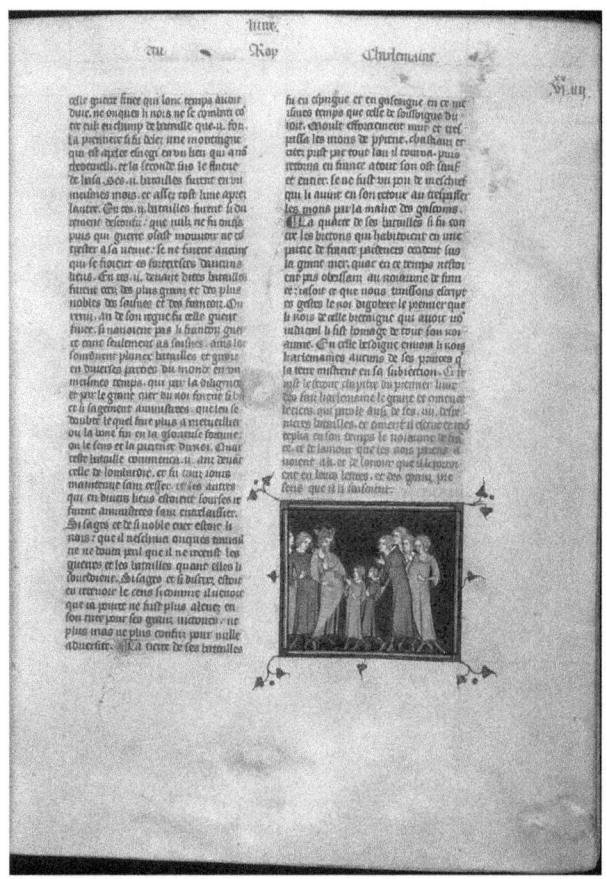

FIGURE 7.3: Charlemagne receives hostages of Tassilo of Bavaria. Manuscript miniature from Paris, France, 1332–50. London, British Library, MS Royal 16 G VI fol. 126r. Public domain image available from the British Library: http://www.bl.uk/catalogues/illuminatedmanuscripts/ILLUMINBig.ASP?size=big&IllID=43782.

people living on the fringes of western Europe. Such agreements almost invariably treated the defeated as an inferior party who had to give hostages to ensure their future compliant behavior. The logic behind this was simple: hostages were intended to deter conflict through the threat of mistreatment or death (Kosto 2012: 34). In an international context, it was aimed at curtailing a ruler's ability to gather support for waging warfare, and as a consequence, hostages tended to be heirs of rulers and/or heirs of their closest supporters (Benham 2011: 158–63; Kosto 2002:134–5). However, there are examples of treaties (e.g., Milan (1158)), where the hostages were drawn from a wider cross-section of society (Mierow 1994: 221). The implications of giving hostages were perhaps not quite as one-sided as it appears, because maltreatment of hostages, conversely, meant that the giver had no incentive to keep any peace concluded. Hence, as Kosto has concluded, the mistreatment or execution of hostages, even in cases of violations, were rarer than is often thought (Kosto 2012: 36–41).

In the later medieval period, the practice of giving hostages to guarantee peace and security died out except where they were given to secure the release of rulers, and other important men, captured in war. Often referred to as ransom treaties, such agreements enabled a captured king to be released in return for a ransom, and as a security for the payment of this ransom, hostages might be given. One of the best-documented examples comes from the fourteenth century, when King Jean II of France was captured by the Black Prince at the Battle of Poitiers in 1356, arrived as a captive in London in May 1357, and obtained his release some three years later under the terms set out in the Treaty of Bretigny (1360). The king was released against a huge ransom of 3,000,000 écus, some of which was to be paid immediately, whilst forty hostages were to be given for the eventual payment of the full amount (Cosneau 1889: 47–52). Although the logic behind the giving of hostages in ransom agreements was the same as in other instances of hostage-giving, it is evident that the ransoming of high-status individuals as a significant economic driver of warfare in this period gives this type of hostage a slightly different cultural, political, and social context than those of the earlier period. For instance, Kosto has observed that agreements often evolved; the hostages could be returned, replaced or exchanged, the debt remitted, and sometimes the captive himself could even turn into a hostage (Kosto 2012: 163–98). Hostages, specifically those in ransom treaties, in many ways show the relationship between conflict and conflict resolution; between enforcing peace and curtailing violence; and between guaranteeing peace as deterrence and incentivising warfare.

The complexity involved in using hostages to secure peace and act as a deterrent to conflict may explain why rulers developed a variation of this practice, namely the use of sureties and conditional hostages. These were pledges of property (real sureties) or people (personal sureties), which, like hostages, were not direct subjects of the agreement but, unlike hostages, only had to be handed over if the terms of an agreement were breached (Benham 2011: 165–6). These practices reflected the use of sureties in dispute settlement at the lower levels of society, but only emerge clearly as means by which to secure peace in an international context in the twelfth century. For instance, the Anglo-Flemish alliance of 1101 records that the count of Flanders, when requested, would supply 1,000 knights to the king of England, for use against his enemies, in return for the annual sum of £500. The sureties given as guarantors of the treaty show that, in case of violation, they could be expected to work in three different ways: by persuading the violator to make amends; by each surety paying his share of a specified fine; and, if the first two failed, by each surety presenting himself for imprisonment at a specified location (Van Houts 1999:170–3). The second of these became common in agreements for debts of the later

FIGURE 7.4: In the margin to the left of this historiated initial 'D', a seated King John II "le Bon" (the Good) of France, held hostage in London, hands his sword to King Edward III of England, mounted on a lion below. Manuscript illumination made within 20 years after the battle of Poitiers (1356). London, British Library, MS Egerton 3277, fol. 68v. Public domain image available from the British Library: https://www.bl.uk/catalogues/illuminatedmanuscripts/ILLUMIN.ASP?Size=mid&IllID=55847

medieval period (Kosto 2012: 130–1), while the last dominated how such sureties were used in treaties between rulers throughout the twelfth century. By the last decade of that century, property usually accompanied the person who promised to hand himself into captivity if the treaty was breached (Delaborde 1916: 464–6; Benham 2011: 166–8). This variation seems to have been specifically developed between adversaries, such as the kings of England and France, who were frequently in conflict with each other and where both sides—kings as well as supporters—could draw upon different familial, economic, legal, and social bonds (Kosto 2012: 156; Power 2001). It is no accident that those named as sureties in such treaties tended to be those whose support was fiercely contested and/or whose property was located in a disputed area. Here, it is clear that engaging and incentivizing nobles was seen as a crucial part of the process by which peace and order was restored, presumably because of the capacity of some of these men to wage war but also because it might have been less intrusive than punishing any of their misdemeanors. However, this particular variation, developed in the late twelfth century, does not seem to have survived the loss of most of the English king's continental lands in 1204. Subsequent Anglo-French treaties, if they have sureties, do not contain a combination of real and personal sureties. For instance, the Treaty of Paris (1259) has no named sureties and, in case of breaches, these promised only to "help the king of France and his heirs against us [the king of England] and our heirs until this thing is sufficiently amended in the opinion of the court of the king of France" (Rothwell 1996: 378–9). This shows that some systems and practices were created or adapted for very specific circumstances and lapsed when those no longer applied.

It thus seems evident that guaranteeing and enforcing peace, as well as achieving deterrence, required striking a balance between multiple—sometimes conflicting, sometimes cooperating—concepts and practices. Political and cultural contexts could, furthermore, hinder or facilitate processes of peace and security and, at different times, render a particular practice as a deterrent to, or a driver of, conflict, or render it obsolete.

DIPLOMACY AND FOSTERING PEACEFUL RELATIONS

Consensus—the need to agree, confirm, guarantee, and enforce peace collectively—was one of the cornerstones to resolving conflict in the medieval period. As medieval political entities were usually centered on a ruler (or a ruling council) and a small number of advisers or supporters, face-to-face meetings were intended to foster cordial relations by plugging into the wider cultural and social context of the period in which men showed their honor and status through feats of war and displays of camaraderie and largesse. The surest way to secure and maintain peace and to prevent future conflict was for rulers to foster personal relations with each other and their followers at these gatherings (Benham 2011: 36).

One of the best descriptions of this can be found in the *Five Books of Histories* by the eleventh-century Burgundian monk, Ralph (*Rodulfus*) Glaber, in which he describes the peace conference of 1023 between the German Emperor Henry II (r. 1002–1024) and the king of the Franks, Robert II "the Pious" (r. 996–1031). Glaber records how the two kings "came together for a meeting on the river Meuse, which forms the frontier between their kingdoms" (*Rodulfus Glaber Opera* 1989: 108–9). Sites on river borders seem to have been common meeting places, with favored locations including bridges, islands, trees, and even boats, anchored in the middle (Benham 2011: 21–37; Dalton 2005: 14–15; Voss 1987: 38–87; Kolb 1988: 58–71; Ganshof 1971: 127). Rulers could also opt for neutral locations, for example churches—a general promoter of peace—or in spaces that had not been involved in the conflict. The best such example is probably the Peace of Venice of 1177, which brought an end to nearly two decades of strife between the papacy and its allies and the Holy Roman Empire, and which was accompanied by the conclusion of several separate treaties between the various parties. Venice became the chosen location for this peace conference—on a scale perhaps comparable to more modern events such as Vienna in 1815 or Versailles in 1919—after the parties had rejected the initial suggestion of the small north Italian city of Bologna, deeming it too involved in the conflict between the papacy, the various city states of the region, and the Emperor, Frederick Barbarossa (Benham 2018). All these locations reflect the fact that the participants claimed equal status in their negotiations with each other, but that they also feared entering another ruler's territory. Diplomacy was not always so straightforward, however, and there are numerous examples of smaller powers negotiating with more powerful neighbors on their own territory, often under military threat, or in the territory of their larger neighbors, as a voluntary admission of their inferior status. The most frequently recorded evidence of this includes Anglo-Saxon and later English rulers' diplomacy with their British neighbors, and on the Continent, the Frankish and later "German" kings' relations with the people living on their furthest frontiers (e.g., the Bretons, the Danes, and the Slavs (Benham 2011: 44–62; Reuter 1992: 24, 27–8, 64)).

That face-to-face meetings between rulers were seen as an important aspect in securing peace is clear from the fact that princes often fiercely defended their right to attend or hold them. There are plenty of references to such practices being customary (Stevenson 1875: 135–6; John of Worcester 1998: 64–5; Edwards 1935: 2) and that this was not mere words is evident from the fact that, occasionally, meetings are also outlined in legal texts (Jenkins 1986: 5; Henderson 1905: 203). From the evidence, it is further clear that largesse—exchanging of gifts and communal feasting—always accompanied such meetings, together with a host of other different rituals, gestures, and ceremonies. The account of Ralph Glaber again serves as an example:

> The emperor rose at dawn, and, taking with him only a small escort, crossed the river to the king of the French; they embraced warmly and kissed, heard Mass celebrated by the bishops, and decided to take breakfast together. When the meal was over King Robert offered to Henry vast presents of gold and silver and precious stones, together with one hundred splendidly caparisoned horses each bearing a cuirass and a helmet; he proclaimed that if the emperor refused any of these, then by so much would their friendship be diminished. Henry understood how enormously generous his friend was, but he chose from all this only a gospel-book set with gold and precious stones, and a similar reliquary containing the tooth of St Vincent, deacon and martyr; his wife would take only a pair of golden vessels. The rest he refused graciously and took his leave. The following day, in his turn, King Robert with his bishops crossed the river and went to the camp of the emperor, who received him with great honour, and, when a meal had been taken, offered him one hundred pounds of pure gold, but the king would only take a pair of gold vessels. When they had confirmed their friendship they returned to their own lands.
> —*Rodulfus Glaber Opera* 1989: 108–9

Many of these acts were clearly aimed at honoring or engaging each other in a game of one-upmanship, but also at manifesting friendship and reconciliation. Other acts and ceremonies symbolized or confirmed the agreement concluded, or parts of it, or conferred specific legal status or rights. For instance, following his capture at the Battle of Alnwick in 1174, the king of Scots, William I, was forced to make a humiliating treaty in which his inferior status was confirmed when he became "the liege man of the [English] king against all men, for Scotland, and for all his other lands" and he "swore fealty to him [the English king] as his liege lord in like manner as his other men are accustomed to do to him" at a ceremony in Valognes in the English king's lands in Normandy (Stones 1965: 3). Most commonly across the period, medieval writers report on the oath-swearing ceremony, noting particularly that it was done by free will and with the hand of the oath-taker touching the object on which the oath was sworn (Benham 2011: 145–53). Gestures and ceremonies, and their execution at large gatherings, hence had an importance beyond mere symbolism and the fostering of cordial relations as it was the witnessing of these acts that made an agreement and all its constituent parts legally binding (Althoff 2002: 71–4).

FIGURE 7.5: Drawing up of a treaty between France and England. Miniature in a manuscript of Jean Froissart's *Chronique*, vol. IV, part 2, made in the Southern Netherlands (Bruges), *c.* 1470–72. London, British Library, Harley 4380, fol. 10v. Public domain image available from the British Library: http://www.bl.uk/catalogues/illuminatedmanuscripts/ILLUMIN.ASP?Size=mid&IllID=22201

PEACE, DETERRENCE, AND LAW IN THE MIDDLE AGES AND BEYOND

It is important to recognize that our picture of peace, security, and deterrence in the Middle Ages is incomplete. Lots of questions about the ways and means by which peace was secured and maintained remain unanswered; partly because of the nature of our sources but partly because a scholarly tradition in which a cross-disciplinary approach to the study of medieval international relations, such as that which has broadened the discussion of diplomatic issues for later historical periods, is only slowly emerging (Watkins 2008: 1). This gap in our knowledge has become more evident over the last decade or so with renewed interest among the scholarly community working on more recent history and events in how conflicts were resolved in a period before fully-fledged nation-states. For instance, Jakub Grygiel has recently argued that in an age of globalization, asymmetric problems (e.g., cyber security), and the proliferation of non-state actors in conflicts, pre-modern history could "greatly improve our understanding of current and future strategic challenges" (2013: 1). His argument is underpinned by the assertion that, in pre-modern societies, diplomacy and deterrence were weak and lacked effectiveness, and violent confrontations were not constrained by international law and institutional arrangements as they are in the modern period (Grygiel 2013: 14–17). Grygiel was, of course, making generalizations and not referring specifically to medieval conditions, yet it is important to tackle his assertions because they capture long-standing misconceptions among scholars and the general public alike about how medieval people resolved conflict, maintained peace and security, and prevented war and violence. Here, for brevity and relevance, I will focus on two specific issues: effectiveness (or enforcement) and deterrence.

Effectiveness of peace and conflict resolution in the medieval period is frequently interlinked with the notion of international law, institutions, and organizations, or rather the lack of them. However, for the medieval period, the study of international law has rarely moved beyond the contribution of canon law and even the best treatments of the topic tend to leave a gap from the end of the western Roman Empire to the revival of Roman and canon law in the twelfth and thirteenth centuries—nearly 800 years (Lesaffer 2012: 72–6). Furthermore, two of the most important sources of international law—treaties and customs (or legal practice)—have never received a full scholarly treatment for the period *c.* 500–*c.* 1500. Hence, any assertion that the medieval period saw no international law is currently not based on an examination of the available evidence (Benham 2013a). Nevertheless, briefly outlining what international law is and how it applies to the Middle Ages can be instructive and go some way towards answering the question about enforcement and effectiveness.

In his textbook on international law, Martin Dixon outlines that "the most cogent argument for the existence of international law as a *system of law* is that members of the international community recognize that there exists a body of rules binding upon them as law" (2013: 4). Evidence of this belief can be cited in three ways. First, that it is practiced on a daily basis "in foreign offices, national courts and other governmental institutions, as well as in international organisations" (Dixon 2013: 4). As discussed above, in the medieval period we see this best through diplomacy, arbitration, and displacement of people, where specific practices engaged and made use of domestic institutions and actors. For instance, courts and royal officials for chasing those expelled for crimes; envoys, arbitrators, and mediators to negotiate disputes or ensure payment of restitution awarded; or using the Church or papacy to muster international condemnation and shame to effect a judgment or agreement. Secondly, that there is a reliance upon justification of action. We meet this clearly through the development of the "just war" doctrine, which in the medieval period was based primarily on the thoughts of St Augustine but also had Roman, non-Christian, precedents as seen through the works of, amongst others, Cicero (Russell 1975). Furthermore, insistence upon rights and customs, such as those relating to face-to-face meetings, could also be used to justify actions during a dispute. Thirdly, that the majority of international legal rules are consistently obeyed—a notion that goes right to the heart of the question about effectiveness or enforcement. Clearly, this is difficult to assess. Medieval writers, like their modern counterparts, were often more interested in law-breaking because obedience was not newsworthy. In the ecclesiastical thought-world inhabited by chroniclers, writing providential history was the order of the day and the breaking of oaths is frequently commented upon because it was followed by divine retribution. Hence, to take one famous example, the defeat of Harold Godwineson at the Battle of Hastings was depicted by Norman sources as divine retribution for having broken his promise to Duke William with regard to the English succession (Davis and Chibnall 1998: 20–1, 68–71, 76–7, 120–1; Van Houts 1995: 158–61). The problem with our evidence aside, we need to consider carefully how useful the notion of effectiveness or enforcement is with regards to international law because, even in the modern period, it is not the only facilitator or controller of state conduct, nor is it designed to be. The practice of international law, whether in the medieval or modern period, is fundamentally linked to diplomacy, politics, and the conduct of foreign relations. As remarked by Dixon:

> International law does not operate in a sterile environment and international legal rules may be just one of the factors which a state or government will consider before deciding whether to embark on a particular course of action. In fact, in many cases, legal considerations will prevail, but it is perfectly possible that a state may decide to forfeit legality in favour of self-interest, expediency or "humanity".
>
> —2013: 3–4

Thus, the effectiveness of any peace is in many ways dependent on the immediate circumstances in which it was concluded; how its success was viewed at the time; and how it has come to be perceived in light of subsequent events. This is a task that is highly subjective and, as a consequence, is not always a good yardstick by which to measure success or effectiveness (Benham 2011: 201–12). Furthermore, if we are looking for effectiveness in terms of enforcement, this is tricky to find evidence for even with regards to domestic law and justice: there are lots of laws but little evidence that the majority of those clauses were ever put into practice. Nevertheless, with regard to peace and security, one could point to certain enforcement procedures, such as loss of legal rights and privileges. One of the best examples of this is the termination of trade relations between Charlemagne, king of the Franks, and Offa, king of the Mercians, in the 790s. When their negotiations about a marriage alliance broke off, the author of the *Gesta* of St Wandrille records how Charlemagne had imposed an embargo on traders from Britain (Lohier and Laporte 1936: 86). The existence of the trade embargo is confirmed in the letters of Alcuin, who further notes that Offa imposed his own embargo on traders from Francia and now "on both sides the passage of ships has been forbidden to merchants and is now ceasing" (Whitelock 2004: 841).

Grygiel claimed that pre-modern agreements primarily came after conflict and frequently simply rubber-stamped the results of war rather than representing a compromise reached at the negotiating table (2013: 15). However, the vast majority of agreements that have survived from the medieval period are not concerned with final peace after conflict, but rather with deterrence or prevention of conflict. As discussed above, this could be achieved in a number of ways and is most clearly seen in the myriad purposes of the agreements and the clauses within them. Arguing that medieval deterrence was weak, a "sometime thing," and often unenforceable due to the difficulties of making threats credible in some ways misses the point about medieval efforts to secure and maintain peace and security. As shown in many of the examples above, medieval efforts were often targeted at creating shared cultural values, and fostering personal relationships of togetherness and friendships. Ideas of honor and masculinity were central to this, as were more religious ideas, such as charity, which linked directly to the medieval concept of peace. Deterrents hence focused on breaches of these cultural values—breaking one's oath, forsaking hostages, failing in communal obligations—all of which could result in exclusion from the community in this life or the next. Of course, there were threats that adhere to the more traditional principle of deterrence, that is, that it could "credibly threaten to impose costs" (Grygiel 2013: 15). Military action through the use of mercenaries or counter-piracy are such examples. To some extent, we can also find them in agreements that followed submissions or defeats where payments of tribute, for instance, threatened the economic basis of the defeated community or ruler (Pryce 2005: 387–8). But even then, the threats were often mitigated by efforts to include not exclude, by resorting to fostering good relations and thereby those shared cultural values through gestures, ceremonies, and communal obligations (Benham 2011: 90–106, 156–71). Deterrence was, in other words, multi-faceted, flexible, and tailored to particular circumstances—the kind of strategic approach scholars often argue is needed to meet contemporary demands because "one-size fits all" solutions are no longer viable (Morgan 2012: 103).

None of this is to say that deterrence, or securing and maintaining peace, in the medieval period was particularly easy or effective. As this study highlights, they were, nonetheless, goals that could be pursued in many different ways, and rulers frequently did so using well-known institutions (e.g., sureties, arbitration, or expulsion), a plethora of customs and legal practices (e.g., face-to-face meetings, giving of gifts), and a combination of domestic and international legal instruments (e.g., laws, charters, and treaties). Rulers, their supporters, and whole communities not only considered themselves bound by this system, such as it was, but also bore testament to its success, however small, as is evidenced by its frequent and sustained use throughout the medieval period.

CHAPTER EIGHT

Peace as Integration: The Many Sides of Medieval Peace

GEOFFREY KOZIOL

A PROTEAN TERM

For well over 150 years, historians have repeatedly identified "peace" as a central, enduring category of medieval law and political order, only they have vastly disagreed on its defining content—the peace of the king, the peace of the kindred, or the peace of the Church, an Augustinian peace emphasizing obedience of inferiors to superiors or a Germanic peace founded on the autonomy of the free. All such attempts have been failures. The older ones used later medieval legal sources to create early medieval institutions that never existed (these were largely based on a discredited nineteenth-century German historiography: Goebel 1976: 7–61; Kershaw 2011: 68–70). The more recent ones attributed to Augustine an authority he did not possess until the eleventh century, or treated one particular expression of peace as if it represented the whole (Malegam 2013).[1] The result has been to flatten our understanding of medieval ideas of peace, to make them more coherent and uniform than they actually were, thereby enabling generalizations about kingship, law, and the Church that do not stand up against the variegated realities. Broad generalizations about medieval peace have allowed medieval kings to appear much more powerful than they really were, the medieval Church more monolithic and univocal than it ever was. They assigned kindreds an autonomous reality they never possessed and turned violence and feuding into the ordinary state of social relations (for kindreds, see Hummer 2018: 36–37, 41–42, 51, 72); for feuds and violence, see Brown 2011, Halsall 1998 with the response of Hyams 2010). Re-examining peace in the Middle Ages therefore challenges our understanding of the fundamental institutions of medieval society. But we cannot begin with historiographical and sociological models or statements by supposedly authoritative authors. We must begin with the myriad ways the word "peace" was actually deployed.

In reality, "peace" was one of the period's most protean of terms. To take only the Carolingian era, "peace" was often deployed merely as a catch-word in encomia for kings, as in a praise-poem written for Charles the Bald (840–77) calling him "a peacemaker, like Solomon" (Kershaw 2011: 2–3). Ninth-century legislation of Carolingian rulers and Church councils repeatedly admonished kings, bishops, and counts to work for "the peace and salvation of the people," while also demanding that there be "peace and concord" between bishops and counts (*Capitularia Regum Francorum* 1883–97, 2: 168, 170). The same legislation stated that travelers should always go "with peace," that those traveling to judicial courts should "remain in peace," that all residing at or journeying to and from the palace should "live peacefully" (*Capitularia Regum Francorum* 1883–97, 2: 71, 87, 284–85, 372). Royal armies were told to observe "peace," meaning that, while marching to the front, they were to refrain from the exaction of improper requisitions (Magnou-Nortier 1980, 1992). One synod declared that monks and clerics who spread false teachings among the people were to be regarded as "disturbers of ecclesiastical peace" (*Capitularia Regum Francorum* 1883–97, 2: 122). Such a diversity of usages is a warning: in the early Middle Ages "peace" never denoted a fixed, definable institution or idea. On the contrary, the word was useful partly because peace was an undeniable social, political, and ecclesiastical good that *resisted* precise definition. Every faction, polemicist, ideologue, and encomiast could claim that they or their heroes stood for peace, while their enemies worked against it (De Jong 2009; Booker 2009). In this respect, "peace" worked a little like "the common good" of the later Middle Ages (Najemy 2000).

Nevertheless, a substratum of assumptions gave consistency to at least some of these diverse usages. The single most important was that "peace" (*pax*) was established by a "pact" (*pactio*). Indeed, Roman jurisprudents believed (correctly) that etymologically *pax* (the abstraction) was derived from *pactio* (the specific) (*Thesaurus Linguae Latinae* 2006: 10.1.863; *The Theodosian Code* 1952: 45–6 [II.9]; *The Digest* 1985: 2.14.1; Weinstock 1960: 44–5). Broadly speaking, a pact was a voluntary agreement between two legally autonomous parties. More technically (and the technicality was usually adhered to in practice), a pact was a voluntary agreement between two legally autonomous parties that amended a legal form to suit their particular needs while still respecting the law that the legal form implemented. Though pacts had begun as an institution of Roman law, they quickly attracted to themselves a rich Christian vocabulary of love, concord, and spiritual brotherhood. Accordingly, we already find such Christianized pacts in late sixth-century formularies that provided templates for different types of legal transactions. Above all, we find them in treaties between Merovingian kings as early as *c*. 525 (Koziol 2018: 3–5; Murray 1988: 75–7, 80–3; Kosto 1998: 1–16, 32–6).

A second important deployment of early medieval peace language was what one might call "ecclesial peace." This applied the idea of the pact to the Church as a whole. Its first key expression came in the pseudo-Pauline Letter to the Ephesians (4:3), which promoted "the unity of the Spirit in the bond of peace." Such language was severely tested during the great doctrinal disputes of the fourth and fifth centuries, when highly factionalized ecclesiastical councils tended to coerce unity while demonizing opponents as servants of the Devil (MacMullen 2006; Malegam 2013: 81–93). However, the Pauline formulation returned to prominence in episcopal councils of fifth- and sixth-century Gaul, which masked coercion behind the language of agreement. To understand why, one should remember that, during the early Middle Ages, the pope had a position of honor as the successor of Peter at Rome but no real jurisdictional superiority over other bishops (unless it momentarily benefited a group of them to assign it to him). For the most part, the early medieval Church was an episcopal church and bishops regarded each other as equals who made decisions collectively, in councils comprising bishops of one or more ecclesiastical provinces. Accordingly, bishops meeting in councils cast themselves as brothers (*fratres*) united not by blood but by the Holy Spirit and deciding issues of order and precedence not by legal judgments but out of love for each other (Moore 2011: 21–84; Koziol 2018: 4–5).

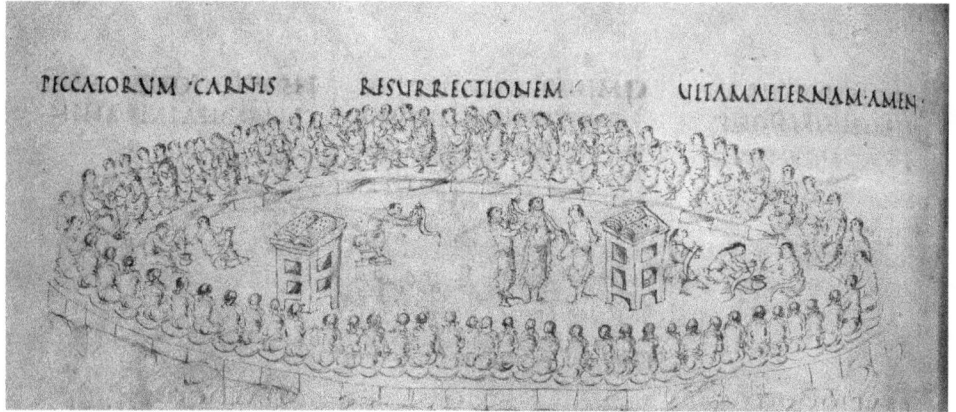

FIGURE 8.1: The Utrecht Psalter of c. 830: "Quicumque vult" (the "Athanasian Creed"). An idealized depiction of an ecclesiastical council. Universiteitsbibliotheek Utrecht, the Netherlands, MS. I 32, fol. 90v. Photo reproduced by permission of the Universiteitsbibliotheek Utrecht.

A final venue of early medieval peace language was the guild, which might be seen as a pact agreed to on oath by a small association of individuals. Guilds first appear in our sources in 786 and only sporadically thereafter. Carolingian references to them are brief and invariably hostile, for the only oaths Carolingian rulers permitted were oaths made in courts of law and oaths of loyalty made by inferiors to superiors (Depreux 2009). In contrast, guilds entailed oaths by individuals to each other, creating an association of horizontal loyalties. The Carolingians classed them as "conspiracies" (*conjurationes*). Nonetheless, they clearly existed on the continent, particularly on the northern coast, as self-help associations against pirates. They, too, deployed a vocabulary of brotherhood, and if they were not led by priests, priests were clearly involved in their formation, suggesting that guilds had already developed an array of quasi-sacramental paraliturgies and salvational aims (Oexle 1985). Certainly these characteristics are all apparent in the best attested early medieval guild. In England, a regulation incorporated into the laws of Athelstan (924–39) established a "peace-guild" (*friðgegyldum*) by the bishops and reeves of the territory of London, acting with the king's explicit authorization (Liebermann 1903–16, 1: 173–83, translated in Whitelock 1955: 387–91). Although the text is quite detailed, the details only generate more puzzles (Keynes 1990: 235–41; Wormald 1999: Ch. 3, Table 3 and 296–8; context in Loyn 1984: 131–71). Still, the basics are clear enough. The peace-guild incorporated both nobles and free commoners (*ge eorlisce ge ceorlisce*). Its purpose was to punish crime—particularly theft of cattle, personal property, and slaves. The guild divided its members into groups of 100, each group of 100 further divided into groups of ten (a tithing). Whenever a theft was committed, an individual was to raise a hue and cry, requiring every member of the tithing to assemble and track the thief. A convicted thief lost all his property. The property remaining after compensating the victim was shared out in three parts: two parts for the king and the victim's wife, the third for "the fellowship" (*ferscipe*). Every member of the guild was to contribute fourpence yearly "for our common needs" (*to ure gemæne þearfe*). Once a month, the men of the hundred were to "gather" (*gegaderian*) and "take note of how our agreement (*ure gecwydræddene*) is being observed." At that time all were to dine together, apparently quite well, leftovers being distributed to the needy. On the death of a member, all his fellow guildsmen (*æle gegilda*) were to give a loaf of bread and other food for his soul and, in addition, sing or have sung fifty psalms.

One should not reify these three discourses of peace into fixed, distinct, exclusive categories. They are presented here only as ideal types that bring some conceptual order to a multiplicity of variations and hybrids. For example, there was the "association" (*societas*), which might be seen as a guild without the oath or as a pact with multiple partners or as a limited ecclesial brotherhood. One of the best-documented types from the earlier Middle Ages was the prayer fellowship, such as that established at the synod of Attigny in 762: on the death of any of its members, forty-four bishops and abbots of the nascent Carolingian empire obligated themselves to personally perform 100 masses and to have the priests of their communities sing 100 psalters and 100 masses (Schmid and Oexle 1974). One should also underscore that when dealing with early medieval peace, one cannot limit oneself solely to instances of the word "peace." Instead, one must include what Reinhard Schneider called *Caritas-Terminologie*, a rich semiotic field vibrating with ideas of peace, unity, and consensus: thus not only "peace" and "pact" but also brotherhood (*fraternitas*), friendship (*amicitia*), treaty (*foedus*), love (*caritas*), and any number of terms for agreement (*concordia, conventum, convenientia*) (Schneider 1964).

A POLITICS OF PACTS

What all these expressions shared was the assumption that peace was fundamentally a voluntary agreement of individuals acting cooperatively to some definite end that either supplemented law and judgment or did away with the need for them. This assumption formed the basis for all the different kinds of peace that developed in the Middle Ages. It is worth asking why. The simple answer is that early medieval kings lacked the material resources to establish military and administrative systems which they fully controlled. Particularly in Italy and the Gauls, when kings arrived they entered a world in which there were already powerful aristocrats and, above all, a very powerful episcopate which was used to acting independently and collectively (Wickham 2005: 155–78; Rapp 2005; Heinzelmann 1976: 211–32). In order to rule, kings had to develop means of establishing consensus with these powerful groups, so that, from the very beginning, politics became highly consensual and required constant negotiation. The fact that armed force on the ground was actually in the hands of local leaders (including bishops) further embedded consensus and negotiation in European political discourses and institutions. Finally, the practice of law privileged self-help. This was not only the case with tracking cattle rustlers and executing them on the spot when captured. It was true of every aspect of law, which depended on public, performative actions to work. Thus, for a party to assert a claim required him to actually publicly execute that claim (e.g., plowing land, cutting down and hauling away timber, collecting a rent) and meet resistance with force. To deny the claim required one to publicly and forcefully resist its execution by the opposing party. As a result, "legal" procedures in courts coexisted with and even promoted consensual resolutions; for if prosecuting a dispute meant violence, there was a certain amount of pressure to negotiate a settlement before violence occurred or worsened (Geary 1995; Koziol 2012: 42–52, 340–52; White 1978).

One of the results of these conditions was that early medieval kings had an equivocal relationship with peace. Quite simply, they were ideologically held to be responsible for it yet, practically speaking, could not enforce it—because "peace" was ultimately an agreement between individuals that had nothing to do with kings. To take the starkest example, Charlemagne (768–814) and Louis the Pious (814–40) demanded that those who committed homicide "make peace" by paying compensation to the victim's family who, in turn, were to "make peace" by accepting the offer; but the two emperors reiterated the demand so frequently and experimented with so many different "sanctions" against those who would not "accept peace" that it seems clear that even these two strongest of Carolingian rulers were having trouble not just enforcing their wills but even conceptualizing a policy. And no wonder: if "peace" were fundamentally an agreement willingly entered into by individuals, then for a king to openly outlaw self-help and impose "peace" on the unwilling was easily seen as a violation of the rights of individuals, indeed, a violation of law itself. As a result, the only consistent sanction a king or a court could impose for a failure to make peace was exile, intended less as a punishment than as a practical means of preventing contact and continued hostilities between opponents (the sources are listed in Le Jan 1995: 64–72).

Thus, every association of a king with "peace" can be shown, on closer inspection, to be ambivalent. When Sedulius Scottus called Charles the Bald "a peacemaker, like Solomon," his intent was less to praise Charles's peacemaking than to compare him with Solomon, who was famous not only for his wise judgments but even more so for building the Temple of Jerusalem; and the context of Sedulius's paean was to celebrate Charles's building of a palace at Compiègne, which Sedulius was likening to Solomon's Temple (Herren 1996). When Louis the Pious's enemies denounced him as a "disturber of peace" (*perturbator pacis*), they meant that he had broken apart the bonds of peace that maintained the unity of the Christian people of the empire; for he had unilaterally abrogated the terms of an 817 agreement that established harmonious relations among his sons in anticipation of the imperial succession, thereby causing strife between his sons and their supporters (De Jong 2009; Booker 2009).

This agreement of 817 is known as the *Ordinatio imperii*—not an "ordinance" in the modern sense but rather an "ordering" (*Ordinatio imperii* 1883, transl. Dutton 1993: 176–79). Its terms return us to the first two ideal types of peace discussed above. One reason the ecclesial peace of fifth- and sixth-century Gallic councils was so important is because the Carolingians turned it into a template for their empire. The most vibrant expression of this ideal came at the very beginning of the enterprise, in a capitulary known as the *Admonitio generalis*. Its most important article (c. 61) reads as follows:

> That there be peace and concord and unanimity among all the Christian people between bishops, abbots, counts, judges, and all everywhere, whether greater or lesser, since nothing is pleasing to God without peace, not even the gift of the holy offering at the altar, as we read in the Gospel, where the Lord himself commands it, for this is the second command in the Law: "You shall love your neighbor as yourself."
> —Mk 12:30; Mt. 22:39; *Admonitio generalis* 2012

This was ecclesial peace on a grand scale, uniting all the faithful of the entire empire in peace undergirded by love between all the faithful of the empire, seen as equals under God regardless of differences in social rank and legal status. There was a reason this particular vision of peace appeared at this particular moment. In 789, Charlemagne was just completing the first stage of the creation of an empire. Some regions had been taken over by conquest, some by alliance, some by cunning political maneuvering. The fact remained that the empire was multi-ethnic, and its creation had required the suppression of formerly autonomous political communites. The empire comprised Lombards, Saxons, Frisians, Bretons, Aquitainians, Bavarians, and Alamannians, each a separate people with its own laws and political traditions. All now found themselves ruled by Franks. To express the unity of the empire in terms of subjection to a single foreign people was to accentuate the empire's divisibility, its fundamental lack of unity, even its grounding in force. Increasingly, therefore, the Carolingians emphasized the fundamental unity of the empire as a Christian entity that brought together all its peoples not through war but in peace (Reimitz 2015: 335–59; McKitterick 2008: 292–380). This was the ideal vision of the *Admonitio generalis* in 789. It was also that of the *Ordinatio imperii* in 817, proclaimed after three days of fasting, prayer, and almsgiving in what was essentially a combined ecclesiastical and imperial council. The purpose was to devise a succession plan that would maintain the unity of an ecclesial empire while also respecting the rights of each of Louis the Pious's sons to some share of royal authority. The solution adopted was to award Louis's eldest son, Lothar, the title of emperor and the two "imperial" capitals of Rome and Aachen, while establishing Lothar's two younger brothers as kings, each ruling his own own kingdom under Lothar's authority. In this way, the empire's unity was doubly guaranteed: first by the recognition of Lothar's singular imperial authority; second, and more important, by the "perpetual peace" that was to exist between the three brothers, who were required to meet once a year "for the sake of discussing in mutual fraternal love what pertains to perpetual peace."

The effort ultimately failed. After Louis's death the empire's territories were divided among his sons, who divided their shares among their sons. By the early tenth century the empire had fragmented into a number of effectively separate kingdoms and principalities, none of them lastingly ruled by Carolingians. The imperial title came to be reserved for whatever king managed to control Rome and get himself crowned "emperor" by the pope. But that title gave him no authority over other kings, at least not in their own eyes. This situation—the equality of kings who ruled separate kingdoms and had to deal with each other as equals—led to a growing reliance on pacts to regulate political affairs. In the ninth century, when Carolingians still ruled, conflicts and alliances between different kings were habitually regulated by pacts often called "brotherhoods" (*fraternitates*), entailing joint agreements and statements of policy, combined assemblies, and reciprocal gift-giving. The pattern continued into the tenth, eleventh, and twelfth centuries—and well beyond—with agreements called "friendships" (*amicitiae*) or "treaties" (*foedera*) (Althoff 2004; Schneider 1964; Voss 1987). For example, in 921, the West Frankish king and the king of Germany, along with their respective entourages, gathered on either side of the Rhine at Bonn, while legates passed back and forth across the river to negotiate protocol and policy. After several days of this, each king climbed into a boat and was rowed out to a third boat, anchored in the middle of the river, where they made "a pact of unanimity and a friendship of association" and swore identical binding oaths to each other "for the sake of peace" (Schmid 1984). The same thing happened a century later, in 1023: the king of France Robert the Pious and the king of Germany Henry II met at Ivois, on the Meuse, the river that formed the boundary between their two kingdoms. Again negotiations emphasized protocols (more troublesome because Henry bore the imperial title). Eventually Henry crossed the river first. The two kings embraced and kissed and shared a meal. Robert offered Henry countless priceless gifts, but Henry accepted only a gospel book, a reliquary, and two vessels of gold. The next day Robert crossed the river and was similarly received by Henry, who offered his counterpart 100 pounds of gold; but Robert accepted only two vessels of gold. They then "each confirmed [by oath] the pact of friendship" and departed

(*Rodulfus Glaber Opera* 1989: 109–11 [III.8]; *Gesta episcoporum Cameracensium* 1846: 480 [III.37]; Voss 1992).

Pacts thus became the basis for all west European politics, not only between kings but also between magnates, and even in some kingdoms (such as France) between kings and magnates (Koziol 2012: 213–313; Magnou-Nortier 1976). How deeply embedded a politics of treaties became can easily be judged by the edited "constitutions" of one of the greatest of German emperors, Frederick I Barbarossa. Of those acts defined by the editors as "peaces" (*pacta*) and "agreements" (*conventiones*) a large number were really treaties between the ruler and northern Italian cities (*Constitutiones* 1893: nos. 150, 172, 174, 205, 211–14, 218, 221, 229, 238, 242–45, 247–48, 251, 259–74, 276, 284–91, 293–95, 303). The reason Frederick was brought to this impasse was because the cities had established pacts with each other, creating associations or leagues that were collectively so powerful that they were ultimately able to defeat his army and force him to negotiate (Raccagni 2010). When Frederick was buying the loyalty of cities allied with him, the award was usually cast as a gracious ruler's beneficent reward for the loyal service of subjects. Even so, the terms of the grant still recognized and favored the cities' effective autonomy. And when he was forced to accede to the demands of the cities associated in the famous Lombard League and its antecedents, these peaces were framed, as such peaces usually were, as bilateral agreements beween de facto equals, as in a peace of 1175, which begins: "This is the agreement (*concordia*) made between Lord Frederick, by the grace of God emperor of the Romans, and the Lombards, Anconans, Venetians, Romagnans, and all their association." As was also normal practice, the first requirement of the agreement was to to set up a procedure to finalize a peace, the procedure itself enshrining the equality of the two sides: each was to elect three persons who, on oath and acting together, were to negotiate terms "congruent to peace and concord between the lord emperor and the cities and all their association" (*Constitutiones* 1893: nos. 242–45, quotations from p. 339). Dante's *De Monarchia* is often held up to illustrate the importance of a single empire to the European ideal of peace, but Dante's vision was both utopian and polemical. The reality of European politics was completely different.

THE PEACE OF GOD AND ASSOCIATIVE PEACES

As for the ecclesial ideal of peace, its history was more complex. In a way, its finest formulation in the *Admonitio generalis* was also its last. Although mixed assemblies of laity and clergy continued to be held regularly throughout Catholic western Europe during the ninth century, there were subtle, but noticeable and important changes. References to "peace between all Christians, greater and lesser," became less common. Instead, emphasis was placed increasingly on peace between those who were classed as "sharers" in the royal "ministry," meaning bishops and counts, who together were to rule a Christian people now seen as subject to them. In such contexts, we begin to find a different deployment of "peace": peace was protection of the defenseless by counts and bishops. In particular, the defenseless required protection from the elite's abuse of its military perquisites. Since those perquisites were frequently exactions imposed on the lands of churches, the demand for this sort of peace was asserted with special force by ecclesiastical leaders, of whom Archbishop Hincmar of Reims (r. 845–82) was only the most adamant. And so, this change was accompanied by another: as prelates like Hincmar became more concerned with the protection of ecclesiastical lands from usurpation and their protection from military exactions, bishops resurrected the custom of meeting in exclusively ecclesiastical assemblies to regulate the affairs of the churches subject to them (Koziol 2018; Patzold 2008; Magnou-Nortier 1980).

During the last decade of the tenth century, all these aspects of peace fused in a program known as the Peace of God (for all that follows, see Koziol 2018; Barthélemy 1999; Goetz 1983). It was first established in councils led by bishops but normally acting in close cooperation with high-ranking members of the lay aristocracy. One of its primary goals was to limit the destruction caused when members of the military aristocracy prosecuted their private wars (*werrae*) to advance their political agendas and legal claims. The means by which limits were accepted came in the form of pacts of peace. A handful of statements suggest that the pacts were actually imagined as being sworn with God; whether or not that was really how they were regarded, the results were horizontal associations of peace-swearers who bound themselves on oath to respect the articles of the Peace. In this regard, the Peace associations were very much like the *conjurationes* Carolingian rulers had so strongly opposed. However, the Peace of God also resurrected some aspects of ecclesial peace. For although elites were the primary articulators of the articles of Peace and normally the primary swearers of its oaths, monastic writers promoted the movement by presenting it as inaugurating a new age of Christian brotherhood that united all the faithful, and so described the Peace councils as vast assemblies that brought together the Christian people of both sexes and every status.

The first declarations of the Peace of God appeared across a broad swathe of Aquitaine. Like southern France generally, Aquitaine lacked any single strong princely authority. Given a vacuum of secular leadership, bishops had come to play an unusually prominent role in constructing stabilizing political alliances, and pacts became a very common means of settling political and legal conflicts. The program was then adopted and adapted by the king of France, Robert the Pious, to aid his takeover of the duchy of Burgundy, as his lieutenant there held a series of assemblies that united the regional aristocracy in agreements to respect the articles of the Peace. During the 1020s and 1030s the Peace arrived in northern France, entering not only royal lands but also the principalities of Normandy and Flanders. It also reached the far southern provinces of Roussillon and Catalonia, where beginning in 1027, the bishop of Vic created a major amendment to the articles of the Peace, known as the Truce of God. By the 1040s, all known declarations of the Peace also entailed the Truce.

During the 1020s, the terms of the Peace of God stabilized into a fairly standardized set of articles, a *forma pacis* sworn by its adherents under the aegis of bishops. All those who were unarmed were protected by the terms of the Peace: that is, clerics and monks, peasants, women, and merchants. The goods of all these classes of persons were also protected, as were the agricultural implements of peasants. The protection meant that both during times of *werrae* and when merely advancing ordinary legal claims, neither these persons nor their goods could be attacked or seized. The Truce of God absolutely prohibited all acts of violence (and often even the carrying of weapons) during certain specified, sanctified, periods of the year: for example, the feast days of the Apostles and any number of other locally prominent saints, but above all throughout the seasons of Advent, Easter, and Pentecost, and every week of the year from sundown on Wednesday to sunrise on Monday—these being the days and liturgical periods that recalled Christ's Incarnation, Passion, and Resurrection and the descent of the Holy Spirit on the Church after Christ's Ascension. Violations of the Peace and Truce were met with excommunication, which was not the empty threat it has sometimes been thought. Excommunication, if enforced, did not so much mean that an individual was ipso facto damned (such

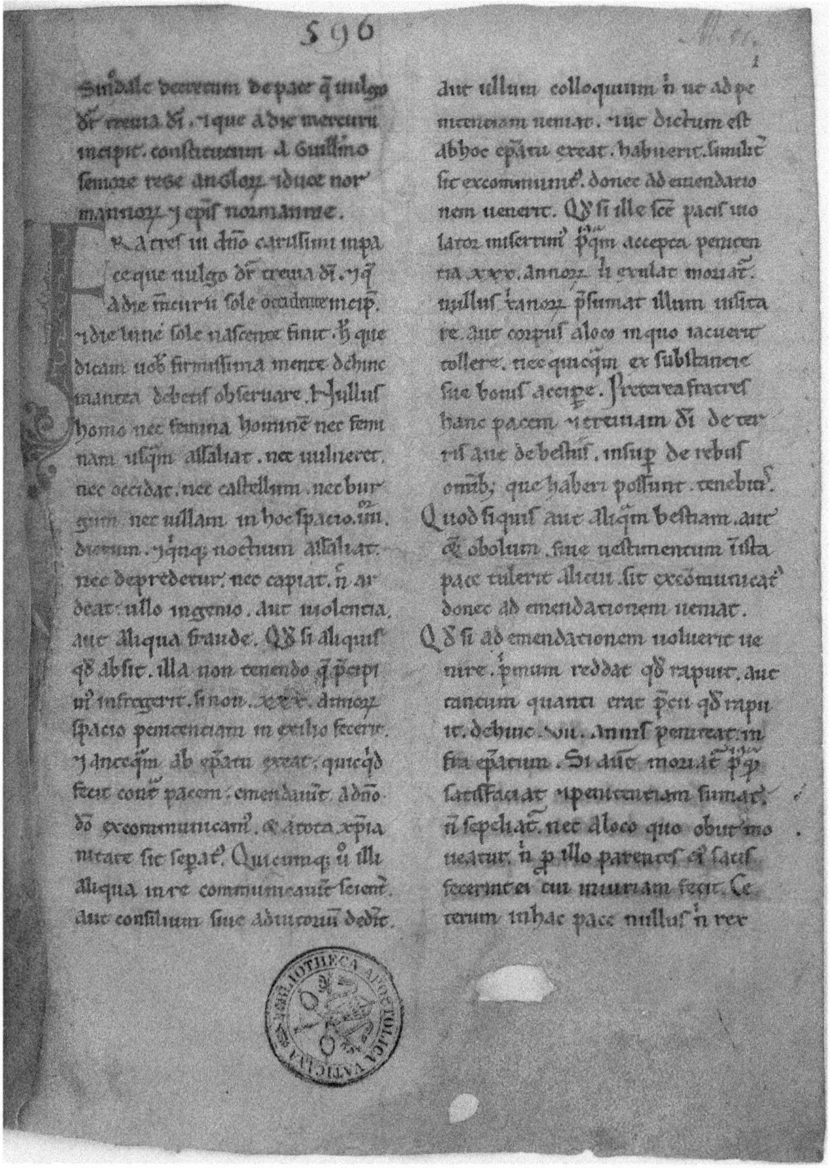

FIGURE 8.2: The Peace and Truce of Lillebonne, Normandy (1080). Rome, Vatican Library, MS Reg. lat. 596, fol. 1r. © 2020 Biblioteca Apostolica Vaticana. Photo reproduced by permission of the Biblioteca Apostolica Vaticana, with all rights reserved.

punishment was reserved for anathema) (Jaser 2013: 43–4; Little 1993: 30–40). Excommunication meant that an individual could not enter a church or receive the sacraments, including the viaticum at the time of death, the social exclusion lasting until the excommunicate had done what was needed to amend the wrong and be reconciled. It also meant that all Christians in good standing were prohibited from socializing with the excommunicate—from eating and drinking or transacting business with them—on pain of falling under the same excommunication. The goal of such social excommunication was to put pressure on individuals to make amends for their misdeeds. That was the real, implicit, goal of the Peace: to create positive pressures for a peaceful resolution of conflicts before they reached the stage of armed self-help or before self-help turned into open *werrae*. For the same reason some Peace councils required individuals who had grievances with each other to bring their case before a bishop or a count, who would try to reconcile the parties peacefully, through compromise, before they resorted to violence (e.g., councils of Poitiers in 1000–1014, Amiens and Corbie in 1033, Arles in 1037–1041, Narbonne in 1054, and so forth). One might thus think of the Peace of God as a Christian peace association that relied on Christian pacts to end disputes and restore ecclesial peace to a Christian society.

The history of the Peace and Truce of God is often written as if it were no more than a relatively brief movement that had little practical effect, but that is not true. The Peace and Truce continued to be proclaimed throughout the eleventh century. In 1095, the Truce of God was declared by Pope Urban II at the proclamation of the First Crusade at Clermont, and later by Pope Innocent II during his tour of France. Given this papal imprimatur, the Truce passed into the decrees of the first three Lateran councils (Koziol 2018: 33; Carraz 2013: 527–8). In the thirteenth century, the great compilation of Saxon custom known as the *Sachsenspiegel* still assumed that the days of the Truce of God were "bound" or "covenanted" days on which all violence was prohibited (*Sachsenspiegel Landrecht* 1955: 135 [II.10]). The first true legislation of the kings of France in the thirteenth century was still wrapped around the Peace of God in its explicit protection of

FIGURE 8.3: Swearing an oath on a reliquary (1336). Oldenburger Bilderhandschrift des Sachsenspiegels, Landesbibliothek Oldenburg, Germany, Cim 410 I, fol 38v. Leihgabe der Niedersächsischen Sparkassenstiftung. Source: https://digital.lb-oldenburg.de/ihd/content/pageview/192505.

peasants and their agricultural implements from the harms of private war (Firnhaber-Baker 2006). However, the real legacy of the Peace and Truce was not simply in these late ripples. Their real importance came in the ways they were institutionalized over time, in different regions, for different purposes.

The first important aspect of this institutionalization was the fundamental fact that neither the Peace nor the Truce actually outlawed *werrae* or aggressive self-help. Quite the contrary, *werra* and self-help continued to be fully legitimate outside the periods of the Truce, and in cases where negotiations of legal claims failed to produce a pact, and when a party to a dispute was required to defend himself against an opponent who refused to accept a court's judgment. What the Peace and Truce did was limit the destructive effects of self-help on those who were not directly involved in a conflict; put certain places and persons off limits from all acts of legitimate violence; and create rules that promoted the peaceful settlement of disputes. Nevertheless, self-help remained a right, and a potent threat when asserting legal claims. Equally important, the Peace and Truce made no attempt to outlaw the rights of lords over their own dependents. On the contrary, after the 1020s, most *formae pacis* actually institutionalized rights of lordship over dependents, as when they stated that someone who swore the Peace could not seize the goods of a peasant and hold them for redemption—save for his own peasants or peasants over whom he was enforcing a valid legal claim.[2] Significantly, such power belonged not only to lay lords but also to ecclesiastical lordships, whether those of bishops, cathedral chapters, or monasteries. In this way, the Peace of God was an important aspect of a larger process occurring throughout western Europe: the precipitation of coherent lordships, both secular and ecclesiastical, such that a variety of lords came to exercise more or less exclusive jurisdictional power within territories subject to them, and all lords had control, backed up by courts and force, over the peasants subject to them (West 2013: 173–97, 228–52; Bisson 2009: 1–83; Mazel 2007; Mazel 2008: 29–61; Mazel 2016: 237–306; Rosenwein 1999: 156–83; Lauwers 2013).

This process of nucleation also affected towns, which often received qualified rights of jurisdictional autonomy from their lords. Here, too, the language of peace had a role. For example, in 1114, the count and countess of Hainaut granted a charter of privileges to the inhabitants of Valenciennes (*La Paix de Valenciennes de 1114* [1981]). It is extant only in much later versions, so we cannot know exactly what rights the original grant comprised; but certain key elements were certainly present from the beginning. The inhabitants of Valenciennes formed "a peace" (*pax*). The peace was administered by "lords of the peace" chosen by the "men of the peace." Merchants traveling to and from Valenciennes were protected from seizures of their persons and property by neighboring lords, who themselves swore to observe the peace. Disputes between men of the peace were to be adjudicated by the lords of the peace. Those accused of violating the peace could be convicted on the sworn testimony of two men of the peace. Everything was done to ensure that before disputes reached a point of self-help, reconciliations were attempted by the lords of the peace. All reconciliations that resulted required fines to the lords of the peace (generally shared with the count's local agent) and also amends made to the aggrieved party. Those who were found guilty of violating the peace were punished by hanging or mutilation.

One of the most interesting aspects of the Peace of Valenciennes was its pointed references to those excluded from it. For example, at the time it was established, the counts of Hainaut and Flanders were at war with each other. As a result, the protection of merchants and their merchandise did not extend to merchants of Douai, which was part of Flanders (c. 1). Rules governing imprisonment and corporal punishment were also much harsher for "outsiders" (*extranei*) (cc. 2, 19, 23, 61). There was a corresponding insistence on the duties of those who were "men of the peace," particularly with respect to their military obligations: for the Peace of Valenciennes was also a military association, to benefit both the townspeople of Valenciennes and the count of Hainaut. The Peace therefore required the formation of a militia. Whenever there was a "great cry" (*clamor magnus*), the town bell was to be rung, and immediately, on penalty of a fine, every "man of the peace" was to run to the location of the cry bearing their arms, and all were to march out together behind their assigned banners (c. 24). All of which, of course, made the Peace of Valenciennes a more effective institution of mobilization for war.

The military aspect of the Peace of Valenciennes was very common during the period. Indeed, the Peace of God itself not only assumed the correctness of warfare but demanded warfare to enforce the Peace. Some of its very first declarations required swearers to aid each other in a military alliance not only against those who had sworn and violated its terms but even against those who had merely refused to swear them—these latter often being called "rebels against the peace" (Mansi 1759–98, 19: 827–32, c. 4 [Narbonne, 1054]). The obligation was often spelled out in the *formae pacis*. The most famous example was the very first to be described in detail. In 1038, Archbishop Aimo of Bourges established a Peace of God for his own archdiocese, to be implemented also by the other bishops of his province. Most of its terms were fairly standard. But Aimo appears to have done something somewhat different from previous bishops by requiring all males in his archdiocese, aged fifteen and older, to swear the Peace oath; and part of their oath required them to gather under the priests of their parishes when summoned and to fight together as an army against those who violated the peace or refused to swear it. The reason we know so much about this case is because Aimo actually used his militia against the most powerful lord of his archdiocese, Ebbo of Déols, and Ebbo's family, clients, and allies. Aimo set his militia against Ebbo's party not because they had violated the peace but because they had refused to swear it at all, thereby becoming "rebels against the peace," probably because they recognized Aimo's innovation for what it was: a means by which the archbishop and his viscount could assert authority over the lands controlled by Ebbo and his allies (Koziol 2018: 28–29; Barthélemy 1999: 404–16).

In time, Aimo's policy came to be quite widespread: peace militias appeared throughout much of northern France during the second half of the eleventh century (Vermeesch 1966; Barthélemy 2014). Nor were they always formed by bishops. In Le Mans, the people of the city formed their own militia, then demanded that their bishop accept it. The result was an army of peace-swearers who marched behind the banners of the saints of local churches—as in 1038 not against peace-breakers but against "rebels" who refused to swear the oaths (Koziol 2018: 39; *Actus pontificum Cenomannis* 1901: 81–7).

In the south of France, such militias were especially long lived, continuing well into the thirteenth century. But then, the entire organization of the Peace became more and more finely structured here and continued to be organized largely by bishops. The reason appears to be that the Languedoc was a region of extremely fragmented lordships, which, as in Aquitaine when the Peace first formed, lacked any coherent princely leadership. On the contrary, the region was torn between two competing princely houses (the counts of Barcelona and the counts of Toulouse), their conflict leading to widespread hostilities among other lords, who gravitated to one or the other camp depending on which benefited them more against their own rivals. In any case, the Peace and Truce of God not only continued to be proclaimed by bishops acting in councils and demanding the swearing of peace oaths. They also continued to establish peace militias, funded by the imposition of a tax on livestock (helpfully collected by the Templars and Hospitallers). And within every diocese officials, called *paziers* or *paciarii*, were appointed whose primary task was to hear disputes before they passed into violence and, when disputants violated the Peace and Truce, to gather the local militia and lead it against the peace-breakers (Carraz 2013; Koziol 2018: 44–6).

In Germany, the situation was a little different. There the Peace and Truce of God first appeared in 1082 and 1083 at Liège and Cologne, in more or less the form usual in France (Goetz 1984). Very quickly, however, the *forma pacis* developed into what German historians call the *Landfrieden* and *Reichsfrieden*—territorial peaces and royal or imperial peaces (Wadle 2001; Koziol 2018: 41–3; Harding 2002: 79–98). The most important difference between them was simply that *Reichsfrieden* were issued by the king (or emperor), often (but not invariably) for the entire kingdom, while *Landfrieden* were issued for territories by consortia of lords, including both bishops and lay magnates. Otherwise, the two were quite similar and certainly shared the same principles and tendencies. Yet both were quite different from the French Peace of God and even from the developing peaces issued by territorial rulers like the counts of Flanders and Barcelona. *Landfrieden*, for example, said nothing about excommunication: the sanctions were fines, amends, and not least, corporal and capital punishment. Protection of the unarmed was not a particular concern. Instead, the peaces covered all individuals within a territory, with slightly different punishments and proofs required for free and unfree. Mostly, the territorial peaces present lists of what we would call crimes and torts, and the procedures and punishments attaching to them. Above all, as the name suggests, *Landfrieden* did not cover territories defined in terms of ecclesiastical dioceses. Instead, early *Landfrieden* were established for Alsace, Alamannia, Bavaria, and Saxony. Later others were established for the counties of Valais and Hainaut or for territories delimited by natural boundaries or by the limits and intersections of dioceses and counties. As a result, *Landfrieden* established frameworks within which distinct regional German customary laws developed. But *Landfrieden* were always sworn. All of them put a great deal of emphasis on the hue and cry, that is, the responsibility of every member of the territorial peace to raise a clamor upon evidence of a crime and to pursue the criminal. One of the standard punishments besides mutilation and death was "proscription," meaning exile and outlawry.

A VERY EUROPEAN IDEA OF PEACE

These were the most important types of "peace" one finds in practice during the largest portion of the Middle Ages. The question remains, were they forces of integration?

Harry Truman once threw up his hands in exasperation and exclaimed, "Give me a one-handed economist!" because every time he asked an economist for advice the answer was invariably, "On the one hand . . ., but on the other hand . . ." It is a very academic sort of response, equally common among historians. Administrators need to make decisions. Amateurs assume that there are true and false facts. Historians know that reality was complicated, that many variables affected the course of events, and that any given society holds contradictions. So were medieval forms of peace integrative? It depends. The ecclesial ideal of peace expressed by Alcuin was beautiful but utopian. It offered an ideal (or perhaps ideology) of integration for a subcontinental empire, but it was impossible to institutionalize. Its vision of universal Christian brotherhood went against the embeddedness of conflict in political relations. It also went against the increasing stratification of social relations, which was why in the ninth century "peace" came to be cast as protection offered by the strong to the weak. Ecclesial peace also went against western Europe's inability to create institutions of empire, that is, institutions that concentrated authority in a single, continent-wide court. As a result, even under Louis the Pious there was tension and conflict between Louis's sons, and after Louis's death the empire fragmented into smaller entities, all functionally autonomous. Relations between those entities were established by treaties between their kings. Relations within them were established by agreements between kings and magnates and between magnates themselves.

The result was to embed the structures of "peace" ever more deeply into European political discourse. Whether they were called "pacts," "conventions," "brotherhoods," "friendships," "treaties," or "concords," all assumed that a peace derived from an agreement between autonomous individuals acting freely. "Peace" as "pact" was therefore not integrative at all, save for one important facet: in Europe, since pacts became the most durable and pervasive framework for settling political and legal conflicts, a language of pacts came to be a trait shared by all European societies. In this respect, the European Economic Community as it was established after the Second World War was very typically European, its foundations profoundly medieval.

As for the peace of the London guild, the peace of the Peace of God, the peace of the *Landfrieden*, the peace of the communes of Le Mans and Valenciennes, these were also founded on the agreement of individuals acting (in theory) autonomously. They were highly integrative. Every individual who swore the oath had an obligation to the community and to each other. They had an obligation to fight alongside each other against enemies, to avoid doing harm to each other, to make peaceful settlements with each other in cases of conflict. But one can speak of the integrative capacity of such peaces only with two important caveats. First, peace associations hardly created happy, harmonious communities of equals. In Aimo of Bourges' 1038 Peace League and in the 1114 Peace of Valenciennes, every male over a certain age was required to swear the articles of peace. If he did not, he became a "rebel against the peace," and liable to all the sanctions the Peace could marshal. Furthermore, as is well known, the communities and associations who articulated their obligations in terms of peace were composed of men of different statuses and widely varying degrees of wealth and power, differences that became more extreme over the course of the twelfth century. The equality and mutuality of peace associations were an ideological fiction. Second, insofar as these kinds of "associative" peace did serve to integrate communities, they did so by defining those communities in terms of enemies. Thus, these first come into view as institutions to pursue and punish thieves; to pursue and punish those who did not abide by the rules of the peace; to pursue and punish those who refused to swear the peace; to oppose the German emperor and his Italian allies. The inclusiveness of peace that bounded communities was not just predicated upon but, in fact, generated the exclusion of "outsiders," "enemies," and "rebels" against the peace to be excommunicated and proscribed.

On the one hand, medieval peace was strongly integrative. On the other hand, the integration was not wholly real, and the construction of the fiction required an equal emphasis on exclusion and enmity. That, too, was a medieval legacy to later Europe.

NOTES

Introduction

1. *Francis of Assisi* (2001), 3, p. 482, note *a*, indicates that the story of St Francis and the wolf is older than historians generally assumed.
2. Rosenwein (2006) and Rosenwein (2016) are especially critical of Elias's work.

Chapter 1

1. These wars were seen as exceptional situations: neither Alcuin nor Paul the Deacon would join the king in these war zones even when specially summoned: see Bullough (2003): 367.
2. While Nelson (1992) has shown that the disorder of Charles the Bald's kingdom may have been exaggerated, it is worth remembering where his most prolific interlocutor Hincmar of Reims had his bishopric: Reims, vulnerable to Viking as well as Lotharingian incursions. See Morrison (1964) and Kershaw (2011): 221–22.
3. On *deditio*, see recently Roach (2012); also Reuter (1991), Koziol (1992), Althoff (1997): 99–125, and Buc (2001): 60. As Roach and Buc suggest, given its variations and borrowings from both secular ritual and religious liturgy, the performance can be considered an array of symbolic gestures strategically deployed—by petitioner or chronicler—rather than a single specific ceremony.
4. This is consistent with the argument in Fasoli (1968) that *pax* read through the Germanic *pak* meant a new undertaking after the conclusion of hostilities.
5. As a corollary to this image, some scholastics described the individual self as a kingdom in which perfect peace meant a correct sequence of order and command. For Hugh of Saint-Victor, writing *c*. 1130, the body was a subject populace whose actions and responses could only mirror decisions made by one of two leaders: reason, the rightful ruler, or carnality, which more often than not, had usurped control, see Malegam (2013): 113.
6. See Reichberg (2011) for a comprehensive discussion. This does not mean warfare in the interests of securing quiescence, as tenth-century peace discourse would have it, but rather force applied under the aegis of peace (i.e., by legitimate authority and for the right reasons). Aquinas and later political theorists such as Marsilius of Padua argued that with concord as the desired outcome (or proximal end, in Aristotelian terms), fighting must follow norms that would ensure the possibility for reconciliation (i.e., proportional, not total war). See also Malegam (2013): 299–302.
7. For Marsilius, priests had no coercive authority, merely a mandate to express coercive divine judgment through performance or withholding of the sacrament.

Chapter 2

1. Thomas Aquinas (1895): I–II.q. 70, a. 3. See also Thomas Aquinas (1950): ch. 11, §885: "[A]d rationem pacis, duo concurrunt: primo quidem, quod aliqua sint unita; secondo, quod concordant ad unum."

2. Thomas Aquinas (1950): ch. 11, §885: "Ad rationem pacis, duo concurrunt: primo quidem, quod aliqua sint unita; secondo, quod concordent ad unum"; see also §896: "Unitio . . . ad rationem pacis pertinent," hence (§901) "haec unitio [of peace] distinctiones rerum non tollit."
3. As used by Aristotle (1984b): bk. III, ch. 1, 1110b1: "violence" is compulsory action (in Latin, *violentum*); it designates the movement by which a thing is impelled toward an end by an extrinsic principle, without there being a corresponding internal tendency toward the end in question.
4. Aquinas writes that "peace includes concord and adds something thereto . . . For concord is properly between, properly speaking is between one human being and another, insofar as the wills of various hearts agree together in consenting to the same thing" (1895: II–II, q. 29, a. 1).
5. Thomas Aquinas (1895): II–II, q. 29, a. 1, ad 1. In this respect, Aquinas would not be at ease with the Roman conception of peace (*pax*), which (deriving as it did from the root noun of the verb *pacisci*) signified the pact that ended a war. This peace "did not presume that the pact was made between equals," as it often proceeded from unconditional surrender, such that the verb *pacere* could refer to conquest, as when we today speak of "pacification"; see Shogimen (2010): 873–4.
6. Thomas Aquinas (1895): II–II, q. 29.a. 2 ad 4: "true peace (*pax vera*) is twofold. One is perfect (*perfecta*) . . .The other is imperfect (*imperfecta*), and it is had in this world."
7. In Thomas Aquinas (1965): 25: 2 Thomas adds additional levels of "perfect peace": First, there is the peace that characterizes the "higher intellectual substances [angels] who live in supreme concord" (*in summa concordia vivunt*). Wholly without the indigence (*absque miseria*) of lower creatures and participating to a greater degree in the unity of the divine power, "they are preserved in a condition of supreme peace" (in *summa pace eas conservans*). Second, there is the concord of the heavenly bodies, which undergo no contrariety, neither of generation or corruption, as is found in lower bodies, nor discord of wills, as among human beings (pp. 142–3, lines 20–40).
8. Thomas Aquinas (1979): II, p. 205, lines 476–7: "that state [heaven] will not be subject to the attack of any enemy" (*per alicuius hostes impugnationem*). In his commentary to Isaiah 26:12 (Thomas Aquinas 1974), Thomas notes how our future peace in eternal life results from (i) abundance of goods, (ii) assurance against evils, and (iii) immutability.
9. Thomas Aquinas (1895): II–II, q. 29, a. 3, ad 2. He adds in the commentary to Isaiah 26:12 (Thomas Aquinas 1974) how peace in this life results from (i) contempt of opulence, (ii) submission of carnal desires, and (iii) contemplation of divine wisdom.
10. See Thomas Aquinas (1895): II–II, q. 29, a. 4. In his discussion of the beatitudes (ibid. I–II.69.3), Aquinas notes how "peace" has a special connection with the "active life": "As regards the virtues . . . whereby a person is perfected in relation to his neighbor, the effect of the active life is peace . . . hence the seventh beatitude *Blessed are the Peacemakers*" (Mt. 5:9).
11. See, for instance, Shogimen (2010): 876, who writes that by drawing "a sharp distinction between Christians and non-Christians," Aquinas thereby rejected "the possibility of the latter attaining . . . true peace. Peace was therefore impossible without grace."

Chapter 3

1. Since the *Chronicles* of Jean le Bel and Jean Froissart are available in different editions and translations, with different pagination, page references to a specific edition will be followed by reference to the standard chapter and/or paragraph numbers in square brackets.

2. Kimberly LoPrete has noted that Orderic Vitalis used the term *viriliter* 100 times, always for men (2005: 38).
3. This episode appears in an early thirteenth-century account, but the event took place in the twelfth century (Nicholson 1997: 337).
4. Georges Duby, the French doyen of the study of medieval nobility, wrote, "It is true that some chronicles refer to women who took up arms in defense of the rights of their husbands or sons. But this seemed abnormal, even scandalous" (1995: 73).
5. A later chronicle is more forthcoming about this episode, describing her involvement in much more detail, see *Istore et croniques de Flandre* (1879): 219.

Chapter 4

1. For example, Qur'ān 49:13: "O mankind! We created you from a single [pair] of a male and a female, and made you into nations and tribes, that you may come to know one another. Verily the most honored among you in the sight of God is the most righteous of you" (Funk and Said 2009: 125).
2. This is discussed in the last section of *Mishneh Torah* 11: 4, which Eisen says is "censored out of most printed editions" (2011: 116, n. 11).
3. Indeed, he explicitly connected *concordia* and *pax* in *Summa Theologiae* II–II, q. 29, a. 1, where he wrote, "Peace includes concord and adds something thereto . . . Concord denotes a union of appetites among various persons, while peace denotes, in addition to this union, the union of appetites even in one man." See Reichberg (2017): 25, n. 30.
4. This text has sometimes been attributed to Hugh of St. Victor, including by Siberry (1985): 209, but Leclerq (1957, with edition of the letter and the section translated here on p. 87) argued for Hugh of Payns as the author. I am grateful to Walter Simons for this clarification.

Chapter 5

1. Although innovative and influential, the treatment of premodern millenarianism in Cohn (1970) is often uncritical in its use of primary sources; for a more measured introduction to some of the issues, see Lerner (2004).
2. See Montemaggi (2015) for more on Dante's theological argument in the *Divine Comedy*, as well as Kempshall (2015), who draws attention to Aristotelian elements in Dante's understanding of politics and justice. For Dante's possible influence on visions of peace by the French author, Christine de Pizan (1364–1430), see *Book of Peace* (2008): 127.
3. Both Petkov and Jansen, in different ways, assume that the practice of kissing to seal the peace crossed from the Christian, religious realm into secular rituals. For interesting nuances and further interpretations of the Italian evidence, see Kumhera (2017), 132–5. More broadly, see also Offenstadt (2007) and Chapter Six in this volume.
4. See also Chapter Six in this volume.

Chapter 7

1. There is a wealth of literature on these trends and on some of the analogies to premodern societies. For brief introductions, see Watkins (2008), Kaldor (2013), and Grygiel (2013).

Chapter 8

1. The classic example is Bonnaud-Delamare (1939). For the early Middle Ages' misunderstanding of Augustine's political ideas, see Arquillière (1934); for doubts about his influence generally, Leyser (2012); for doubts about knowledge of his ideas of peace specifically, Kershaw (2011): 64–8, 150–1.
2. Thus Verdun-sur-le Doubs (1021?), Compiègne (1023), Vienne (early eleventh century), Laon (1030s?), Douai (1036?), Caen (1040s?), and others.

BIBLIOGRAPHY

Abels, Richard (1991), "King Alfred's Peace-making Strategies with the Vikings," *Haskins Society Journal*, 3 (1991): 23–34.
Abels, Richard (2008), "Paying the Danegeld: Anglo-Saxon Peacemaking with the Vikings," in Philip de Souza and John France (eds), *War and Peace in Ancient and Medieval History*, 173–192, Cambridge: Cambridge University Press.
Actus pontificum Cenomannis in urbe degentium (1901), ed. G. Busson and A. Ledru, Archives historiques du Maine, 2, Le Mans: Société des Archives historiques du Maine.
Admonitio Generalis (2012), ed. H. Mordek, K. Zechiel-Eckes and M. Glatthaar, in MGH, Fontes Iuris Germanici Antiqui, vol. 16, 179–239, Hanover: Hahn.
Afterman, Adam and Gedaliah Afterman (2012), "'Rise up and kill him first': On Modern Attempts to Create a Jewish Ethics of War," *Nova et Vetera* (English edition), 10, 4: 1183–1213.
Agobard of Lyons (1981), *De divisione imperii*, ed. L. van Acker, *Corpus Christianorum, Continuatio Mediaeualis*, 52, Turnhout, Belgium: Brepols.
Alberic of Trois-Fontaines (1874), "Chronicon," ed. Paulus Scheffer-Boichorst in MGH Scriptores in folio, vol. 23, 674–950, Hanover: Hahn.
Alfred the Great (1983), transl. S. Keynes and Michael Lapidge, London: Penguin.
Alger of Liège (1855), *De sacramentis corporis et sanguinis Dominici*, in *PL*, vol. 180, 739C–854C.
Allmand, Christopher (1971), "The War and Non-Combatants," in Kenneth Fowler (ed.), *The Hundred Years War*, 163–83, London: Macmillan.
Althoff, Gerd (1997), *Spielregeln der Politik im Mittelalter*, Darmstadt: Wissenschaftliche Buchgesellschaft.
Althoff, Gerd (2002), "The Variability of Rituals in the Middle Ages," in Gerd Althoff, Johannes Fried and Patrick J. Geary (eds), *Medieval Concepts of the Past: Ritual, Memory, Historiography*, Cambridge: Cambridge University Press.
Althoff, Gerd (2004), *Family, Friends and Followers: Political and Social Bonds in Medieval Europe*, trans. Christopher Carroll, Cambridge: Cambridge University Press.
Althoff, Gerd (2006), *Heinrich IV*, Darmstadt: Wissenschaftliche Buchgesellschaft.
Álvarez Gómez, Mariano (1999), "Hacia los fundamentos de la paz perpetua en la religión según Nicolás de Cusa," *La ciudad de Dios*, 212(2): 299–340.
Analectica Hymnica (1886–1922), ed. Guido M. Dreves and Clemens Blume, Leipzig: Reisland, 55 vols.
Andersen, Per, *et al.* eds. (2013), *Law and Disputing in the Middle Ages*, Copenhagen, Djøf Publishing.
Appelt, H., ed. (1985–90), *Die Urkunden Friedrichs I*, vols 3–4, Hanover: Hahn.
Aristotle (1984a), *Metaphysics*, in Jonathan Barnes (ed.), *The Complete Works of Aristotle*, vol. 2, 1552–1728, Oxford: Oxford University Press.
Aristotle (1984b), *Nicomachean Ethics*, in Jonathan Barnes (ed.), *The Complete Works of Aristotle*, vol. 2, 1729–1867, Oxford: Oxford University Press.

Arnold, John H. (2005), *Belief and Unbelief in Medieval Europe*, London: Hodder Arnold.
Arquillière, H.-X. (1934), *L'augustinisme politique: Essai sur la formation des théories politiques du moyen-âge*, Paris: J. Vrin.
Aurell, Martin (2005), "Les femmes guerrières (XIe et XIIe siècles)," in Martin Aurell and Thomas Deswarte (eds), *Famille, violence et christianisation au Moyen Age. Mélanges offerts à Michel Rouche*, 319–30, Paris: Presses de l'Université de Paris-Sorbonne.
Augustin d'Hippone (1966), *Sermons pour la Pâque*, ed. Suzanne Poque, Sources Chrétiennes, 116, Paris: Éditions du Cerf.
Averroës (1978), *Tahafut al-tahafut* [*The Incoherence of the Incoherence*], trans. Simon Van Den Bergh, London: E.J.W. Gibb Memorial Trust.
Avicenna (2005), *The Metaphysics of "The Healing." A Parallel English-Arabic text*, ed. and trans. M.E. Marmura, Provo, Utah: Brigham Young University Press.
Bagge, Sverre (1996), "Ideas and Narrative in Otto of Freising's Gesta Frederici," *Journal of Medieval History*, 22(4): 345–77.
Baird, Joseph, Giuseppe Baglivi, and John Robert Kane, eds. (1986), *The Chronicle of Salimbene de Adam*, Binghamton, NY: Medieval & Renaissance Texts & Studies.
Bange, P. (1995), "The Image of Women of the Nobility in the German Chronicles of the Tenth and Eleventh Centuries," in Adelbert T. Davids (ed.), *The Empress Theophano: Byzantium and the West at the Turn of the First Millenium*, 150–68, Cambridge: Cambridge University Press.
Barber, Richard (1997), *Life and Campaigns of the Black Prince*, Woodbridge: Boydell.
Barlow, Frank (1983), *William Rufus*, London: Methuen.
Barrow, R.H. (1950), *Introduction to Saint Augustine, The City of God*, London: Faber and Faber.
Barthélemy, Dominique (1999), *L'An mil et la paix de Dieu: La France chrétienne et féodale, 980–1060*, Paris: Fayard.
Barthélemy, Dominique (2004), *Chevaliers et miracles. La violence et le sacré dans la société féodale*, Paris: Armand Colin.
Barthélemy, Dominique ([1997] 2009), *The Serf, the Knight and the Historian*, Ithaca, NY: Cornell University Press.
Barthélemy, Dominique (2014), "Paix de Dieu et communes dans le royaume capétien, de l'an mil à Louis VI," *Comptes-rendus des séances de l'Académie des inscriptions et Belles-Lettres*, 1 [janvier-mars]: 207–41.
Bartlett, Robert ([1998] 2010), "'Mortal Enmities': The Legal Aspect of Hostility in the Middle Ages," in B.S. Tuten and T.L. Billado (eds), *Feud, Violence and Practice: Essays in Medieval Studies in Honor of Stephen D. White*, 197–212, Burlington: Ashgate.
Barton, Richard E. (1998), "Zealous Anger and the Renegotiation of Aristocratic Relationships in Eleventh- and Twelfth-century France," in Barbara H. Rosenwein (ed.), *Anger's Past: The Social Uses of an Emotion in the Middle Ages*, 153–70, Ithaca: Cornell University Press.
Bejczy, István (1994), *Pape Jansland en Utopia. De verbeelding van de beschaving van middeleeuwen en renaissance*, Nijmegen, the Netherlands: Universitair publikatiebureau.
Bellaguet, Louis, ed. and trans. (1839–1855), *Chronique du religieux de Saint-Denys, contenant le règne de Charles VI de 1380 à 1422*, vol. 5, Paris: Imprimerie de Crapelet.
Benham, Jenny (2011), *Peacemaking in the Middle Ages: Principles and Practice*, Manchester: Manchester University Press.
Benham, Jenny (2013a), "Law or Treaty? Defining the Edge of Legal Studies in the Early and High Medieval Periods," *Historical Research*, 86: 487–97.
Benham, Jenny (2013b), "Perceptions of War and Peace: The Role of Peace Treaties from the Tenth to the Early Thirteenth Century," in L. Beach and K. Borrill (eds), *Battle and Bloodshed: The Medieval World at War*, 217–29. Newcastle-upon-Tyne: Cambridge Scholars Publishing.

Benham, Jenny (2018), "The Peace of Venice, 1177," in Gordon Martel (ed.), *Encyclopedia of Diplomacy*, Chichester: Wiley-Blackwell.

Bennett, Judith M. and Ruth Mazo Karras, eds. (2013), *The Oxford Handbook of Women and Gender in Medieval Europe*, Oxford: Oxford University Press.

Biblia sacra iuxta Vulgatam versionem (1994), ed. Robert Weber, revised 4th edn Roger Gryson, Stuttgart: Deutsche Bibelgesellschaft.

Biechler, James (1991), "A New Face Toward Islam: Nicholas of Cusa and John of Segovia," in Gerald Christianson and Thomas M. Izbicki (eds), *Nicholas of Cusa in Search of God and Wisdom. Essays in Honor of Morimichi Watanabe by the American Cusanus Society*, 185–202, Leiden: Brill.

Bisson, Thomas N. (1994), "The Feudal Revolution," *Past & Present*, 142: 6–42.

Bisson, Thomas N. (2009), *The Crisis of the Twelfth Century: Power, Lordship, and the Origins of European Government*, Princeton: Princeton University Press.

Blockmans, Frans (1935), "Een patricische veete te Gent op het einde der XIIIe eeuw (vóór 1293 tot 10 juni 1306)," *Bulletin de la Commission royale d'histoire*, 99: 573–692.

Blockmans, Wim (1998), "Representation (Since the Thirteenth Century)," in Christopher Allmand (ed.), *The New Cambridge Medieval History. Volume VII c. 1415–c. 1500*, 29–64, Cambridge: Cambridge University Press.

Blumenthal, Uta-Renate (1988), *The Investiture Controversy: Church and Monarchy from the Ninth to the Twelfth Century*, Philadelphia: University of Pennsylvania Press.

Blythe, J. M. (2001), "Women in the Military: Scholastic Arguments and Medieval Images of Female Warriors," *History of Political Thought*, 22(2): 242–70.

Bonino, Serge-Thomas (2006), "'Toute vérité, quel que soit celui qui la dit, vient de l'Esprit-Saint': Autour d'une citation de l'*Ambrosiaster* dans le corpus Thomasien," *Revue thomiste*, 106 (1–2): 101–47.

Bonizo of Sutri (1891), *Liber ad amicum*, ed. Ernst Dümmler, in MGH, Libelle de Lite, vol. 1, 568–620, Hanover: Hahn.

Bonnaud-Delamare, Roger (1939), *L'idée de paix à l'époque carolingienne*, Paris: Domat-Montchrestien.

The Book of Peace by Christine de Pizan (2008), ed. and transl. Karen Green et al., University Park, PA: The Pennsylvania State University Press.

Booker, Courtney (2009), *Past Convictions: The Penance of Louis the Pious and the Decline of the Carolingians*, Philadelphia: University of Pennsylvania Press.

Boone, Marc (2010), *A la recherche d'une modernité civique. La société urbaine des anciens Pays-Bas au bas Moyen Age*. Brussels: Éditions de l'Université de Bruxelles.

Born, Gary B. (2015), *International Arbitration: Cases and Materials*, 2nd ed., Alphen aan den Rijn, the Netherlands: Wolters Kluwer.

Bornstein, Daniel (1994), *The Bianchi of 1399: Popular Devotion in Late Medieval Italy*, Ithaca, NY: Cornell University Press.

Boucheron, Patrick (2005), "'Tournez les yeux pour admirer, vous qui exercez le pouvoir, celle qui est peinte ici': La fresque du Bon Gouvernement d'Ambrogio Lorenzetti," *Annales. Histoire, Sciences Sociales*, 60(6): 1135–99.

Bowlus, Charles R. (2008), "The Early Hungarians as Mercenaries 860–955," in John France (ed.), *Mercenaries and Paid Men. The Mercenary Identity in the Middle Ages*, 193–204, Leiden: Brill.

Brett, Annabel S., ed. (2005), *Defensor Pacis, by Marsilius of Padua*, New York: Cambridge University Press.

Breviarium Parisiense (1680), *Pars Hyemalis*, Paris: Sumptibus Federici Leonard.

Brown, Warren C. (2011), *Violence in Medieval Europe*, New York: Longman.
Brunner, Otto (1992), *Land and Lordship: Structures of Governance in Medieval Austria*, trans. Howard Kaminsky and James van Horn Melton, Philadelphia: University of Pennsylvania Press.
Buc, Philippe (2001), *The Dangers of Ritual: Between Early Medieval Texts and Social Scientific Theory*, Princeton, NJ: Princeton University Press.
Bull, Marcus (2009), "Crusade and Conquest," in Rubin and Simons, *Christianity in Western Europe c. 1100–c. 1500*, 340–52.
Bullough, Donald A. (2003), "Was there a Carolingian anti-war movement?," *Early Medieval Europe*, 12(4): 365–76.
Capitularia regum Francorum (1835), ed. Georg Heinrich Pertz, vol. 1, in MGH, Leges in folio, vol. 3, Hanover: Hahn.
Capitularia Regum Francorum (1883–97), ed. Alfred Boretius and Victor Krause, in MGH, Legum Sectio II, Hanover: Hahn.
Caputo, Nina (2008), *Nahmanides in Medieval Catalonia: History, Community, and Messianism*, Notre Dame, IN: University of Notre Dame Press.
Carraz, Damian (2012). "Un *revival* de la paix de Dieu? Les paix diocésaines du XIIe siècle dans le Midi," in *La réforme "grégorienne" dans le Midi*, 523–58, Cahiers de Fanjeaux, 48, Toulouse: Privat.
Cassell, Anthony K. (2004), *The Monarchia Controversy: An Historical Study with Accompanying Translations of Dante Alighieri's Monarchia, Guido Vernani's Refutation of the Monarchia by Dante and Pope John XXII's bull, Si fratrum*, Washington, DC: Catholic University of America Press.
Chambers, John David (1877), *Divine Worship in England in the Thirteenth and Fourteenth Centuries, Contrasted with and Adapted to That in the Nineteenth*. London: Basil Montagu Pickering.
Charte communale de Laon ([1885] 1974), in Arthur Giry (ed.), *Documents sur les relations de la royauté avec les villes en France de 1180 à 1314*, 14–20, Geneva: Slatkine-Megariotis Reprints.
Chazan, Robert (2004), *Fashioning Jewish Identity in Medieval Western Christendom*, New York: Cambridge University Press.
Chazan, Robert (2010), *Reassessing Jewish Life in Medieval Europe*, New York: Cambridge University Press.
Chronica Rogeri de Houedene (1869–70), ed. William Stubbs, vols 2–3, London: Longman.
Chronicon sancti Huberti Andaginensis (1848), ed. L.C. Bethmann and W. Wattenbach, in MGH, Scriptores in folio, vol. 8, 565–630, Hanover: Hahn.
Clausewitz, Carl von (1984), *On War*, trans. Michael Howard and Peter Paret, rev. ed. Princeton: Princeton University Press.
Cobianchi, Roberto (2009), "Franciscan Legislation, Patronage Practice, and New Iconography in Sassetta's Commission at Borgo San Sepolcro," in Machtelt Israëls (ed.), *Sassetta: The Borgo San Sepolcro Altarpiece*, vol. 1, 107–16, Florence: Villa I Tatti.
Codagnelli, Giovanni (1901), *Annales Placentini*, ed. O. Holder-Egger, MGH, Scriptores in Rerum Germanicarum in usum scholarum separatim editi, 23, Hanover: Hahn.
Cohn, Norman (1970), *The Pursuit of the Millennium: Revolutionary Millenarians and Mystical Anarchists of the Middle Ages*, rev. ed. Oxford: Oxford University Press.
Coleman, Edward (2013), "Bishop and commune in twelfth-century Cremona: the interface of secular and ecclesiastical power," in Frances Andrews and Maria Agata Pincelli (eds), *Churchmen and Urban Government in Late Medieval Italy, c. 1200–c.1450, Cases and Contexts*, 25–42, Cambridge: Cambridge University Press.

Colish, Marcia L. (1997), *Medieval Foundations of the Western Intellectual Tradition 400–1400*, New Haven and London: Yale University Press.

Concilium Lateranense III (1973), in J. Alberigo et al. (eds), *Conciliorum oecumenicorum decretali*, 205–25, Bologna: Istituto per le scienze religiose.

Constitutiones et Acta Publica Imperatorum et Regum (1893), vol. I, ed. L. Weiland, in MGH, Legum Sectio IV, Hanover: Hahn.

Cosneau, E., ed. (1889), *Les grand traités de la guerre de cent ans*, Paris: Alphonse Picard.

Cottiaux, Jean (1995), "Un plaidoyer liégeois du XIIIe siècle en faveur de la non-violence et de la tolerance religieuse. Une initiative à portée européenne?" *Bulletin de la Société d'art et d'histoire du diocèse de Liège* 60: 1–45.

Cowdrey, H.E.J. (1968), "The Papacy, the Patarenes, and the Church of Milan," *Transactions of the Royal Historical Society*, ser. 5, 18: 25–48.

Curry, Anne (2009), "Soldiers' Wives in the Hundred Years' War," in Peter Coss and Christopher Tyerman (eds), *Soldiers, Nobles and Gentlemen. Essays in Honour of Maurice Keen*, 198–214, Woodbridge, Suffolk: Boydell Press.

Dalton, Paul (2005), "Sites and Occasions of Peacemaking in England and Normandy, c. 900–c. 1150," *Haskins Society Journal*, 16: 12–26.

Dante (1995), *Monarchia*, trans. Prue Shaw, Cambridge: Cambridge University Press.

Dante Alighieri (1870), *The Divine Comedy*, trans. Henry Wadsworth Longfellow, vol. 3, Boston: Fields, Osgood & Co.

Dante Alighieri (1916), *De monarchia*, ed. E. Moore, Oxford: Clarendon Press.

Davis, Jennifer R. (2015), *Charlemagne's Practice of Empire*, Cambridge: Cambridge University Press.

Davis, R.H.C. and M. Chibnall, eds. and trans. (1998), *The Gesta Guillelmi of William of Poitiers*, Oxford: Oxford University Press.

Dean, Trevor (2001), *Crime in Medieval Europe, 1200–1500*, London: Longman.

Dean, Trevor (2004), "The Rise of the *Signori*," in David Abulafia (ed.), *Italy in the Central Middle Ages, 1000–1300*, 104–24, Oxford: Oxford University Press.

Decrees of the Ecumenical Councils (1990), ed. and trans. Norman P. Tanner, Washington, DC: Georgetown University Press, 2 vols.

De Jong (2009), Mayke, *The Penitential State: Authority and Atonement in the Age of Louis the Pious, 814–840*, Cambridge: Cambridge University Press.

Delaborde, H.F. (1916), *Recueil des actes de Philippe Auguste*, vol. 1, Paris: Imprimerie Nationale.

Delcorno, Pietro (2015), "'Quomodo discet sine docente?' Observant Efforts towards Education and Pastoral Care," in *A Companion to Observant Reform in the Late Middle Ages and Beyond*, James D. Mixson and Bert Roest (eds), Leiden: Brill, 147–84.

Depreux, Philippe (2009), "Les Carolingiens et le serment," in Marie-France Auzépy and Guillaume Saint-Guillain (eds), *Oralité et lien social au Moyen Âge (Occident, Byzance, Islam): Parole donnée, foi jurée, serment*, 63–80, Paris: Association des amis du Centre d'histoire et civilisation de Byzance.

Desnouelles, Jean (1855), "Extraits de la chronique attribuée à Jean Desnouelles, abbé de Saint Vincent de Laon," in *Recueil des historiens des Gaules et de la France*, ed. Joseph-Daniel Guigniaut and Natalis de Wailly, vol. 21, 181–97, Paris: Imprimerie royale.

Dessì, Rosa Maria (2007), "L'invention du 'bon gouvernement'. Pour une histoire des anachronismes dans les fresques d'Ambrogio Lorenzetti (XIVe–XXe siècle)," *Bibliothèque de l'École des Chartes*, 165(2): 453–504.

DeVries, Kelly (1999), *Joan of Arc: A Military Leader*, Stroud: Sutton.

Dickson, Gary (1989), "The Flagellants of 1260 and the Crusades," *Journal of Medieval History* 15(3): 227–67.
The Digest of Justinian (1985), ed. Paul Krueger, trans. Alan Watson, Philadelphia: University of Pennsylvania Press.
Dixon, Martin (2013), *Textbook on international Law*, 7th edn, Oxford: Oxford University Press.
Douët-d'Arcq, Louis-Claude, ed. (1857–62), *La chronique d'Enguerran de Monstrelet, en deux livres, avec pièces justificatives 1400–1444*, vol. 2, Paris: Société de l'histoire de France.
Douglas, David Charles (1999), *William the Conqueror*, New Haven, CT: Yale University Press.
Dubois, Adrien (2004), "Femmes dans la guerre (XIVe-XVe siècles): un rôle caché par les sources?" *Tabularia*, 4: 39–51.
Duby, Georges (1953), *La société aux XIe et XIIe siècles dans la région mâconnaise*, Paris: Armand Colin.
Duby, Georges (1990), *The Legend of Bouvines. War, Religion and Culture in the Middle Ages*, London: Polity Press.
Duby, Georges (1995), "Women and Power," in Thomas N. Bisson (ed.), *Cultures of Power: Lordship, Status, and Process in Twelfth-Century Europe*, 69–85, Philadelphia: University of Pennsylvania Press.
Dunn, Diana (2000), "The Queen at War: The Role of Magaret of Anjou in the Wars of the Roses," in Diana Dunn (ed.), *War and Society in Medieval and Early Modern Britain*, 141–61, Liverpool: Liverpool University Press.
Dutton, Paul E. (1993), *Carolingian Civilization: A Reader*, Peterborough, Ont.: Broadview.
Eads, Valerie (2003), "The Geography of Power: Matilda of Tuscany and the Strategy of Active Defense," in Donald Joseph Kagay and L.J. Andrew Villalon (eds), *Crusaders, Condottieri, and Cannon: Medieval Warfare in Societies Around the Mediterranean*, 355–85, Leiden: Brill.
Earenfight, Theresa (2007), "Without the Persona of the Prince: Kings, Queens and the Idea of Monarchy in Late Medieval Europe," *Gender & History*, 19(1): 1–21.
Eco, Umberto (1988), *The Aesthetics of Thomas Aquinas*, Cambridge, MA: Harvard University Press.
Edgington, Susan, and Sarah Lambert, eds. (2001), *Gendering the Crusades*, Columbia University Press.
Edwards, J.G., ed. (1935), *Calendar of Ancient Correspondence Concerning Wales*, Cardiff: University Press Board.
Einhard, *Vita Karoli Magni* (1911), ed. O. Holder-Egger, MGH, Scriptores in Rerum Germanicarum in usum scholarum separatim editi, vol. 25, Hanover: Hahn.
Eisen, Robert (2011), *The Peace and Violence of Judaism: From the Bible to Modern Zionism*, Oxford: Oxford University Press.
Elias, Norbert ([1939] 2000), *The Civilizing Process: Sociogenetic and Psychogenetic Investigations*, trans. Edmund Jephcott; ed. Eric Dunning, Johan Goudsblom, and Stephen Mennell, rev. ed., Malden, MA: Blackwell.
Erb, Heather McAdam (2007), "Interior Peace," in Peter A. Kwasniewski (ed.), *Wisdom's Apprentice: Essays in Honor of Lawrence Dewan*, 260–81, Washington, DC: Catholic University of American Press.
Eshelman, Lori (2000), "Weavers of Peace, Weavers of War," in Diane Wolfthal (ed.), *Peace and Negotiation: Strategies for Coexistence in the Middle Ages and the Renaissance*, 15–37, Turnhout: Brepols.
Esposito, John L. (1998), *Islam: The Straight Path*, 3rd edn, New York: Oxford University Press.

Fanjoux, G. (1849), "Notice archéologique et historique sur la ville de Jaligny et sur ses seigneurs," *L'art en province: histoire, littérature, voyages*, nouvelle série, 10: 12–19.

Fasoli, Gina (1968), "Pace e guerra nell'alto medioevo," in *Ordinamenti militari in Occidente nell'alto Medio Evo*, Settimane di Studio del Centro Italiano di Studi sull'Alto Medioevo, vol. 15(1), 15–47, Spoleto: Centro Italiano di Studi sull'Alto Medioevo.

Fenster, Thelma S., and Daniel Lord Smail, eds. (2003), *Fama: The Politics of Talk and Reputation in Medieval Europe*, Ithaca, NY: Cornell University Press.

Field, Sean (2019), *Courting Sanctity: Holy Women and the Capetians*, Ithaca, NY: Cornell University Press.

Firnhaber-Baker, Justine (2006), "From God's Peace to the King's Order: Late Medieval Limitations on Non-Royal Warfare," *Essays in Medieval Studies*, 23: 19–30.

Firnhaber-Baker, Justine (2010), "Seigneurial War and Royal Power in Late Medieval Southern France," *Past and Present*, 208: 37–76.

Firnhaber-Baker, Justine (2014), *Violence and the State in Medieval Languedoc, 1240–1400*, Cambridge: Cambridge University Press.

Fisch, J. (2012), "Peoples and Nations," in Fassbender B. and Peters A. (eds), *Oxford Handbook of the History of International Law*, Oxford: Oxford University Press.

Fisher, P. and Friis-Jensen, Karsten, ed. and trans. (2015), *Saxo Grammaticus, Gesta Danorum: The History of the Danes*, Oxford: Oxford University Press, 2 vols.

Flori, Jean (2007), *Eleanor of Aquitaine: Queen and Rebel*, trans. Olive Casse, Edinburgh: Edinburgh University Press.

Fortin, John R. (2008), "Saint Anselm on the Kingdom of Heaven: A Model of Right Order," *The Saint Anselm Journal*, 6(1): 1–10.

France, John (1999), *Western Warfare in the Age of the Crusades 1000–1300*, Ithaca, NY: Cornell University Press.

France, John (2008), "Introduction," in John France (ed.), *Mercenaries and Paid Men. The Mercenary Identity in the Middle Ages*, 1–13, Leiden: Brill.

Francis of Assisi: Early Documents (2001), ed. Regis L. Armstrong, J.A. Wayne Hellmann, and William J. Short, New York: New City Press, 3 vols.

Friedman, Yvonne (1995), "Women in Captivity and their Ransom During the Crusader Period," in Michael Goodich, Sophia Menache, and Sylvia Schein (eds), *Cross-cultural Convergences in the Crusader Period: Essays Presented to Aryeh Grabois on His Sixtieth Birthday*, 75–87, New York: Peter Lang.

Friedman, Yvonne (2002), "Captivity and Ransom: The Experience of Women," in Susan B. Edgington and Sarah Lambert (eds), *Gendering the Crusades*, 121–39, New York: Columbia University Press.

Froissart (1867), *Oeuvres de Froissart. Tome deuxième, 1322–1339: Chroniques*, ed. J. B. Kervyn de Lettenhove and Charles-François Férand, Brussels: Victor Devaux.

Froissart (1873), *Chroniques de J. Froissart. Tome quatrième, 1346–1366*, ed. Siméon Luce, Paris: Jules Renouard.

Funk, Nathan C. and Abdul Aziz Said (2009), *Islam and Peacemaking in the Middle East*, Boulder CO: Lynne Rienner Publishers.

Ganshof, François-Louis (1967), "The Treaties of the Carolingians," *Medieval and Renaissance Studies*, 3: 23–52.

Ganshof, François-Louis (1971), *The Middle Ages: A History of International Relations*, New York: Harper & Row.

Gaposchkin, M. Cecilia (2017), *Invisible Weapons: Liturgy and the Making of Crusade Ideology*, Ithaca, NY: Cornell University Press.

Gauvard, Claude (1991), *"De Grace especial." Crime, état et société en France à la fin du Moyen Age*, Paris: Publications de la Sorbonne.

Gauvard, Claude (1993), "Violence citadine et réseaux de solidarité: L'exemple français aux XIVe et XVe siècles," *Annales. Histoire, Sciences Sociales*, 48(5): 1113–26.

Gauvard, Claude (1999), "Violence licite et violence illicite dans le royaume de France à la fin du moyen âge," *Memoria y civilización*, 2: 87–115.

Geary, Patrick J. (1986), "Vivre en conflit dans une France sans état: typologie des méchanismes de règlement des conflits, 1050–1200," *Annales. Économies, Sociétés, Civilisation*, 41: 1107–33.

Geary, Patrick J. (1995), "Extra-Judicial Means of Conflict Resolution," in *La Giustizia nell'alto Medioevo (secoli V–VIII)*, vol. 1, 569–605, Settimane di studio del Centro italiano di studi sull'alto medioevo, 42, Spoleto: Centro italiano di studi sull'alto medioevo.

Gennaro, Clara (1975), "Gli ideali di pace nei movimenti religiosi del '300," in *La Pace nel pensiero, nella politica, negli ideali del Trecento*, 13–16 ottobre 1974, Convegno del centro di studi sulla spiritualità medievale nr. 15, 93–112, Todi: Presso l'Accademia tudertina.

Gergen, Thomas (2002), "The Peace of God and Its Legal Practice in the Eleventh Century," *Cuadernos de Historia de Derecho*, 9: 11–27.

Gershenzon, Shoshanna, and Jane Litman (1995), "The Bloody 'Hands of Compassionate Women': Portrayals of Heroic Women in the Hebrew Crusade Chronicle," in Menahem Mor (ed.), *Crisis & Reaction: The Hero in Jewish History*, 73–91, Omaha, NE: Creighton University Press.

Gesta Ambaziensium Dominorum (1913), in Louis Halphen and René Poupardin (eds), *Chroniques des Comtes d'Anjou et des Seigneurs d'Amboise*, 74–132, Paris: Auguste Picard.

Gesta domni Arnaldi (1901), in A. Ledru and G. Busso (eds), *Actus pontificum Cenomannis in urbe degentium*, 376–81, Le Mans: Société des Archives historiques du Maine.

Gesta episcoporum Cameracensium (1846), ed. L.C. Bethmann, in MGH, Scriptores in folio, vol. 7, 393–525, Hanover: Hahn.

Gesta episcoporum Mettensium (1852), ed. D.G. Waitz, in MGH, Scriptores in folio, vol. 10, 531–51, Hanover: Hahn.

Gesta regis Henrici secundi Benedicti abbatis (1867), ed. William Stubbs, London: Longman, 2 vols.

Gibbons, Rachel (1996), "Les conciliatrices au bas Moyen Âge: Isabeau de Baviére et la guerre civile," in Philippe Contamine and Olivier Guyotjeannin (eds), *Guerre, la violence et les gens au Moyen Age*, vol. 2: *Guerre et gens*, 23–34, Paris: Éditions du CTHS.

Gilbert, James E. (2005), "A Medieval 'Rosie the Riveter'? Women in France and Southern England during the Hundred Years War," in L.J. Andrew Villalon and Donald J. Kagay (eds), *The Hundred Years War: A Wider Focus*, 333–63, Leiden: Brill.

Giraudo, Stefania (2013), "La devozione dei Bianchi del 1399: analisi politica di un movimento di pacificazione," *Reti Medievali Rivista* 14.1: 167–95.

Gislebert of Mons (1904), *La chronique de Gislebert de Mons*, ed. Léon Vanderkindere, Brussels: Kiessling.

Gluckman, M. (1955), "The Peace in the Feud," *Past & Present*, 8: 1–14.

Gobillot, Geneviève (2000), *La conception originelle: ses intreprétations et fonctions chez les penseurs musulmans: la fitra*, Cairo: Institut français d'archéologie orientale.

Goebel, Julius, Jr. (1976), *Felony and Misdemeanor: A Study in the History of Criminal Law*, Philadelphia: University of Pennsylvania Press.

Goetz, Hans-Werner (1981), *Strukturen der spätkarolingischen Epoche im Spiegel der Vorstellungen eines zeitgenössischen Mönchs: Eine Interpretation der "gesta Karoli" Notkers von Sankt Gallen*, Bonn: Habelt.

Goetz, Hans-Werner (1983), "Kirchenschutz, Rechtswahrung und Reform: Zu den Zielen und zum Wesen der frühen Gottesfriedensbewegung in Frankreich," *Francia*, 11: 193–239.

Goetz, Hans-Werner (1984), "Der Kölner Gottesfriede von 1083: Beobachtungen über Anfänge, Tradition und Eigenart der deutschen Gottesfriedensbewegung," *Jahrbuch des Kölnischen Geschichtsverein*, 55: 39–76.

Gregory of Tours (2006), *The Merovingians*, ed. and trans. Alexander Callander Murray, Readings in Medieval Civilizations and Cultures, X, Peterborough, Ont.: Broadview Press.

Grosseteste, Robert (1918), *Le Château d'Amour*, ed. J. Murray, Paris: Champion.

Grygiel, Jakub (2013), "The Primacy of Premodern History," *Security Studies*, 22:1: 1–32.

Guibert of Nogent (1981), *Autobiographie (Monodies)*, ed. Edmond-René Labande, Paris: Les Belles Lettres.

Guibert of Nogent (1984), *Self and Society in Medieval France: The Memoirs of Abbot Guibert of Nogent*, trans. John F. Benton, Toronto: University of Toronto Press.

Guillaume, Tudela (1996), *The Song of the Cathar Wars: A History of the Albigensian Crusade*, trans. Janet Shirley, Burlington, VT: Ashgate.

Guillaume de Deguileville (1992), *The Pilgrimage of Human Life (Le Pèlerinage de la vie humaine)*, trans. Eugene Clasby, Garland Library of Medieval Literature 76, New York: Garland.

Halsall, Guy (1998), "Violence and society in the early medieval west: An introductory survey," in Guy Halsall (ed.), *Violence and Society in the Early Medieval West*, 1–45, Woodbridge: Boydell.

Hamilton, Bernard (2003), *Religion in the Medieval West*, 2nd edn, London: Hodder Arnold.

Hamilton, Sarah (2001), *The Practice of Penance, 900–1050*, Rochester: Boydell Press.

Harding, Alan (2002), *Medieval Law and the Foundations of the State*, Oxford: Oxford University Press.

Hay, David J. (2004), "Canon Laws Regarding Female Military Commanders up to the Time of Gratian: Some Texts and Their Historical Contexts," in Mark D. Meyerson, Daniel Tiery, and Oren Falk (eds), *A Great Effusion of Blood? Interpreting Medieval Violence*, 287–313, Toronto: University of Toronto Press.

Hay, David J. (2008), *The Military Leadership of Matilda of Canossa, 1046–1115*, Manchester: Manchester University Press.

Head, Thomas, and Richard Allen Landes eds. (1992), *The Peace of God: Social Violence and Religious Response in France around the Year 1000*, Ithaca, NY: Cornell University Press.

Heinrici Chronicon Lyvonie (1874), ed. Wilhelm Arndt in MGH, Scriptores in folio, vol. 23, Hanover: Hahn.

Heinzelmann, Martin (1976), *Bischofsherrschaft in Gallien: Zur Kontinuität römischer Führungsschichten vom 4. bis zum 7. Jahrhundert. Soziale, prosopographische und bildungsgeschichtliche Aspekte*, Munich: Artemis Verlag.

Henderson, E.F. (1905), *Select Historical Documents of the Middle Ages*, London: George Bell and Sons.

Heng, Geraldine (2018), *The Invention of Race in the European Middle Ages*, Cambridge: Cambridge University Press.

Herren, Michael (1996), "Eriugena's 'Aulae Sidereae,' the 'Codex Aureus,' and the Palatine Church of St. Mary at Compiègne," *Latin Letters in Early Christian Ireland*, 593–608, Aldershot: Variorum.

Heyn, Udo (1997), *Peacemaking in Medieval Europe: A Historical and Bibliographical Guide*, Guides to Historical Issues 7, Claremont, CA: Regina Books.

Hill, B.E. (2013), *Charles the Bald's 'Edict of Pîtres' (864): A Translation and Commentary*, MA thesis, University of Minnesota, Minneapolis.
Histoire des ducs de Normandie et des rois d'Angleterre (1840), ed. Francisique Michel, Paris: Jules Renouard.
Hodgson, Natasha R. (2007), *Women, Crusading and the Holy Land in Historical Narrative*, Woodbridge: Boydell Press.
Hoffmann, Hartmut (1964), *Gottesfriede und Treuga Dei*, Stuttgart: Anton Hiersemann.
Holmbäck, Å. and Wessén, E. (1933), *Svenska landskapslagar: tolkade och förklarade för nutidens svenskar. Ser. 1, Östgötalagen och Upplandslagen*, Stockholm: Geber.
Hoose, Adam L. (2010), "Francis of Assisi's Way of Peace? His Conversion and Mission to Egypt," *Catholic Historical Review*, 96(3): 449–69.
Hopkins, Jasper, ed. (1994), *Nicholas of Cusa's "De pace fidei" and "Cribratio alkorani": Translation and Analysis*, Minneapolis, MN: Arthur J. Banning Press.
Howell, Margaret (2002), "Royal Women of England and France in the Mid-Thirteenth Century: A Gendered Perspective," in Björn Weiler (ed.), *England and Europe in the Reign of Henry III (1216–1272)*, 163–81, Burlington, VT: Ashgate.
Hugh of Poitiers (1992), *The Vézelay Chronicle and Other Documents from MS. Auxerre 227 and Elsewhere*, ed. and trans. John Scott and John O. Ward, Binghamton, NY: Medieval and Renaissance Text and Studies.
Hummer, Hans (2018), *Visions of Kinship in Medieval Europe*, Oxford: Oxford University Press.
Huneycutt, Lois (1995), "Intercession and the High Medieval Queen: The Esther Topos," in Jennifer Carpenter and Sally-Beth MacLean (eds), *Power of the Weak: Studies on Medieval Women*, 126–46, Urbana, IL: University of Illinois Press.
Hyams, Paul R. (2003), *Rancor and Reconciliation in Medieval England*, Ithaca: Cornell University Press.
Hyams, Paul R. (2010), "Was There Really Such a Thing as Feud in the High Middle Ages?" in Susanna A. Throop and Paul R. Hyams (eds), *Vengeance in the Middle Ages: Emotion, Religion and Feud*, 151–75, Burlington, VT: Ashgate.
Imperiale di Santangelo, C. (1936), *Codice diplomatico della repubblica di Genova*, vol 1, Rome: Tipografia del Senato.
Iogna-Prat, Dominique (2002), *Order and Exclusion: Cluny and Christendom Face Heresy, Judaism, and Islam (1000–1150)*, trans. Graham Edwards, Ithaca, NY: Cornell University Press.
Istore et croniques de Flandre (1879), ed. J.B. Kervyn de Lettenhove, Brussels: Commission royale d'Histoire.
Ivo of Chartres (1854), *Epistolae*, in *PL*, vol. 162, 11D–287B.
Izbicki, Thomas M. (1991), "The Possibility of Dialogue with Islam in the Fifteenth Century," in Gerald Christianson and Thomas M. Izbicki (eds), *Nicholas of Cusa in Search of God and Wisdom. Essays in Honor of Morimichi Watanabe by the American Cusanus Society*, 175–83, Leiden: Brill.
Jamison, Carol Parrish (2004), "Traffic of Women in Germanic Literature: The Role of the Peace Pledge in Marital Exchanges," *Women in German Yearbook*, 20: 13–36.
Jansen, Katherine Ludwig (2018), *Peace and Penance in Late Medieval Italy*. Princeton: Princeton University Press.
Jaser, Christian (2013), *Ecclesia maledicens: Rituelle und zeremonielle Exkommunikationsformen im Mittelalter*, Tübingen: Mohr Siebeck.
Jenkins, D. (1986), *The Law of Hywel Dda*, Llandysul: Gomer Press.

Jestice, Phyllis (1997), *Wayward Monks and the Religious Revolution of the Eleventh Century*, Leiden: Brill.
Jochens, Jenny M. (1986), "The Medieval Icelandic Heroine: Fact or Fiction?" *Viator*, 17: 35–50.
John of Salisbury (1855), *Policraticus sive de nugiis curalium et vestigiis philosophorum*, in PL, vol. 199, 379–822D.
John of Worcester (1998), *The Chronicle of John of Worcester*, ed. P. McGurk, vol. 3, Oxford: Clarendon Press.
Jones, Philip (2010), "Communes and Despots: The City State in Late-Medieval Italy," in Bernadette Paton and John E. Law (eds), *Communes and Despots in Medieval and Renaissance Italy*, 3–24, Farnham: Ashgate.
Jouet, Roger (1969), *La résistance à l'occupation anglaise en Basse Normandie (1418–1450)*, Cahiers des Annales de Normandie, 5, Caen: Musée de Normandie.
Kaldor, M. (2013), "In Defence of New Wars," *Stability*, 2: 1–16.
Kantorowicz, Ernst ([1957] 1997), *The King's Two Bodies: A Study in Medieval Political Theology*, Princeton: Princeton University Press.
Karras, Ruth Mazo (2003), *From Boys to Men: Formation of Masculinity in Late Medieval Europe*, Philadelphia: University of Pennsylvania Press.
Katzenellebogen, Adolf ([1939] 1989), *Allegories of the Virtues and Vices in Medieval Art: From Early Christian Times to the Thirteenth Century*, Medieval Academy Reprints for Teaching, 24, Toronto: University of Toronto Press.
Kempshall, Matthew S. (2015), "The Utility of Peace in 'Monarchia'," in John C. Barnes and Daragh O'Connell (eds), *War and Peace in Dante: Essays Literary, Historical and Theological*, 141–72, Dublin: Four Courts Press.
Kennelly, Dolorosa (1962), "Medieval Towns and the Peace of God," *Medievalia et humanistica*, 15: 35–53.
Kershaw, Paul J.E. (2011), *Peaceful Kings: Peace, Power, and the Early Medieval Political Imagination*, Oxford: Oxford University Press.
Keynes, Simon (1990), "Royal government and the written word in late Anglo-Saxon England," in Rosamond McKitterick (ed.), *The Uses of Literacy in Early Mediaeval Europe*, 226–57, Cambridge: Cambridge University Press.
Kolb, Werner (1988), *Herrscherbegegnungen im Mittelalter*, Bern: P. Lang.
Kosto, Adam (1998), "The *Convenientia* in the Early Middle Ages," *Mediaeval Studies* 60(1): 1–54.
Kosto, Adam J. (2012), *Hostages in the Middle Ages*, Oxford: University Press.
Kosto, Adam J. (2002), "Hostages in the Carolingian World (714–840)," *Early Medieval Europe*, 11: 123–47.
Koziol, Geoffrey (1992), *Begging Pardon and Favor: Ritual and Political Order in Early Medieval France*, Ithaca, NY: Cornell University Press.
Koziol, Geoffrey (2012), *The Politics of Memory and Identity in Carolingian Royal Diplomas: The West Frankish Kingdom (840–987)*, Turnhout: Brepols.
Koziol, Geoffrey (2018), *The Peace of God*, Leeds: ARC Humanities Press.
Kühnel, Bianca (1987), *From the Earthly to the Heavenly Jerusalem: Representations of the Holy City in Christian Art of the First Millennium*, Rome: Herder.
Kumhera, Glenn (2017), *The Benefits of Peace: Private Peacemaking in Late Medieval Italy*, Leiden: Brill.
La Paix de Valenciennes de 1114 (1981), ed. Philippe Godding and Jacques Pycke, Louvain: Institut d'études médiévales.

Lalou, Elisabeth (1991), "Les questions militaires sous le règne de Philippe le Bel," in Philippe Contamine, Charles Giry-Deloison, and Maurice Keen (eds), *Guerre et société en France, en Angleterre et en Bourgogne, XIVe-XVe siècle*, 37–62, Villeneuve d'Ascq: Université Charles de Gaulle (Lille III), Centre d'Histoire de la Région du Nord et de l'Europe du Nord-Ouest.

Lambert of Ardres (1879), *Historia Comitum Ghisnensium*, ed. Johannes Heller in MGH Scriptores in folio, vol. 24, 550–642, Hanover: Hahn.

Lambert of Wattrelos (1859), *Annales Cameracenses*, ed. Georg Heinrich Pertz in MGH Scriptores in folio, vol. 16, 509–54, Hanover: Hahn.

Lansing, Carol (1991), *The Florentine Magnates: Lineage and Faction in a Medieval Commune*. Princeton: Princeton University Press.

Lantschner, Patrick (2015). *The Logic of Political Conflict in Medieval Cities: Italy and the Southern Low Countries, 1370–1440*, Oxford: Oxford University Press.

Larson, L.M. (1917), *The King's Mirror*, New York: Oxford University Press.

Laursen, John Christian, and Cary J. Nederman eds. (1998), *Beyond the Persecuting Society: Religious Toleration before the Enlightenment*, Philadelphia: University of Pennsylvania Press.

Lauwers, Michel (2013), "De l'incastellamento à l'inecclesiamento: Monachisme et logiques spatiales du féodalisme," in Dominique Iogna-Prat, Michel Lauwers, Florian Mazel and Isabelle Rosé (eds), *Cluny: Les moines et la société au premier âge féodal*, 315–38, Rennes: Presses universitaires de Rennes.

Le Baud, Pierre (1907–22), *Chronicques et Ystoires des Bretons*, ed. Charles de la Lande de Calan, Rennes: Société des Bibliophiles des Bretons.

Le Bel, Jean (1904–1905), *Chronique de Jean le Bel*, ed. Jules Viard and Eugène Déprez, Paris: Société de l'histoire de France, 2 vols.

Leclerq, Jean (1957), "Un document sur les débuts des Templiers," *Revue d'Histoire Ecclésiastique*, 52(1): 81–91.

Le Jan, Régine (1995), "Justice royale et pratiques sociales dans le royaume franc au IXe siècle," in *La Giustizia nell'alto medioevo (secoli IX–XI)*, vol. 1, 47–90, Settimane di studio del Centro italiano di studi sull'alto medioevo 44:1-2, Spoleto: Centro italiano di studi sull'alto medioevo.

Lerner, Robert (2004), "Medieval Millenarianism and Violence," in *Pace e guerra nel basso medioevo: Atti del XL Convegno storico internazionale, Todi, 12–14 ottobre 2003*, 37–52, Spoleto: Accademia Tudertina.

Lesaffer, Randall (2012), "Peace Treaties and the Formation of International Law," In B. Fassbender and A. Peters (eds), *Oxford Handbook of the History of International Law*, Oxford: Oxford University Press.

Lett, Didier (2012), "Genre et paix. Des mariages croisés entre quatre communes de la Marche d'Ancône en 1306," *Annales–Histoire, Sciences Sociales*, 67(3): 620–55.

The Letters of Abelard and Heloise (2003), trans. Betty Radice, rev. ed. M.T. Clanchy, London: Penguin.

Leyser, Conrad (2012), "Augustine in the Latin West, 430–ca. 900," in Mark Vessey (ed.), *A Companion to Augustine*, 450–64, Chichester: Wiley-Blackwell.

Leyser, Karl (1979), *Rule and Conflict in an Early Medieval Society: Ottonian Saxony*, Bloomington, IN: Indiana University Press.

Liebermann, Felix, ed. (1903–16), *Die Gesetze der Angelsachsen*, 3 vols, Halle: Max Niemeyer.

Lilley, Keith (2006), *City and Cosmos: The Medieval World in Urban Form*, London: Reaktion Books.

Limor, Ora, (2009), "Christians and Jews," in Rubin and Simons, *Christianity in Western Europe c. 1100–c. 1500*, 135–48.

Linklater, Andrew (2016), *Violence and Civilization in the Western States-Systems*, Cambridge: Cambridge University Press.
Little, Lester K. (1978), *Religious Poverty and the Profit Economy in Medieval Europe*. Ithaca, NY: Cornell University Press.
Little, Lester K. (1993), *Benedictine Maledictions: Liturgical Cursing in Romanesque France*, Ithaca, NY: Cornell University Press.
Liudprand of Cremona (2007), *The Complete Works*, ed. and trans. Paolo Squatriti, Washington, DC: Catholic University of America.
Lohier, F. and J. Laporte, eds. (1936), *Gesta sanctorum patrum Fontanellis coenobii*, Rouen: Lestringant.
LoPrete, Kimberly A. (2005), "Gendering Viragos: Medieval Perceptions of Powerful Women," in Christine Meek and Catherine Lawless (eds), *Studies on Medieval and Early Modern Women 4: Victims or Viragos*, 17–38, Dublin: Four Courts Press.
Lord, Carla (2002), "Queen Isabella at the Court of France," *Fourteenth Century England* 2: 45–52.
Loyn, H.R. (1984), *The Governance of Anglo-Saxon England*, Stanford, CT: Stanford University Press.
Lull, Ramon (2004), *The Book of the Order of Chivalry*, ed. Alfred T.P. Byles, London: Kegan Paul.
MacEvitt, Christopher (2008), *The Crusades and the Christian World of the East: Rough Tolerance*, Philadelphia: University of Pennsylvania Press.
MacMullen, Ramsay (2006), *Voting About God in Early Church Councils*, New Haven, CT: Yale University Press.
Magnou-Nortier, Élisabeth (1976), *Foi et fidélité: Recherches sur l'évolution des liens personnels chez les Francs du VIIe au IXe siècle*, Toulouse: Association des publications de l'Université de Toulouse-Le Mirail.
Magnou-Nortier, Élisabeth (1980), "Les mauvaises coutumes en Auvergne, Bourgogne méridionale, Languedoc et Provence au XIe siècle: un moyen d'analyse sociale," in *Structures féodales et féodalisme dans l'Occident méditerranéen (X^e–XIIIe siècles): Bilan et perspectives de recherches*, 135–72, Collection de l'École française de Rome, 44, Rome: École française de Rome.
Magnou-Nortier, Élisabeth (1992), "The Enemies of the Peace: Reflections on a Vocabulary, 500–1100," in Head and Landes (eds), *The Peace of God*, 58–79.
Maier, Christoph T. (2004), "The Roles of Women in the Crusade Movement: A Survey," *Journal of Medieval History*, 30(1): 61–82.
Malegam, Jehangir Y. (2008), "No Peace for the Wicked: Conflicting Visions of Peacemaking in an Eleventh-Century Monastic Narrative," *Viator*, 39(2): 23–49.
Malegam, Jehangir Y. (2011), "Love between Peace and Violence: Not a Crisis but a Critique of Fidelity after 1000," *Quaestiones medii aevi novae*, 16: 321–36.
Malegam, Jehangir Y. (2013), *The Sleep of Behemoth: Disputing Peace and Violence in Medieval Europe, 1000–1200*, Ithaca: Cornell University Press.
Mansi, J.D. et al. eds. (1759–98), *Sacrorum conciliorum nova amplissima collectio*, 31 vols., Florence and Venice: Antonii Zatta (Available at: www.documentacatholicaomnia.eu).
Márkus, Gilbert, trans. (2008), *Cáin Adomnán: A Seventh-Century Law for the Protection of Non-Combatants*, Kilmartin, Ireland: Kilmartin House Museum.
Marsilius of Padua (1928), *Defensor Pacis*, ed. C.W. Previté-Orton, Cambridge: Cambridge University Press.
Mastnak, Tomaž (2002), *Crusading Peace: Christendom, the Muslim World, and Western Political Order*, Berkeley, CA: University of California Press.

Mazeika, Rasa J. (1998), "'Nowhere Was the Fragility of Their Sex Apparent': Women Warriors in the Baltic Crusade Chronicles," in Alan V. Murray (ed.), *From Clermont to Jerusalem: The Crusades and Crusader Societies, 1095–1500*, 229–48, Turnhout: Brepols.

Mazel, Florian (2007), "Des familles de l'aristocratie locale en leurs territoires: France de l'Ouest, du IXe au XIe siècle," in Philippe Depreux, François Bougard and Régine Le Jan (eds), *Les élites et leurs espaces: Mobilité, rayonnement, domination (du VIe au XIe siècle)*, 361–98, Turnhout: Brepols.

Mazel, Florian (2008), *La noblesse et l'Église en Provence, fin X{e} –début XIVe siècle: L'exemple des familles d'Agoult-Simiane, de Baux et de Marseille*, Paris: CMTH.

Mazel, Florian (2016), *L'évêque et le territoire: L'invention médiévale de l'espace*, Paris: Seuil.

McAlpine, Monica A. (1997), "The Burghers of Calais: Chapters in a History," in Thomas Hahn and Alan Lupack (eds), *Retelling Tales: Essays in Honor of Russell Peck*, 231–58, Woodbridge: D.S. Brewer.

McAuliffe, Mary (1996), "The Lady in the Tower: The Social and Political Role of Women in Tower Houses," in C.E. Meek and M.K. Simms (eds), *"The Fragiligy of Her Sex"?: Medieval Irish Women in Their European Context*, 153–62, Portland, OR: Four Courts Press.

McGinn, Bernard, ed. (1979). *Apocalyptic Spirituality: Treatises and Letters of Lactantius, Adso of Montier-en-Der, Joachim of Fiore, the Franciscan Spirituals, Savonarola*, Mahwah, NJ: Paulist Press.

McKitterick, Rosamond (2008), *Charlemagne: The Formation of a European Identity*, Cambridge: Cambridge University Press.

McLaughlin, Megan (1990), "The Woman Warrior: Gender, Warfare and Society in Medieval Europe," *Women's Studies*, 17: 193–209.

McMillin, Linda A. (1989), "Women on the Walls: Women and Warfare in the Catalan Grand Chronicles," *Catalan Review: International Journal of Catalan Culture*, 3 (July): 123–36.

McRee, Ben R. (1994), "Peacemaking and Its Limit in Late Medieval Norwich," *The English Historical Review* 109(433): 831–66.

Meens, Rob (2014), *Penance in Medieval Europe, 600–1200*, Cambridge: Cambridge University Press.

Meersseman, G. G. (1962), "Disciplinati e penitenti nel duecento," in *Il movimento dei disciplinati nel vii centenario dal suo inizio*, 43–72, Perugia: Deputazione di storia patria per l'Umbria.

Méhu, Didier (2001), *Paix et communautés autour de l'abbaye de Cluny, X{e}-XVe siècle*, Lyon: Presses universitaires de Lyon.

Michetti, Raimondo (2005), "François d'Assise et la paix révélée. Réflexions sur le mythe du pacifisme franciscain et sur la prédication de paix dans la société communale du XIIIe siècle," in Rosa Maria Dessì (ed.), *Prêcher la paix et discipliner la société*, 279–312, Turnhout: Brepols.

Mienert, John (2016), "*Alimentum Pacis*: The Eucharist and Peace in St. Thomas Aquinas," *Nova et Vetera* (English Edition): 14(4): 1193–1212.

Mierow, C.C. (1994), *The Deeds of Frederick Barbarossa*, Toronto: University of Toronto Press.

Miller, William Ian (1990), *Bloodtaking and Peacemaking: Feud, Law, and Society in Saga Iceland*, Chicago, IL: University of Chicago Press.

Minstrel of Reims (1876), *Récits d'un ménestrel de Reims au treizième siècle*, ed. Natalis de Wailly, Paris: Librairie Renouard.

Miracula sancti Benedicti (1858), ed. E. de Certain, Paris: Jules Renouard.

Mixson, James D. and Bert Roest, eds. (2015), *A Companion to Observant Reform in the Late Middle Ages and Beyond*. Leiden: Brill.

Montemaggi, Vittorio (2015). "'E'n la sua volontade è nostra pace': Peace, Justice and the Trinity in the *Commedia*," in John C. Barnes and Daragh O'Connell (eds), *War and Peace in Dante: Essays Literary, Historical and Theological*, 195–225, Dublin: Four Courts Press.

Moore, Michael Edward (2011), *A Sacred Kingdom: Bishops and the Rise of Frankish Kingship, 300–850*, Washington, DC: The Catholic University of America Press.

Moore, Robert I. ([1987] 2007), *The Formation of a Persecuting Society: Power and Deviance in Western Europe, 950–1250*, 2nd edn, Oxford: Blackwell.

Moore, Robert I (2016), "The Weight of Opinion: Religion and the People of Europe from the Tenth to the Twelfth Century," in Kate Cooper and Conrad Leyser (eds), *Making Early Medieval Societies: Conflict and Belonging in the Latin West, 300–1200*, 202–19, Cambridge: Cambridge University Press.

Moravsik, G. and Jenkins, R.J.H., eds. (1962), *De Administrando Imperio*, vol. 1, London: Athlone Press.

Mordek, Hubert, et al., eds. (2012), *Die Admonitio generalis Karls des Großen*, MGH, Fontes Iuris Germanici Antiqui in usum scholarum separatim editi, 16, Hanover: Hahn.

Morgan, P.M. (2012), "The State of Deterrence in International Politics Today," *Contemporary Security Policy*, 33: 85–107.

Morice, Dom Pierre-Hyacinthe (1744), *Mémoires pour servir de preuves à l'Histoire ecclésiastique et civile de Bretagne*, vol. 2, Paris: Charles Osmont.

Mormando, Franco (1999a), "'Just as your lips approach the lips of your brothers': Judas Iscariot and the Kiss of Betrayal," in Franco Mormando (ed.), *Saints and Sinners: Caravaggio and the Baroque Image*, 179–90, Chestnut Hill, MA: McMullen Museum of Art, Boston College.

Mormando, Franco (1999b), *The Preacher's Demons: Bernardino of Siena and the Social Underworld of Early Renaissance Italy*, Chicago IL: University of Chicago Press.

Morrison, Karl F. (1964), *The Two Kingdoms: Ecclesiology in Carolingian Political Thought*, Princeton: Princeton University Press.

Muchembled, Robert ([2008] 2012), *A History of Violence: From the End of the Middle Ages to the Present*, trans. Jean Birrell, Cambridge: Polity Press.

Muessig, Carolyn, George Ferzoco and Beverly Kienzle (eds) (2011), *A Companion to Catherine of Siena*, Brill's Companions to the Christian Tradition, 32, Leiden: Brill.

Mulder-Bakker, Anneke B. (2003), "Jeanne of Valois: The Power of a Consort," in Kathleen Nolan (ed.), *Capetian Women*, 253–69, Basingstoke: Palgrave Macmillan.

Muldoon, James (1979), *Popes, Lawyers, and Infidels: The Church and the Non-Christian World 1250–1550*, Philadelphia: University of Pennsylvania Press.

Muldoon, James (2001), "Tolerance and Intolerance in the Medieval Canon Lawyers," in Michael Gervers and James M. Powell (eds), *Tolerance and Intolerance: Social Conflict in the Ages of the Crusades*, 117–23, Syracuse, NY: Syracuse University Press.

Murata, Sachiko, and William C. Chittick (1994), *The Vision of Islam*, St. Paul, MN: Paragon House.

Murray, Alexander Callander (1988), "From Roman to Frankish Gaul: 'Centenarii' and 'Centenae' in the Administration of the Merovingian Kingdom," *Traditio*, 44: 59–100.

Musto, Ronald G. (2003), *Apocalypse in Rome: Cola di Rienzo and the Politics of the New Age*. Berkeley CA: University of California Press.

Muzzarelli, Maria Giuseppina. "Pawn Broking between Theory and Practice in Observant Socio-Economic Thought," in James D. Mixson and Bert Roest (eds), *A Companion to Observant Reform in the Late Middle Ages and Beyond*, 204–29, Leiden: Brill.

Najemy, John M. (2000), "Civic Humanism and Florentine Politics," in James Hankins (ed.), *Renaissance Civic Humanism: Reappraisals and Reflections*, 75–104, Cambridge: Cambridge University Press.

Najemy, John M. (2006), *A History of Florence, 1200–1575*, Malden, MA: Blackwell.

Nederman, Cary J. (2000), *Worlds of Difference: European Discourses of Toleration, c. 1100–1550*, University Park, PA: Penn State University Press.

Nederman, Cary J. (2013), "Toleration in Medieval Europe: Theoretical Principles and Historical Lessons," in James Muldoon (ed.), *Bridging the Medieval-Modern Divide: Medieval Themes in the World of the Reformation*, 45–64, Farnham: Ashgate.

Nelson, Janet L. (1987), "The Lord's Anointed and the People's Choice: Carolingian Royal Ritual," in David Cannadine and Simon Price (eds), *Rituals of Royalty*, 137–80, Cambridge: Cambridge University Press.

Nelson, Janet L. trans. (1991), *The Annals of St.-Bertin*, Manchester: Manchester University Press.

Nelson, Janet L. (1992), *Charles the Bald*, London: Longman.

Newman, Barbara (2003), *God and the Goddesses: Vision, Poetry, and Belief in the Middle Ages*, Philadelphia: University of Pennsylvania Press.

Nicholas, David (2003), *Urban Europe, 1100–1700*, Basingstoke and New York: Palgrave Macmillan.

Nicholson, Helen J. trans. (2005), *Chronicle of the Third Crusade: A Translation of the Itinerarium Peregrinorum et Gesta Regis Ricardi*, Aldershot: Ashgate.

Nicholson, Helen J. (2015), "Women's Involvement in the Crusades," in Adrian Boas (ed.), *The Crusader World*, 54–67, New York: Routledge.

Nightingale, John (2001), *Monasteries and Patrons in the Gorze Reform: Lotharingia, c. 850–1000*, Oxford: Oxford University Press.

Nirenberg, David (1996), *Communities of Violence: Persecution of Minorities in the Middle Ages*, Princeton: Princeton University Press.

Nirenberg, David (2009), "Christendom and Islam," in Rubin and Simons, *Christianity in Western Europe c. 1100–c. 1500*, 149–69.

Nithard's Histories (1972), trans. B.W. Scholz, in *Carolingian Chronicles*, Ann Arbor, MN: University of Michigan Press.

Norwich, J.J. (1967), *The Normans in the South 1016–1130*, London: Longman.

Nugent, S. Georgia (2000), "*Virtus* or *Virago*? The Female Personifications of Prudentius's *Psychomachia*," in Colum Hourihane (ed.), *Virtue & Vice. The Personifications in the Index of Christian Art*, 13–28, Princeton: Index of Christian Art and Princeton University Press.

Oexle, Otto Gerhard (1985), "Conjuratio und Gilde im frühen Mittelalter: Ein Beitrag zum Problem der sozialgeschichtlichen Kontinuität zwischen Antike und Mittelalter," in Berent Schwineköper (ed.), *Gilden und Zünfte: Kaufmännische und gewerbliche Genossenschaften im frühen und hohen Mittelalter*, 151–214, Vorträge und Forschungen 29, Sigmaringen: J. Thorbecke.

Oexle, Otto G. (2001), "Peace through Conspiracy," in Bernhard Jussen (ed.), *Ordering Medieval Society: Perspectives on Intellectual and Practical Modes of Shaping Social Relations*, 285–322, Philadelphia: University of Pennsylvania Press.

Offenstadt, Nicolas (2001), "Les femmes et la paix à la fin du moyen âge: genre, discours, rites," in *Le règlement des conflits au Moyen Âge. Actes du XXXIe Congrès de la SHMESP (Angers, 2000)*, 317–33, Paris: Publications de la Sorbonne.

Offenstadt, Nicolas (2002), "Paix de Dieu et paix des hommes. L'action politique à la fin du Moyen Age," *Politix*, 15(58): 61–81.

Offenstadt, Nicolas (2007), *Faire la paix au Moyen Âge: Discours et gestes de paix pendant la guerre de Cent Ans*, Paris: Odile Jacob.

O'Loughlin, Thomas, ed. (2001), *Adomnán at Birr, A.D. 697: Essays in the Commemoration of the Law of the Innocents*, Dublin: Four Courts Press.

Orderic Vitalis (1969–80), *The Ecclesiastical History of Orderic Vitalis*, ed. and trans. Marjorie M. Chibnall, Oxford: Clarendon Press, 6 vols.

Ordinatio imperii (1883), ed. A. Boretius in *Capitularia regum Francorum*, vol. 1, 270–73, Hanover: Hahn.

Otto of Freising (1912), *Chronica sive historia de duabus civitatibus*, ed. A. Hofmeister, MGH, Scriptores in Rerum Germanicarum in usum scholarum separatim editi, 45, Hanover: Hahn.

Otto of Freising and Rahewin ([1912] 1978), *Gesta Friderici I Imperatoris*, (ed.) G. Waitz and B. von Simson, MGH, Scriptores in Rerum Germanicarum in usum scholarum separatim editi, 46, Hanover: Hahn.

Palmer, James A. (2014), "Piety and Social Distinction in Late Medieval Roman Peacemaking," *Speculum* 89(4): 974–1004.

Palmer, James A. (2019), *The Virtues of Economy: Governance, Power, and Piety in Late Medieval Rome*, Ithaca: Cornell University Press.

Parker, Geoffrey, ed. (2008), *The Cambridge Illustrated History of Warfare: The Triumph of the West*, rev. ed. Cambridge: Cambridge University Press.

Parsons, John Carmi (1995), "The Queen's Intercession in Thirteenth-Century England," in Jennifer Carpenter and Sally-Beth MacLean (eds), *Power of the Weak: Studies on Medieval Women*, 147–77, Urbana, IL: University of Illinois Press.

Paton, Bernadette (1992), *Preaching Friars and the Civic Ethos: Siena, 1380–1480*, London: Centre for Medieval Studies, Queen Mary and Westfield College, University of London.

Patzold, Steffen (2008), *Episcopus: Wissen über Bischöfe im Frankenreich des späten 8. bis frühen 10. Jahrhunders*, Ostfildern: Thorbecke.

Paul of Bernried (1862), *Vita Gregorii papae*, ed. J.M. Watterich, *Pontificum Romanorum vitae*, 474–545, Leipzig: Engelmann.

Pelikan, Jaroslav (1993), *Christianity and Classical Culture: The Metamorphosis of Natural Theology in the Christian Encounter with Hellenism*. New Haven: Yale University Press.

Perella, Nicolas James (1969), *The Kiss Sacred and Profane: An Interpretative History of Kiss Symbolism and Related Religio-Erotic Themes*. Berkeley, CA: University of California Press.

Petit-Dutaillis, Charles ([1947] 1970), *Les communes françaises: Caractéres et évolution des origines au XVIIIe siécle*, Paris: Albin Michel.

Petkov, Kiril (2003), *The Kiss of Peace: Ritual, Self and Society in the High and Late Medieval West*, Leiden: Brill.

Phillips, L. Edward (1996), *The Ritual Kiss in Early Christian Worship*, Cambridge: Grove Books.

Pinker, Steven (2011), *The Better Angels of Our Nature: Why Violence Has Declined*, New York: Viking Penguin.

Pizan, Christine de (1989), *A Medieval Woman's Mirror of Honor: The Treasury of the City of Ladies*, trans. Charity Cannon Willard, New York: Persea Books.

Pizan, Christine de (1998), *The Book of the City of Ladies*, trans. Earl Jeffrey Richards, rev. ed., New York: Persea Books.

Poeta Saxo (1890), *Annalium de gestis Caroli magni imperatoris libri quinque*, ed. Paul von Winterfeld, MGH, Poetae Latini Aevi Carolini, IV, 1, Berlin: Weidmann.

Polecritti, Cynthia (2000), *Preaching Peace in Renaissance Italy: Bernardino of Siena and his Audience*, Washington, DC: Catholic University of America Press.

Powell, James M. (1992), *Albertanus of Brescia: The Pursuit of Happiness in the Early Thirteenth Century*, Philadelphia: University of Pennsylvania Press.

Powell, James M. (2007), "Saint Francis of Assisi's Way of Peace," *Medieval Encounters*, 13: 271–80.

Powell, James M. (2008), "Mendicants, the Communes, and the Law," *Church History* 77(3): 557–73.

Power, D.J. (2001), "L'aristocratie Plantagenêt face aux conflits capétiens-angevins: l'example du traité de Louviers," in M. Aurell (ed.), *Noblesses de l'espace Plantagenêt (1154–1224)*, 121–39, Poitiers: Centre d'études supérieures de civilisation médiévale.

Prester John: The Legend and Its Sources (2015), ed. and trans. Keagan Brewer, Farnham: Ashgate.

Prestwich, Michael (1999), *Armies and Warfare in the Middle Ages: The English Experience*, New Haven: Yale University Press.

Prevenier, Walter (2010), "The Two Faces of Pardon Jurisdiction in the Burgundian Netherlands: A Royal Road to Social Cohesion and an Effectual Instrument of Princely Clientelism," in Peter Hoppenbrouwers, Antheun Janse and Robert Stein (eds), *Power and Persuasion: Essays in the Art of State Building in Honor of W.P. Blockmans*, 177–95, Turnhout: Brepols.

Prudentius (1966), *Psychomachia*, ed. M.P. Cunningham, Corpus Christianorum Continuatio Mediaeualis, 126, Turnhout: Brepols.

Pryce, Huw (2005), *The Acts of Welsh Rulers 1120–1283*, Cardiff: University of Wales Press.

Raccagni, Gianluca (2010), *The Lombard League, 1167–1225*, Oxford: Oxford University Press.

Rapp, Claudia (2005), *Holy Bishops in Late Antiquity: The Nature of Christian Leadership in an Age of Transition*, Berkeley: University of California Press.

Ralph of Diceto (1876), *Radulfi de Diceto decani Lundoniensis opera historica. The Historical Works of Master Ralph de Diceto, Dean of London*, ed. William Stubbs, Rerum britannicarum medii ævi scriptores, vol. 68, London: Longman.

Reimitz, Helmut (2015), *History, Frankish Identity and the Framing of Western Ethnicity, 550–850*, Cambridge: Cambridge University Press.

Reichberg, Gregory M. (2003), "Philosophy Meets War: Francisco de Vitoria's *De Indis* and *De jure belli relectiones* (1557)," in J. Gracia, G. Reichberg, and B. Schumacher (eds), *The Classics of Western Philosophy*, Oxford: Blackwell, 197–204.

Reichberg, Gregory M. (2011), "Aquinas' Moral Typology of Peace and War," *The Review of Metaphysics*, 64(3): 467–87.

Reichberg, Gregory M. (2017), *Thomas Aquinas on War and Peace*, Cambridge: Cambridge University Press.

Reichberg, Gregory M., and Henrik Syse, eds. (2014), *Religion, War, and Ethics: A Sourcebook of Textual Traditions*, Cambridge: Cambridge University Press.

Reichberg, Gregory M., Henrik Syse, and Endre Begby, eds. (2006), *The Ethics of War: Classic and Contemporary Readings*, Maldon, MA: Blackwell.

Remensnyder, Amy G. (1992), "Pollution, Purity, and Peace: An Aspect of Social Reform between the Late Tenth Century and 1076," in Head and Landes (eds), *The Peace of God*, 280–307.

Renna, Thomas (1979), "The Idea of Peace in the Augustinian Tradition, 400–1200," *Augustinian Studies*, 10: 105–11.

Reuter, Timothy transl. (1992), *The Annals of Fulda*, Manchester: Manchester University Press.

Reuter Timothy ([1991] 2006), "Peace-Breaking, Feud, Rebellion, Resistance: Violence and Peace in the Politics of the Salian Era," in *Medieval Polities and Modern Mentalities*, ed. and trans. Janet L. Nelson, 355–87, Cambridge: Cambridge University Press.

Roach, Levi (2012), "Penance, Submission and Deditio: Religious Influences on Dispute Settlement in Later Anglo-Saxon England (871–1066)," *Anglo-Saxon England*, 41: 343–71.

Robert the Monk (2006), *Robert the Monk's History of the First Crusade: Historia Iherosolimitana*, trans. Carol Sweetenham, Aldershot: Ashgate.

Robert of Torigni (1884), *The Chronicle of Robert of Torigni*, ed. Richard Howlett, *Chronicles of the Reigns of Stephen, Henry II, and Richard I*, 4, London: Longman.

Robinson, I.S. (1978), *Authority and Resistance in the Investiture Contest: The Polemical Literature of the Late Eleventh Century*, Manchester: Manchester University Press.

Rodulfus Glaber, *Opera* (1989), ed. and trans. John France, Neithard Bulst and Paul Reynolds, Oxford: Clarendon Press.

Rosenwein, Barbara H. (1999), *Negotiating Space: Power, Restraint, and Privileges of Immunity in Early Medieval Europe*, Ithaca, NY: Cornell University Press.

Rosenwein, Barbara H. (2006), *Emotional Communities in the Early Middle Ages*, Ithaca, NY: Cornell University Press.

Rosenwein, Barbara H. (2016), *Generations of Feeling: A History of Emotions, 600–1700*, Cambridge: Cambridge University Press.

Rothwell, Harry, ed. (1996), *English Historical Documents, Volume 3: 1189–1327*, London: Routledge.

Rousseaux, Xavier (2007), "Politiques judiciaires et resolution des conflits dans les villes de l'Occident à la fin du Moyen Âge," in Jacques Chiffoleau *et al.* (eds), *Pratiques sociales et politiques judiciaires dans les villes du Moyen Âge*, 497–526, Rome: École française de Rome.

Rubin, Miri (1991), *Corpus Christi: The Eucharist in Late Medieval Culture*, Cambridge: Cambridge University Press.

Rubin, Miri, and Walter Simons, eds. (2009), *Christianity in Western Europe c. 1100–c. 1500*, The Cambridge History of Christianity, 4, Cambridge: Cambridge University Press.

Rufinus of Sorrento (1997), *De bono pacis*, ed. Roman Deutinger, MGH, Studien und Texte, 17, Hanover: Hahn.

Rupert von Deutz (1999), *Liber de Divinis Officiis. Der Gottesdienst der Kirche*, ed. and trans. Helmut and Ilse Deutz, Fontes Christiani 33, Freiburg: Herder, 4 vols.

Russell, F.H. (1975), *The Just War in the Middle Ages*, Cambridge: Cambridge University Press.

Sachsenspiegel: Landrecht (1955), ed. K.A. Eckhardt, 2nd edn, MGH, Fontes iuris Germanici, n.s 1.1, Göttingen: Musterschmidt-Verlag.

Sagi, Avi (1994), "The Punishment of Amalek in Jewish Tradition: Coping with the Moral Problem," *Harvard Theological Review*, 87(3): 323–46.

Sbriccoli, Mario (1997), "Legislation, Justice, and Political Power in Italian Cities, 1200–1400," in Antonio Padoa Schioppa (ed.), *Legislation and Justice*, 37–55, Oxford: Clarendon Press.

Sbriccoli, Mario (1998), "'Vidi communiter observari': L'emersione di un ordine penale pubblico nelle città italiane del secolo XIII," *Quaderni fiorentini per la storia del pensiero giuridico moderno* 27: 231–68.

Schmid, Karl (1984), "Unerforschte Quellen aus quellenarmer Zeit: Zur *amicitia* zwischen Heinrich I. und dem westfränkischen König Robert im Jahr 923," *Francia*, 12: 119–47.

Schmid, Karl and Otto Gerhard Oexle (1974), "Voraussetzungen und Wirkung des Gebetsbundes von Attigny," *Francia*, 2: 71–122.

Schmitt, Jean-Claude (2010), *The Conversion of Herman the Jew: Autobiography, History, and Fiction in the Twelfth Century*, Philadelphia: University of Pennsylvania Press.

Schneider, Reinhard (1964), *Brüdergemeine und Schwurfreundschaft: Der Auflösungsprozeß des Karlingerreiches im Spiegel der Caritas-Terminologie in den Verträgen der karlingischen Teilkönige des 9. Jahrhunderts*, Lübeck: Matthiesen.

Schwartz, Daniel (2007), *Aquinas on Friendship*, Oxford: Oxford University Press.

Seabourne, Gwen (2011), *Imprisoning Medieval Women: The Non-Judicial Confinement and Abduction of Women in England, c. 1170–1509*, Burlington: Ashgate.

Shogimen, Takashi (2010), "European Ideas of Peace in the Late Thirteenth and Early Fourteenth Centuries," *The European Legacy*, 15(7): 871–85.

Siberry, Elizabeth (1985), *Criticism of Crusading, 1095–1274*, Oxford: Clarendon Press.

Sigebert of Gembloux (1892), *Epistola Leodicensium adversus Paschalem Papam*, ed. E. Sackur, in MGH, Libelle de Lite, vol. 2, 449–64, Hanover: Hahn.

Skinner, Quentin (1986), "Ambrogio Lorenzetti: The Artist as Political Philosopher," *Proceedings of the British Academy*, 72: 1–56.

Skinner, Quentin (1999), "Ambrogio Lorenzetti's *Buon Governo* Frescoes: Two Old Questions, Two New Answers," *Journal of the Warburg and Courtauld Institutes* 62 (1999): 1–28.

Smail, Daniel L. (2001), "Hatred as a Social Institution in Late Medieval Society," *Speculum*, 76, 1: 90–126.

Spierenburg, Pieter (1991), *The Broken Spell: A Cultural and Anthropological History of Preindustrial Europe*, New Brunswick, NJ: Rutgers University Press.

Stephen of Tournai (1893), *Lettres d'Étienne de Tournai (Epistolae)*, ed. Jules Desilve. Valenciennes: Lemaître; Paris: Alphonse Picard.

Stevenson, J., ed. (1875), *Radulphi de Coggeshall Chronicon Anglicanum*, London: Longman.

Stones, E.L.G. (1965), *Anglo-Scottish Relations 1174–1328: Some Selected Documents*, London: Nelson.

Strayer, Joseph R. (1970), *On the Medieval Origins of the Modern State*, Princeton: Princeton University Press.

Strefling, Sérgio Ricardo (2010), "A concepção de paz na *civitas* de Marsilio de Pádua," *Acta Scientiarum. Education*, 32(2): 153–61.

Strohm, Paul (1992), "Queens as Intercessors," in Paul Strohm, *Hochon's Arrow: The Social Imagination of Fourteenth-Century Texts*, 95–119, Princeton: Princeton University Press.

Stubbs, William, ed. (1921), *Select Charters and other Illustrations of English Constitutional History from the Earliest Times to the Reign of Edward I*, rev. ed. Henry William Carless Davis, Oxford: Clarendon Press.

Thatcher O.J. and McNeal, E.H. eds. (1905), *A Source Book for Mediaeval History. Selected Documents Illustrating the History of Europe in the Middle Age*, New York: Charles Scribner's Sons.

The Theodosian Code and Novels and the Sirmondian Constitutions (1952), trans. Clyde Pharr, Princeton: Princeton University Press.

Thesaurus Linguae Latinae (TLL) Online (2006), Berlin: De Gruyter.

Thomas Aquinas (1895), *Summa theologiae*, in *Sancti Thomae Aquinatis Doctoris Angelici Opera Omnia iussu impensaque Leonis XIII* [Leonine edition], vols 4–12, Rome: Editori di San Tommaso. [English translation: Fathers of the English Dominican Province, *Summa Theologica*, Westminster, MD: Christian Classics, 1981.]

Thomas Aquinas (1950), *In librum Beati Dionysii De divinis nominibus expositio*, Rome: Marietti.

Thomas Aquinas (1953a), *Super Epistolam ad Romanos lectura*, in *Super Epistolas S. Pauli lectura*, vol. 1, 1–230, Rome: Marietti. [English translation: F.R. Larcher, *Commentary on* the Letter of Saint Paul to the Romans, in *Latin/English Edition of the Works of St. Thomas Aquinas*, vol. 37, Lander, WY: The Aquinas Institute for the Study of Sacred Doctrine, 2012.

Thomas Aquinas (1953b), *Super Epistolam ad Philippenses lectura*, in *Super Epistolas S. Pauli lectura*, vol. 2, 89–123, Rome: Marietti. [English translation: F.R. Larcher, *Commentary on the Letters of Saint Paul to the Philippians, Colossians, Thessalonians, Timothy, Titus, and Philemon*, in *Latin/English Edition of the Works of St. Thomas Aquinas*, vol. 40, Lander, WY: The Aquinas Institute for the Study of Sacred Doctrine, 2012.]

Thomas Aquinas (1953c), *Super secundum Epistolam ad Thessalonicenses lectura*, in *Super Epistolas S. Pauli lectura*, vol. 2, 291–99, Rome: Marietti. [English translation: *Commentary on the Letters of Saint Paul to the Philippians, Colossians, Thessalonians, Timothy, Titus, and Philemon*, in *Latin/English Edition of the Works of St. Thomas Aquinas*, vol. 40, Lander, WY: The Aquinas Institute for the Study of Sacred Doctrine, 2012.]

Thomas Aquinas (1953d), *Super primam Epistolam ad Timotheum lectura*, in *Super Epistolas S. Pauli lectura*, vol. 2, 301–26, Rome: Marietti. [English translation: F.R. Larcher, *Commentary on the Letters of Saint Paul to the Philippians, Colossians, Thessalonians, Timothy, Titus, and Philemon*, in *Latin/English Edition of the Works of St. Thomas Aquinas*, vol. 40, Lander, WY: The Aquinas Institute for the Study of Sacred Doctrine, 2012.]

Thomas Aquinas (1965), *Expositio super Iob ad litteram*, in *Sancti Thomae Aquinatis Doctoris Angelici Opera Omnia iussu impensaque Leonis XIII* [Leonine edition], vol. 26, Rome: Ad Sanctae Sabinae. [English translation: Martin D. Jaffe and Anthony Damico, *The Literal Exposition on Job*, Atlanta GA: Scholars' Press, 1989.]

Thomas Aquinas (1969), *Sententia libri Ethicorum*, in *Sancti Thomae Aquinatis Doctoris Angelici Opera Omnia iussu impensaque Leonis XIII* [Leonine edition], vol. 22, Rome: Ad Sanctae Sabinae. [English translation: C.I. Litzinger, *Commentary on Aristotle's Nicomachean Ethics*, Notre Dame, IN: Dumb Ox Books, 1993.]

Thomas Aquinas (1972), *Super Evangelium S. Ioannis lectura*, 6th edn, Rome: Marietti.

Thomas Aquinas (1974), *Expositio super Isaiam ad litteram*, in *Sancti Thomae Aquinatis Doctoris Angelici Opera Omnia iussu impensaque Leonis XIII* [Leonine edition], vol 28. Romae, Ad Sanctae Sabinae.

Thomas Aquinas (1970–76), *Quaestiones disputatae de veritate*, in *Sancti Thomae Aquinatis Doctoris Angelici Opera Omnia iussu impensaque Leonis XIII* [Leonine edition], vol. 22, Rome: Editori di San Tommaso. [English translation: Robert W. Mulligan, *Truth*, Indianapolis: Hackett, 1994.]

Thomas Aquinas (1979a), *Compendium theologiae*, in *Sancti Thomae Aquinatis Doctoris Angelici Opera Omnia iussu impensaque Leonis XIII* [Leonine edition], vol. 42, 75–191, Rome: Editori di San Tommaso. [English translation: Richard J. Regan, *Compendium of Theology*, Oxford: Oxford University Press, 2009.]

Thomas Aquinas (1979b), *De regno ad Regem Cypri*, in *Sancti Thomae Aquinatis Doctoris Angelici Opera Omnia iussu impensaque Leonis XIII* [Leonine edition], vol. 42, 417–71, Rome: Editori di San Tommaso. [English translation: Gerald B. Phelan, *On the Governance of Rulers*, New York: Sheed & Ward, 1938.]

Thomas Aquinas (1996), *Quaestiones de quolibet*, in *Sancti Thomae Aquinatis Doctoris Angelici Opera Omnia iussu impensaque Leonis XIII* [Leonine edition], vol. 25, Rome: Commissio Leonina–Paris: Cerf.

Thompson, Augustine (1992), *Revival Preachers and Politics in Thirteenth-century Italy: The Great Devotion of 1233*, Oxford: Clarendon Press.

Thompson, Augustine (2005), *Cities of God: The Religion of the Italian Communes, 1125–1325*, University Park, PA: Pennsylvania State University Press.

Tolan, John V. (2009), *Saint Francis and the Sultan: The Curious History of a Christian-Muslim Encounter*, Oxford: Oxford University Press.

Truax, Jean A. (1999), "Anglo-Norman Women at War: Valiant Soldiers, Prudent Strategists or Charismatic Leaders?," in Donald J. Kagay and L.J. Andrew Villalon (eds), *The Circle of War in the Middle Ages: Essays on Medieval Military and Naval History*, 111–25, Woodbridge: Boydell Press.

The Travels of Sir John Mandeville (2005), transl. C.W.R.D. Moseley, rev. ed. London: Penguin.

Turner, Ralph V. (2009), *Eleanor of Aquitaine: Queen of France, Queen of England*, New Haven: Yale University Press.

Ullmann, Walter (1976), "The Medieval Papal Court as an International Tribunal," in Walter Ullman, *The Papacy and Political Ideas in the Middle Ages*, London: Variorum Reprints.

Vallerani, Massimo (2005), "Mouvement de paix dans une commune de popolo: les flagellants à Perouse en 1260," in Rosa Maria Dessì (ed.), *Prêcher la paix et discipliner la société: Italie, France, Angleterre (XIIIe-XVe siècle)*, 313–55, Turnhout: Brepols.

Vallerani, Massimo (2012), *Medieval Public Justice*, transl. Sarah Rubin Blanshei, Washington, DC: Catholic University of America Press.

Van Caenegem, Raoul C. (1954), *Geschiedenis van het strafrecht in Vlaanderen van de XIde tot de XIVde eeuw*, Verhandelingen van de Koninklijke Vlaamse Academie voor Wetenschappen, Letteren en Schone Kunsten van België, Klasse der Letteren, XVI, nr. 19, Brussels: Paleis der Academiën.

Van Caenegem, Raoul C. (1956), *Geschiedenis van het strafprocesrecht in Vlaanderen van de XIe tot de XIVe eeuw*, Verhandelingen van de Koninklijke Vlaamse Academie voor Wetenschappen, Letteren en Schone Kunsten van België, Klasse der Letteren, nr. 24, Brussels: Paleis der Academiën.

Vanderputten, Steven (2015), *Imagining Religious Leadership in the Middle Ages: Richard of Saint-Vanne and the Politics of Reform*, Ithaca, NY: Cornell University Press.

Van Engen, John (1983), *Rupert of Deutz*, Berkeley and Los Angeles: University of California Press.

Van Houts, Elisabeth M.C. (1999), "The Anglo-Flemish Treaty of 1101," *Anglo-Norman Studies*, 21: 169–74.

Van Houts, Elisabeth M.C., ed. and trans. (1995), *The Gesta Normannorum Ducum of William of Jumièges, Orderic Vitalis and Robert of Torigni*, vol. 2, Oxford, UK: Oxford University Press.

Vauchez, André (2012), *Francis of Assisi: The Life and Afterlife of a Medieval Saint*, trans. Michael F. Cusato, New Haven, CT: Yale University Press.

Vegetius (2004), *Epitoma rei militaris*, ed. M.D. Reeve, Oxford: Clarendon Press.

Verbruggen, J. F. (2002), *The Art of Warfare in Western Europe During the Middle Ages: From the Eighth Century to 1340*, Woodbridge: Boydell Press.

Vermeesch, Albert (1966), *Essai sur les origines et la signification de la commune dans le nord de la France (XIe et XIIe siècles)*, Heule: UGA.

Vita Leonis noni. La vie du Pape Léon IX (Brunon, évêque de Toul) (1997), ed. Michel Parisse and Monique Goullet, Paris: Les Belles Lettres.

Voss, Ingrid (1987), *Herrschertreffen im frühen und hohen Mittelalter*, Cologne: Böhlau.

Voss, Ingrid (1992), "La rencontre entre le roi Robert II et l'empereur Henri II à Mouzon et Ivois en 1023: Un exemple des relations franco-allemandes au Moyen Age," *Annales de l'Est*, 5 ser. 44: 3–14.

Wadle, Elmar (2001), *Landfrieden, Strafe, Recht: Zwölf Studien zum Mittelalter*, Schriften zur europäischen Rechts- und Verfassungsgeschichte 37, Berlin: Duncker & Humblot.

Warner, G.F., ed. (1891), *Giraldi Cambrensis Opera Omnia, Volume VIII. De Principis Instructione Liber*, London: Eyre and Spottiswoode.

Watkins, J. (2008), "Toward a New Diplomatic History of Medieval and Early Modern Europe," *Journal of Medieval and Early Modern Studies*, 38: 1–14.

Weinstock, Stefan (1960), "Pax and the 'Ara Pacis,'" *Journal of Roman Studies*, 50: 44–58.

West, Charles (2013), *Reframing the Feudal Revolution: Political and Social Transformation Between Marne and Moselle, c. 800–c. 1100*, Cambridge: Cambridge University Press.

White Stephen D. (1978), "'Pactum . . . legem vincit et amor judicium': The Settlement of Disputes by Compromise in Eleventh-Century Western France," *American Journal of Legal History*, 22: 281–308.

White Stephen D. (1995), "Proposing the Ordeal and Avoiding it: Strategy and Power in Western French Litigation, 1050–1110," in Thomas N. Bisson (ed.), *Cultures of Power: Lordship, Status, and Processes in Twelfth-Century Europe*, 89–123, Philadelphia: University of Pennsylvania Press.

White, Stephen D. (1996), "Clotild's revenge: Politics, kinship, and ideology in the Merovingian blood feud," in S.K. Cohn and S.A. Epstein (eds), *Portraits of Medieval and Renaissance Living: Essays in Memory of David Herlihy*, 107–30, Ann Arbor: University of Michigan Press.

White, Stephen D. (2016), "'The Peace in the feud' revisited: Feuds in the peace in medieval European feuds," in Kate Cooper and Conrad Leyser (eds), *Making Early Medieval Societies: Conflict and Belonging in the Latin West, 300–1200*, 220–42, Cambridge: Cambridge University Press.

Whitelock, Dorothy, ed. (1955), *English Historical Documents c. 500–1042*, London: Eyre & Spottiswood.

Whitelock, Dorothy (2004), *English Historical Documents c. 500–1042*, 2nd ed., London: Routledge.

Wickham, Chris (1994), "The Sense of the Past in Twelfth-Century City Chronicles," in Chris Wickham, *Land and Power: Studies in Italian and European Social History, 400–1200*, 295–312, London: British School at Rome.

Wickham, Chris (2005), *Framing the Early Middle Ages*, Oxford: Oxford University Press.

Wickham, Chris (2015), *Sleepwalking into a New World: The Emergence of the Italian City-Communes in the Twelfth Century*, Princeton: Princeton University Press.

Wickham, Chris (2016), *Medieval Europe*, New Haven, CT: Yale University Press.

Widukind of Corvey (1935), *Res gestae Saxonicae*, ed. P. Hirsch and H.-E. Lohmann, MGH, Scriptores in Rerum Germanicarum in usum scholarum separatim editi, 60, Hanover: Hahn.

Wigoder, Geoffrey, ed. (1970), *Hegyon ha-Nefesh ha-'Atsuvah*, by Abraham bar Hiyya, Jerusalem: Mosad Bialik.

Williams, Ann (1997), *The English and the Norman Conquest*, Woodbridge: Boydell & Brewer Ltd.

Wipo (2000), *Deeds of Conrad II*, in T.E. Mommsen and R.L. Benson (eds), *Imperial Lives and Letters of the Eleventh Century*, 52–100, New York: Columbia University Press.

Wolf, Anne Marie (2014), *Juan de Segovia and the Fight for Peace: Christians and Muslims in the Fifteenth Century*, Notre Dame, IN: University of Notre Dame Press.

Wormald, Patrick (1999), *The Making of English Law: King Alfred to the Twelfth Century*, Oxford: Blackwell.

Wright, Nicholas (2000), *Knights and Peasants: The Hundred Years War in the French Countryside*, Woodbridge: Boydell Press.

Wubs-Mrozewicz, J. (2017), "The Late Medieval and Early Modern Hanse as an Institution of Conflict Management," *Continuity and Change*, 32: 59–84.

Zorzi, Andrea, ed. (2009), *Conflitti, paci, e vendetta nell'Italia comunale*, Florence: Firenze University Press.

CONTRIBUTORS

Jenny Benham is Senior Lecturer in Medieval History at Cardiff University. Her research and teaching focus on war, peace, and diplomacy in the period 500–1250. She is the author of *Peacemaking in the Middle Ages: Principles and Practice* (Manchester University Press, 2011) and numerous articles on aspects of medieval diplomacy and law.

Geoffrey Koziol is Professor of History at the University of California, Berkeley. He has written widely on medieval law, ritual, politics, monasticism, and historiography, focusing particularly on settings where religion and power intersect. His latest book is *The Peace of God* (ARC Humanities Press, 2018).

Jehangir Yezdi Malegam is Associate Professor of History at Duke University in Durham, North Carolina, USA. He is the author of *The Sleep of Behemoth: Disputing Peace and Violence in Medieval Europe, 1000–1200* (Cornell University Press, 2013). Recent publications include "Evangelic Provocation: Location of Anger in Medieval Conversion Narratives," *Literature Compass* 13(6) (June, 2016) 372–88 and "Suspicions of Peace in the Middle Ages," *Common Knowledge* 21(2) (May, 2015) 236–52. Currently, he is writing a history of noise and social ordering in medieval Europe.

James A. Palmer is Assistant Professor of History at Florida State University. He is author of *The Virtues of Economy: Governance, Power, and Piety in Late Medieval Rome* (Cornell University Press 2019), which explores how a late-fourteenth-century transformation of Roman political culture enabled the papacy to establish its formal dominion over a city to which it had only recently returned from Avignon. He is interested in the entanglement of lay piety with various discourses of virtue in the context of medieval political societies, as well as in the way these things helped shape late medieval and early modern social, political, and governmental institutions and practices.

Gregory M. Reichberg is Research Professor at the Peace Research Institute Oslo (PRIO) and Adjunct Professor in Political Science at the University of Oslo where he heads the Research School on Peace and Conflict. His recent publications include *Thomas Aquinas on War and Peace* (Cambridge University Press, 2017) and articles in *Ethics and International Affairs*, *Journal of Military Ethics*, *Journal of Religious Ethics*, and *Nova et Vetera* (English edition). He holds a Ph.D. in philosophy from Emory University (1990).

Walter Simons is Professor of History at Dartmouth College in Hanover, New Hampshire. His research deals with religious movements of the central Middle Ages, urban history, gender, and historical methodology. He is the author, among other books, of *Cities of Ladies: Beguine Communities in the Medieval Low Countries, 1200–1565* (University of Pennsylvania Press, 2001) and editor, with Miri Rubin, of *The Cambridge History of Christianity*, vol. 4: *Christianity in Western Europe, c. 1100–c. 1500* (Cambridge University Press, 2009).

Katrin E. Sjursen is an independent scholar and former Associate Professor of Historical Studies at Southern Illinois University, Edwardsville. She researches the political and military activities of northern French medieval noblewomen and has published articles in collected volumes and academic journals such as *The Medieval Feminist Forum* and *The Haskins Society Journal*. In 2013, she won a postdoctoral grant from the American Association of University Women.

Anne Marie Wolf earned her Ph.D. in medieval history at the University of Minnesota and is Professor of History at the University of Maine–Farmington. She is the author of *Juan de Segovia and the Fight for Peace: Christians and Muslims in the Fifteenth Century* (University of Notre Dame Press, 2014). Her current work is toward a comparative and broader study of medieval religious approaches to peace.

INDEX

Page numbers in **bold** refer to figures.

Abbasid period, 73
Abelard, Peter, 10
Abraham bar Hiyya, 74
Adalbero of Metz, Bishop, 21
Adela of Blois, 52
Admonitio generalis, the, 14, 139–40, 141
admonition, culture of, 15
Adomnán, 67
Aethelflaed, King of Mercia, 61
aggressive self-help, outlawed, 145
Agobard of Lyons, 15
Aimo of Bourges, Archbishop, 146, 148
Albigensian Crusade, 9, 58
Alcuin, 147
Alexander III, Pope, 28, 30
Alexander Romances, 93
Alger, Canon, 27
Alice of Montmorency, 58
Alleluia of 1233, the, 102, 106–8
alliances, 20
Alnwick, battle of, 121, 130
Althoff, Gerd, 18, 20
Amalek, 70
Ambrose of Milan, 96–7
amicitia, accords of, 17
Andrea Di Bontaiuto, fresco, **34**
angel of peace, the, 95, 110
Annals of Fulda, 15
Annals of Saint-Bertin, 15
Anselm, St, 89
anti-Muslim tropes, 79
Antiphon for Peace, 84, **85**, 91
anti-Semitism, 93
anti-war movements, xii
apocalyptic theory, 92
apostates, 46
Aquitaine, 56, 142
Arabs, 3
arbitration, 122–4, 125, 132
aristocracy, 9–10
Aristotle, 30, 33, 34, 40–2, **41**, 75–6

associations, 138
associative peace, 141–7, 148
Athelstan, 137
Augustine of Hippo, St, 7, 15, 28, 33, 35, 65–6, 71, 87–8, **88**, 94–5, 102–3, 135
Aurell, Martin, 60
Auxerre, Treaty of, 68
Averroës, 43, **43**
Avicenna, 34

Barton, Richard, 20
Basel, Council of, 78
bath of blood history, ix–x
being, 34
   of God, 37
Benham, Jenny, 18
Bergamo, Venturino da, 102, 111
Bernard of Clairvaux, St, 76–7
Bernardino of Siena, St, 115–16, **117**
Bianchi, the, 102, 113–15, **113**
Black Death, the, 111
Blanche of Castile, 58, 62
Blanche of Naples, 54
Blanche of Navarre, 58
blasphemy, 37–8
bodily compulsion, 46
Bohemia, 9
Bonizo de Sutri, 51
Bosch, Hieronymus, 88, **90**
Bouvet, Honoré, 56
Bretigny, Treaty of, 127
brotherhoods, 140, 148
Brown, Warren C., 6
Bruno of Toul, Bishop, 21–2
Bullough, Donald, 14
Burchard of Worms, 51
Byzantine Empire, 3

Calais, 58
Cambodia, 39
Cambrai, 23

canon law, 132
Caritas-Terminologie, 138
Carolingian empire, 3, 7, 135–6, 139–40
   division of, 14–15, **16**, 17, 140
   governmental structures, 4–5
   guilds, 137
   legacies, 13–15, 17
   royal discourse, 14
   successors, 17
Castile, 124
Cathars, 9
Catherine of Siena, St, 11
Catholic Doctrine, triumph of, **34**
celestial Jerusalem, the, 84–92, **85**, **86**, **87**, **89**, **90**, **91**
ceremonial acts, 18
Cervantes, Juan de, 78–9
charity, 39, 40, 42, 75
Charlemagne, king of the Franks, 3, 7, 14, 31, **126**, 133, 139, 139–40
Charles the Bald, king of the Franks, 15, 17, 135, 139
chiliasm, 92
Christendom, 3
Christian brotherhood, 147–8
Christian tradition, 13
Christianity, xiii, 7, 66
   foundations, 80
   internal peace, 67–9
   offensive wars, 66
   peace across religious traditions, 72–3, 75–80, **77**, **78**
   peace representations, 84–92, **85**, **86**, **87**, **89**, **90**, **91**
   persecution of heretics, 9
   religious tolerance, 75–6, 79
Christine de Pizan, 54, 62
Church, the, 135
   arbitration role, 123–4
   authority, 67–8
   corporate understanding of, 27
   ecclesial peace, 136, 139, 148
   intra-ecclesial conflicts, 22–3
   and peace, 21–3
   and war, 8–9
Church councils, 135–6, **137**
civic friendship, 42, 43
civil society, 31, 36
classical antiquity, 3
Clausewitz, Carl von, 63
Cluny, Peace of, 21
Codagnelli, Giovanni, 26–7

cognitive input, lack of, 20
Cola di Rienzo, 111
collective action, 11
collectively, 27–8
Columbini, 111
common good, the, 5, 36
communes, 11, 23–7, 103–6, **104**, **105**, 106, 112, 115–16, **117**, 118
community, 42
complete peace, 38
conciliators, 56
conflict resolution, and religious belief and practice, 66
coniuratio, 25
connaturaleness, 35–6
Conrad III, King of Germany, 19, 26
consensus, 11, 129, 138
consent, 35
Constantinople, 17
consultative lordship, 18
convenientia, 17, 20
corpora mystica, 27–8
Coulaines, Treaty of, 17
courtly culture, 18
crime, 6, 27
crusades, 9, 44, 45, **53**, 75, 76–7, **77**, **91**, 92
   First, 52, 92, 144
   Second, 61, 76
   Third, 52, 57
   opposition to, 77–80
cultural values, 133–4
culture, definition, x
Cusanus, 79–80
customs, 132

Dante Alighieri, 30, 67, 71, 72, 99, 141
   Divine Comedy, 93–4
De Re Militari, 58
Deguileville, Guillaume de, 88, **89**, 94
Denmark, 122
Dervorgilla, 59
destruction, limitation of, 142, 145
deterrence, xiii, 121–2, 126, 131–4
Dionysius, 35, 37
diplomacy, 129–30, 131, **131**
disorder, usefulness of, 23
displaced people, 120–2, 132
diversity, reduction of, 37
divina pax, 36–8
divine retribution, 10
Dixon, Martin, 132, 133

INDEX 181

Duby, Georges, 4
Durand of Le Puy, 26

Earth, peace on, 92–4
Easter, 86–7, 91, 109
Ebbo of Déols, 146
ecclesial peace, 136, 139, 148
Eco, Umberto, 35
economic expansion, 4
Edward II, King of England, 54
Edward III, King of England, 51
effectiveness, 131–4
Einhard, 14
eirene, 15
Eisen, Robert, 74
Eleanor of Aquitaine, 61
Eleanor of Provence, 63
Elias, Norbert, 5–6
Elizabeth of Jaligny, 53–4, 58
Emma, countess of Norfolk, 63
enforcement procedures, 133
England, 4, 6, 31
equality, 148
Ermesinde of Barcelona, 62
Esplechin, Truce of, 56
ethical dimensions, 33
Eucharistic theology, 27
European Economic Community, 148
evildoers, peace among, 38
Evreux, 59–60
excommunication, 43, 142–4
exile, 120, 139, 147
expulsion, of individuals, 120–1
extra-judicial settlements, 31

Faisani, Rainiero, 109
faith, xii, 8, 43, 46
Fakhr al-Din al-Razi, 73
false peace, 38
familiaritas, 18
femininity, 11
feudal system and the feudal revolution, 4–5
feuding, 10
Firnhaber-Baker, Justine, 31
flagellant movements, 102, 108–10, 111
Florence, 115
Florus of Lyon, 17
forgiveness, 66
formae pacis, 145, 146
France, 4, 31, 144–7
Francis of Assisi, St, 75, **104**, 109
  and the wolf, 1, **2**, 11

Francisco de Vitoria, 46, 47
Franks, the, 3
Frederick Barbarossa, Emperor, 26, 28, **29**, 103, 129, 141
Frederick of Sicily, 56
Friedman, Yvonne, 59
friendship, 41–2, 43, 46, 75–6, 148
Froissart, Jean, 51

Garden of Eden, 88
Gauvard, Claude, 27
gender, xii, 11, 51–63
  blurring, 56–63, **57**, **61**
  and participation in warfare, 52–4, **53**
  peacemaking as feminine, 54, **55**, 56
  roles, 10
  warfare as masculine, 51–4
Gerard of Modena, 26, 106
Germain, Jean, 78
German historiography, 135
Germany, 4, 5, 24, 95, 147
Gerson, Jean, 68
gesture, 18–20
Ghent, 95
Gidinild of Catalonia, 62
Gilbert of Tournai, 27
Giles of Rome, 52
Giotto, *The Exorcism of Arezzo*, **104**
Gislebert of Mons, 54, 62
globalization, xi
Glover, Jonathan, x
God
  action of, 38–9
  being, 37
  the peace said of, 36–8
  and peacemakers, 68
  relations to, 39–40, 69
  worship of, 84–5
  wrath, 111
Good Tree, the, **83**, 84
goodness, 34
Gordimer, Nadine, ix
Gorzian reform, the, 21
Gospels, the, 75, 80
governing authority, 5
grace, 39
Gratian, 77, 78
Great Devotion, the, 26
Gregory of Nazianze, 90
Gregory of Nyssa, 90
Gregory of Tours, Bishop, 11
Gregory VII, Pope, 22, 61

Grosseteste, Robert, 84
Grygiel, Jakub, 131–2, 133
Gubbio, 1, **2**, 11
Guibert, abbot of Nogent, 23
Guibert of Gembloux, 9
guilds, 137–8
Guy of Le Puy, Bishop, 21

Hainaut, 145–6
Hanseatic League, 123
happiness, 65
Harold Godwineson, 132
Hay, David, 60
Heloise, 10
Hennebont, 58
Henry II, Emperor, 18, 129–30, 140–1
Henry II, King of England, 58, 61, 123, 124
Henry III, Emperor, 22
Henry III, King of England, 58, 63
Henry IV, King of Germany, 19–20, 22, **19**
Henry of Suse, 44
Henry the Fowler, 17
Henry V, King of England, 56
Henry VI, King of England, **55**
heretics, 9, 43, 46, 78
Hincmar of Reims, Archbishop, 15, 141–2
history, bath of blood framing, ix–x
Hoffmann, Harmut, 23
Holy Land, the, 45
holy war, 44–6
Homberg, Werner Graf von, **57**
homicide rates, 6
honor, 10, 11, 27
hospitality, 21
hostages, 126–9, **126**, **128**
Hostiensis, 44, 76
Hugh of Auxerre, Bishop, 26
Hugh of Cluny, **19**
Hugh of Lusignan, 59
Hugh of Payns, 76, 78
Hugh of Poitiers, 58
human nature, xi–xii, 30
humanity, ix
Humbert of Silva Candida, 22
Hundred Years' War, **55**, 56, 59, 61, **61**
Hussites, 9

Ibn Qayyim, 47
Ibn Taymihah, 47
Ida of Carinthia, 58
ideal models, 92–3, 103–4
imperfect peace, 30, 38, 39, 68

inclusiveness, 148
individuals
    autonomous, 148
    expulsion of, 120–1
infidels, 44
inner peace, 39
Innocent III, Pope, 46, 144
Innocent IV, Pope, 44–5, **45**
integration, xiii, 135–48
internal peace
    Christianity, 67–9
    Islam, 71–2
    Judaism, 69–71, **70**
international law, 132–3, 134
inter-personal harmony, 39–40
intra-ecclesial conflicts, 22–3
Isabel of Conches, 60
Isabella of France, 54
Isabella of Portugal, 56
Isabelle of Angoulême, 59
Isabelle of Bavaria, 56
Isaiah 26:12, 33
Isidore of Seville, 25
Islam, 7, 66
    definition of word, 71
    grievance courts, 72
    and heretics, 43
    internal peace, 71–2
    jihad, 47
    jurists, 46, 47
    and justice, 71, 72
    legal scholars, 71–2
    peace across religious traditions, 72–3, 73–4
    rationales for waging war, 46–7
    religious tolerance, 46–7, 73
    Sharia law, 71–2
    social order, 71–2
    and unbelievers, 46
Israel, 15
Italy, 4, 5, 102, 141
    the Alleluia of 1233, 102, 106–8
    the Bianchi, 102, 113–15, **113**
    communes, 26, 103–6, **104**, **105**, 106, 112, 115–16, **117**, 118
    flagellant movements, 102, 108–10, 111
    the Observant movement, 116
    politics, 110–13, 116
Ivo of Chartres, 25

Jacqueline of Hainaut, 61
Jalaluddin Rumi, 74
James, William, ix

INDEX

James II of Aragon, 54
James of Vitry, 77–8
Jansen, Katherine, 95
Jean II, King of France, 127, **128**
Jeanne of France, 62
Jeanne of Montfort, 58, 61
Jeanne of Navarre, 61, 62
Jeanne of Valois, 56
Jerusalem, 84–92, **85, 86, 87, 89, 90, 91,** 102
Jesus Christ, 37, 79, 80
Jews, 9, 31, 44, 66, 92
    rationales for waging war, 48–9
jihad, 47
Joan of Arc, xii, 61, **61**
John, King of England, 59, **125**
John XV, Pope, 123
John of Salisbury, 27
John of Vicenza, 26, 106, 107
Judah Halevi, 69
Judaism, 7, 66
    internal peace, 69–71, **70**
    peace across religious traditions, 72–3, 74–5
    rabbinic tradition, 69
    rationales for waging war, 48–9
    relationship with God, 69
    religious tolerance, 74–5
Judas, Kiss of, 96–7, **96**
just war, 68–9, 77
justice, 4, 40, 71, 72, 99, 107, 116

Kantorowicz, Ernst, 27
Kennelly, Dolorosa, 23
Kershaw, Paul, 15
Khmer Rouge, 39
kings
    dual mandate, 32
    inner tranquillity, 15
    limits in power, 13
    lordly prerogatives, 31
    power of discretion, 31–2
    responsibility, 138–9
    as *rex pacificus*, 14
King's Mirror, 120–1
kingship, 4, 18, 67, 135
Kiss of Judas, 96–7, **96**
Kiss of Peace, 94–6, 103, 107, **108**
Knights Templar, 76, 77
Kosto, Adam, 20, 127

Lactantius, 92
Lambert of Ardres, 54, 60

Lambert of St Omer, 84
Lambert of Wattrelos, 53
Landfriede, 24, 28, 31, 147
Laon, 25, 27
Laon Cathedral, **24**
Lateran Council, third, 28, 30, 121
laudes regiae, 14
law, 132–3, 134, 135
Law of the Innocents, 67
le Bel, Jean, 51
Le Mans, 25, 146, 148
Leo III, Pope, 7
Leo IX, Pope, 21–2
Liège, 23
Lille, 25
Lillebonne, Peace and Truce of, **143**
literacy, 102
Liudprand of Cremona, 17
Lombard, Peter, 76
Lombard League, 103, 141
lordly prerogatives, 31
Lorenzetti, Ambrogio, *Peace and War*, 97, **98,** 99–100, **99, 100,** 103
Lothar, king of the Franks, 17, 18, 140
Louis VII, King of France, 123
Louis IX, King of France, 31
Louis the Fat, King of France, 25
Louis the German, 17
Louis the Pious, king of the Franks, 13, 14–15, 17, 18, 32, **120,** 123, 139, 140, 148
Low Countries, the, 4, 95, 102
Ludwig of Bavaria, 31
Lull, Raymond, 52
Lupus of Ferrières, 15

MacEvitt, Christopher, 9
Maimonides, Moses, 48, 70, 70–1, 72, 74–5
Mainz, 52
malice, 39
Malik al-Kâmil, 75
Mandeville, Sir John, 92–3
Margaret of Anjou, **55**
Margaret of Hainaut, 62
Maria of Hungary, 56
marriage, 54, **55,** 56
Marsilius of Padua, 30–1, 68
martial prowess, cultivation of, 9–10
Mass, 84, 94, 95
Matilda, Queen, 62
Matilda de l'Aigle, 63
Matilda of Boulogne, 62
Matilda of Braose, 59

Matilda of Flanders, 60
Matilda of Tuscany, 61
Medieval Age, the, 3–4
Melfi, Treaty of, 126
mercenaries, 121–2
metaphysics, 33, 34–6
Milan, 19, 26–7, 28
military power, male monopoly of, xii
millenarianism, 92
miracle workers, 1
Mohammad, the Prophet, 46–7, 66
monarchy, defense of, 30–1
Monstrelet, Enguerrand de, 68
Monte di Pietà, the, 116
Moore, R.I., 6
moral disciplining, 115
moral reform, **117**
moral uprightness, 38
Muchembled, Robert, 6
Muslims, 3
mutuality, 148

Nachmanides, Moses, 49
Nahmanides, 70
Nantes, Council of, 52
nation states, foundation of early, 4
national state, the, 3
Navarre, 124
Nederman, Cary, 9
negative peace, xi, xii–xiii, 17
Nicene creed, 8
Nicholas of Cusa, 78, 79–80
non-believers, violence against, 9
non-combatants, 56–7, 67
Norway, 120–1
Notker of Saint Gall, 31
Novello, Francesco, 114

oaths, 15, 17, 26, 124–6, 130, 133, **144**, 146
obligations, 126, 148
Observant movement, the, 116
Odo of Toul, Bishop, 24
Oexle, Otto Gerhard, 26
Offa, king of the Mercians, 133
Offenstadt, Nicolas, 56
On the Divine Names, (Pseudo-Dionysius), 33
On the Goodness of Peace (Rufinus of Sorrento), 30
order, 35, 39, 65
Orderic Vitalis, 52, 59–60, 60, 62
Ordinatio, 15
Ordinatio imperii, 139

Otto I, King, 17, 18
Otto of Freising, 28
Ottonian chroniclers, 17
Ottonians, 17–18

pacifism, xii, 77
pacts, 136, 138–41, 142, 148; *see also* treaties
Padua, 114
pagans, 1, 14
papacy, the, 7, 123–4, 136
pardon, power of, 31–2
Paris, Treaty of, 129
Paschal II, Pope, 23
past, the, ix–x
patriarchy, 10
Paul, St, 79, 84, 94
Paupertas, 11
pax, 25, 136
Pax Americana, xiii
pax et amicitia, 14
Pax Romana, xiii
peace, kinds of, 38–9
peace, representations of, xii, 81–100
    Christian imagery, 84–92, **85**, **86**, **87**, **89**, **90**, **91**
    the Good Tree, **83**, 84
    heritage, 81
    the Kiss of Peace, 94–6
    Lorenzetti, 97, **98**, 99–100, **99**, **100**
    peace on Earth, 92–4
    personifications, 84
    pilgrimage, 88, **89**, **90**
    Roman tradition, 81–2, **82**, **83**, 84
peace, zones of, 39–40
peace associations, 142, 148
peace conferences, 129–30, **131**
peace councils, 17, 21
peace history, ix, x, xi
peace language, 135–8, 145–6
Peace League, 24, 148
peace marriages, 54, **55**
peace movements, xii, 101–18
    the Alleluia of 1233, 102, 106–8
    the Bianchi, 102, 113–15, **113**
    flagellant, 102, 108–10, **111**
    the Observant movement, 116
    participation, 101
    politics, 110–13, 116
    processions, 102, 109, 113–15, **113**
    and urban life and a culture, 102, 102–6, **104**, **105**
    waning of, 116, 118

INDEX

Peace of God, 21, 23–5, 56, 67, 101, 141–7, **143, 144**
peace on Earth, 92–4
peace processes, 1–3
peace-guilds, 137–8
peacekeeping, 124–9, **125, 126, 128**
peacemakers
   and God, 68
   women as, 11, 51
peacemaking, 1–3, 10, 13, 139
   civil procedures, 95
   conciliators, 56
   as feminine, 51, 54, **55**, 56
   informal mechanisms, 20
   marriages, 54, **55**
   men's participation in, 54
   performance, 18, 94–7, **96**
   ritualized, 112–13
penance, 103
perfect peace, 38, 39, 68
perpetual peace, 15, 17
personifications, 84
Perugia, 109–10
pessimism, 15
Peter, St, 21, 94
Peter the Hermit, **53**
Petit-Dutaillis, Charles, 25
Petronilla of Grandmesnil, 58
Philip Augustus, King of France, **125**
Philip IV, King of France, 31
Philippa of Hainaut, Queen of England, 51, 54, 62
Phillips, L. Edward, 94
pilgrimage, 88, **90**
Pinker, Steven, x
podestà, the, 106, 107, 109–10
Poitiers, Battle of, 127
political friendship, 33, 42, 76
political legitimacy, xii
political realism, xiii
political theory, secular, 27–8, **29**, 30–1
positive peace, xi, 17
prayer, 92
prayer fellowships, 138
preachers, **105**, 115–16
   the Alleluia of 1233, 106–7
Presles, Raoul de, 87, **88**
Prester John, 92–3
Prevenier, Walter, 31
private warfare, 4
Prudentius, *Psychomachia*, 81–2, **82**, 84
Pseudo-Dionysius, 33, 35

pseudo-Pauline Letter to the Ephesians, 136
Ptolemy of Lucca, 52
public authority, problem of, 4–6
purification, 116

Qur'an, 47, 66, 71, 72, 73, 79

raiding, 121–2
Ralph (*Rodulfus*) Glaber, *Five Books of Histories*, 129–30
ransom, 59, 127
ransom treaties, 127
Raoul de Cambrai, 20
rape, 59
Ravenna, 19
reconciliations, 20
redemption, 31, 69
Reformation, the, 4, 84
Regino of Prüm, 51
Reichberg, Gregory, 68–9, 75–6
Reichsfrieden, 147
religious authority, 7–8, 9
religious belief and practice, 7–9, **8**, 65–80
   Christianity, 66, 67–9, 72–3, 75–80, **77, 78**
   and conflict resolution, 66
   and internal peace, 67–72, **70**
   Islam, 66, 71–2, 72–3, 73–4
   Judaism, 66, 69–71, **70**, 72–3, 74–5
   and war, 8–9
religious deviance, 9
religious enthusiasm, waves of, 102
religious minorities, rough tolerance over, 9
religious tolerance, 75–6, 93
   Christianity, 75–6, 79
   Islam, 46–7, 73
   Judaism, 74–5
   Thomas Aquinas, St, 75–6
religious traditions, peace across, 43–6, 72–80
Renaissance, the, xiii, 4
republicanism, 103
respect, x
rex pacificus, kings as, 14
Richard I, King of England, 57
Richard II, King of England, 56
Richard of Saint-Vanne, Abbot, 21
rights, 132
Robert, King of Naples, 56
Robert II, king of the Franks, 129–30
Robert of Torigny, 54
Robert the Monk, 52
Robert the Pious, King of France, 140–1, 142

Robert the Strong, 17
Roman Empire, 3
Roman law, 4, 5, 136
Roman tradition, peace representations, 81–2, **82**, **83**, 84
Rome, 111, 112, 114, 115
rough tolerance, 9
royal discourse, Carolingian empire, 14
Rufinus of Sorrento, 23, 30
Rupert of Deutz, 86–7, 91–2

sacramental pollution, fears of, 22
Saint-Germain Laprade, 21
Salimbene di Adam, 109
salvation, 7, 94
Sansepolcro Altarpiece, **2**
Saxo Grammaticus, 14, 122
schism, 42
Schneider, Reinhard, 138
scripture, 7
security, xii–xiii, 35, 37
sedition, 42
Sedulius Scottus, 15, 139
Segovia, Juan de, 77–80
self-help, 145
shaming, 52
Shamsuddin Hafiz, 74
Sharia law, 71–2
Shay, Jonathan, x
Shaykh Tusi, 47
Siena, Hall of Peace, 97, **98**, 99–100, **99**, **100**, 103
Sigebert of Gembloux, 23
Simon of Montfort, 58
Simony, 22
sins, 42, 102
skepticism, 111
social goods, 2–3
social peace, 31
social stratification, 148
Song of the Cathar Wars, 58
sovereignty, 31
Spain, 69, 79
species consciousness, xiii
Spierenburg, Pieter, 6
state, the, problem of, 4–6
Stephen of Blois, 52
Stephen of Tournai, 25
stereotypes, 3
Sufism, 73–4
Summa Theologica (Thomas Aquinas), 30, 36, 68–9
sureties, 127–9
Sybil of Anjou, Countess of Flanders, 53
sympathy, x

Talmud, the, 84
temporal peace, 69
theology, 7
Theophano, Empress, 53
Thietmar of Merseberg, 17
Thietmar of Merseburg, 53
Thomas Aquinas, St, 100
   aim, 33
   and Aristotle, 40–2, **41**
   and blasphemy, 37–8
   characteristics of peace, 35
   Christian understanding, 37
   and civil society, 36
   classifications of war, 68–9
   commentary on the *Divine Names*, 37
   and community, 42
   conception of peace, 38–42, 46
   divina pax, 36–8
   and Isaiah 26:12, 33
   and just war, 68–9
   and justice, 40
   kinds of peace, 38–9
   metaphysical background, 34–6
   and the peace said of God, 36–8
   religious tolerance, 75–6
   and the scope of peace, 35–6
   sins, 42
   social and political dimensions, 40–2, **41**
   sources, 33
   Summa Theologica, 30, 36, 68–9
   and unbelievers, 45–6
   zones of peace, 39–40
tolerance, 65
towns, development of, 101–2
tranquillity, 35, 39
translation problem, xi
Travels of Sir John Mandeville, 93
treaties, 121, 125–6, 136, 140–1, 148; *see also* pacts
trial by combat, 18
Truax, Jean, 60
Truce of God, 31, 67, 142, 144, 145, 146–7
Truman, Harry, 147
Truong sisters, xii
tyranny, 39

unemendable crimes, 120
unity, 34, 37

Urban II, Pope, 23, 25, 52, 144
urban life and a culture, and peace movements, 102, 102–6, **104**, **105**
urban populations, 101
Utrecht Psalter, the, **137**

Valenciennes, Peace of, 145–6, 148
Van Engen, John, 92
vassalage, 3–4
Venice, 129
Vercelli, Manfredi da, 114–15
Verdun, Treaty of, 17, 123
Vietnam, xii
Viking literature, 59
Vikings, 121
Vincent of Beauvais, 27
Violante of Hungary, 58–9
violence
   cognitive input, 20
   definition, 20–1
   levels of, x, 6–7
   against non-believers, 9
   state monopoly on, 4, 5–6
virtue, 39, 40, 42, 82, 84, 94
Visconti, Giangaleazzo, 114
Vita Karoli (Einhard), 14

Waldensians, the, 105
Wandrille, St, 133
war and warfare, 42
   classifications of, 68–9
   legitimate, 44–5
   as masculine, 51, 51–4
   private, 4
   and religious belief and practice, 8–9
   religious rationales, 44–9
   scale of, 6–7
   women's incitement of, 59–60
   women's participation, 52–4, **53**, 56–63, **57**, **61**
   women's role, 51
War of the Sicilian Vespers, 54, 56
warring women, 60–3, **61**
warrior code, 9–10
West, Charles, 5
Wickham, Chris, 5, 26
Widukind of Corvey, 17, 18
William, Duke (the Conqueror), 25, 60, 63, 132
William Clito, Count, 25
William of Tyre, **91**
William the Lion, king of Scots, 121, 130
Wipo, 17
women
   active involvement in warfare, 60–3, **61**
   captivity and ransom, 59
   chastity, 59
   education, 62
   honor, 11
   incitement of warfare, 59–60
   as life-givers, xii
   as military advisors, 58
   non-combatants, 56–7
   participation in warfare, 52–4, **53**, 56–63, **57**, **61**
   as peacemakers, 11, 51
   role in warfare, 51
   support activities, 57–8

Yça Gidelli, 79
Yolande of Aragon, Duchess of Anjou, 56